Also by Richard Hyman

THE WORKERS' UNION
MARXISM AND THE SOCIOLOGY OF TRADE
  UNIONISM
STRIKES
DISPUTES PROCEDURE IN ACTION
SOCIAL VALUES AND INDUSTRIAL RELATIONS (*with
  Ian Brough*)
INDUSTRIAL RELATIONS: A Marxist Introduction
TRADE UNIONS AND REVOLUTION (*with James Hinton*)

Also by Robert Price

PROFILES OF UNION GROWTH (*with George Bain*)

THE NEW WORKING CLASS?
WHITE-COLLAR WORKERS
AND THEIR ORGANIZATIONS

A Reader

Edited by
Richard Hyman
and
Robert Price

First published 1983 by
THE MACMILLAN PRESS LTD
London and Basingstoke
Companies and representatives
throughout the world

Hardcover ISBN 0 333 27283 8
Paperback ISBN 0 333 27284 6

Printed in Hong Kong

Contents

v

Contents

Preface

The present century has seen a persistent expansion in the size of the 'white-collar' or 'non-manual' labour force, and more recently a rapid growth in the membership of 'white-collar unions'. There now exists a substantial literature discussing these developments: some reflecting sociologists' concern to relate changes in occupational structure to theories of class; some representing the awareness of 'industrial relations' writers of the importance of organization and collective bargaining among these employee groups; and some stemming from a more general public interest in the economic and and political significance of the rise of what has sometimes been called the 'salariat'.

In compiling our selection from this literature we have aimed to offer both the student and the lay reader a range of approaches which have made a notable contribution to knowledge and understanding. To some extent we have weighted our choice towards less accessible sources such as journal articles and out-of-print publications; but we have decided not to exclude important extracts merely on the grounds of ready availability in their original form. We have also been guided by a desire to maintain some element of thematic unity in our coverage.

While this book as a whole is a collaborative exercise, each of us has assumed primary responsibility for one part. Richard Hyman has arranged the extracts which focus on the meaning and adequacy of the conventional category of white-collar employment, on problems of class identity, and in particular on the appropriateness of such conflicting notions as 'new middle class' and 'new working class'; while Robert Price has organized those which deal with the development of white-collar trade unions and union membership, with the relationship between trade unionism and other forms of collective organization, and with the problem of 'union character'.

Each part of the book is provided with a lengthy introduction which discusses the readings that follow, relating these to each other and to more general issues and approaches in the area. At the same time, these introductions are intended as contributions in their own right to current analysis and debate.

University of Warwick   Richard Hyman
Coventry   Robert Price

Acknowledgements

The editors and publishers wish to thank the following who have kindly given permission for the use of copyright material.

Acta Sociologica, journal of the Scandinavian Sociological Association, for the extract from 'Towards a Structural Theory of the Middle Class' by John Urry, vol. 16, no. 3 (1973).

George Allen & Unwin (Publishers) Ltd for the extract from *The Blackcoated Worker: A Study in Class Consciousness* by David Lockwood (1958).

Basil Blackwell Ltd for the table from *Profiles of Union Growth: A Comparative Statistical Portrait of Eight Countries* by G. S. Bain and R. Price (1980).

British Journal of Industrial Relations for the extracts from 'Who is a White-Collar Employee?' by G. S. Bain and Robert Price, vol. X, no. 3 (November 1972).

The Controller of Her Majesty's Stationery Office for the extracts from *New Earnings Survey* and *Employment Gazette*.

Counter Information Services for the extract from *The New Technology* (1979).

Andre Deutsch Ltd for the extracts from *The New Industrial State* by J.K. Galbraith (1967).

The Editor, *Industrial Relations Journal* (University of Nottingham) for the extracts from 'Attitudes to Work and Trade Unionism Among White-Collared Workers' by D. E. Mercer and D. T. Weir, vol III (summer 1972).

Harvard Business Review for the extract from 'White Collar Unions are Different' by George Strauss (September/October 1954), copyright © 1954 by the President and Fellows of Harvard College, all rights reserved.

Acknowledgements

The Harvester Press Ltd for the extract from *The Division of Labour: The Labour Process and Class Struggle in Modern Capitalism* by Andre Gorz (1976).

Heinemann Educational Books for the extracts from *Reluctant Militants* by B. C. Roberts, Ray Loveridge and John Gennard (1972); from *The Fragmentary Class Structure* by K. Roberts, F. G. Cook, S. C. Clark and Elizabeth Semeonoff (1977); and from *Social Stratification and Trade Unionism* by George Bain, David Coates and Valerie Ellis (1973).

Hutchinson Publishing Group Ltd for the extracts from *The Class Structure of the Advanced Societies* by Anthony Giddens (1975).

Mrs Winifred Klingender for the extract from *The Condition of Clerical Labour in Britain* by the late F. D. Klingender (1935).

The MIT Press for the extracts from *Work in America* (1973).

Monthly Review Press for the extract from *Labor and Monopoly Capital* by Harry Braverman, copyright © 1974 by Harry Braverman.

Oxford University Press Inc for the extracts from *White Collar: The American Middle Classes* by C. Wright Mills, copyright © 1951 by Oxford University Press Inc, renewed 1979 by Yaraslava Mills.

Radical America for the extract from 'The Professional-Managerial Class' by Barbara and John Ehrenreich, vol. II, no. 2 (March–April 1977).

Routledge & Kegan Paul Ltd for the extracts from 'White-Collar Unionization: A Conceptual Framework' by R. M. Blackburn and K. Prandy in *British Journal of Sociology*, vol. XVI, no. 2 (June 1965); from 'On the Economic Identification of the New Middle Class' by G. Carchedi in *Economy and Society*, vol. 4 (May 1975); and from 'What is to Be Known? The Structural Determination of Social Class' by Terence J. Johnson in *Economy and Society*, vol. 6 (March 1977).

Social Science Research Council for the extracts from a paper by Jean-Daniel Reynaud, included in *Social Stratification and Industrial Relations*, the proceedings of an SSRC conference, edited by M. Mann (1969).

Sociological Review for the extract from 'Class Militancy and Union

Acknowledgements

Character: A Study of the Association of Scientific, Technical and Managerial Staffs' by R. Carter in vol. 27 (May 1979).

Sociology, journal of the British Sociological Association, for the extract from 'Approaches to the Study of White-Collar Unionism' by Rosemary Crompton, vol. X (September 1976).

Spokesman for the extracts from *The New Working Class* by Serge Mallet (1975), and Editions du Seuil, Paris, for the extract (translated by Richard Hyman) from *La Nouvelle Class Ouvrière* (1963).

Verso Editions and New Left Books for the extracts from *Late Capitalism* by Ernest Mandel (1975); from *Classes in Contemporary Capitalism* by Nicos Poulantzas (1975); and from *Class, Crisis and the State* by Erik Olin Wright (1978).

C. & J. Wolfers Ltd for the extract from *The Sociology of Industrial Relations* by V. L. Allen.

Part I

The Debate on White-Collar Labour

1 Introduction

White-Collar Workers and Theories of Class

Richard Hyman

'If men define situations as real, they are real in their consequences': it is by now a sociological commonplace that beliefs,
assumptions and frames of reference, even if their foundations are
devoid of substance and logic, can exert substantial influence over
men's (and women's) social relationships. The importance of the
'definition of the situation' is clearly apparent in the context of
white-collar labour and trade unionism. Any notion of a rigid
demarcation between mental and manual work is arbitrary and
artificial. Over a century ago, Mill noted that 'all human exertion
is compounded of some mental and some bodily elements. The
stupidest hodman, who repeats from day to day the mechanical
act of climbing a ladder, performs a function partly intellectual.
. . . On the other hand, there is some bodily ingredient in the
labour most purely mental, when it generates any external
result.'[1] As Bain and Price argue in Chapter 2, none of the many
ingenious attempts to provide a rationale for the conventional
classification of occupations into 'manual' and 'white-collar' have
proved persuasive. Nevertheless, the consequences of the conventional labels are real enough.

The idea of a clearly differentiated class of 'mental' or 'non-
manual' labour has traditionally informed British employment
law, leading to important distinctions in legal rights and pro-
tections,[2] and provides an important basis of classification in
official statistics.[3] It has historically been reflected in a deep-
rooted dichotomy in employer practice, ranging from the contrast
between wages (frequently paid by the piece or the hour, and
subject to reduction in the case of a variety of contingencies) and

3

salaries (paid weekly or monthly on a far less variable basis) on the one hand,[4] to the provision of separate 'staff' and 'works' canteens on the other. Similar distinctions apply in most countries of the world.

Such powerful divisions in conceptual and administrative organization necessarily help shape the attitudes and actions of employees themselves. To the extent that 'manual' and 'non-manual' workers regard each other as qualitatively different, such beliefs are likely to prove self-validating. Conventional assumptions that white-collar status entails a proximity of interests and orientations to those of the employer, must be relevant to the explanation of the relatively low level of unionization traditional in Britain and even more marked in the United States. Elsewhere – notably in such countries as Sweden and Germany, but to a lesser degree in many others – unionized white-collar workers are normally affiliated to different central trade union confederations than their 'manual' counterparts. While in Britain, the predominant organizational framework is the separate 'white-collar union', traditionally regarded as different in 'character' from the mainstream of the labour movement, even though almost all of numerical importance are now members of the Trades Union Congress.

The post-war period in Britain has been marked, first by a rapid expansion (both absolute and relative) of 'white-collar employment'; secondly by the growth, both numerically and (more recently) as a proportion of the eligible workforce, in the membership of 'white-collar unions'. These trends have helped stimulate discussion, in academic analysis and popular commentaries alike, of the changing nature and significance of employment in these occupations, the causes and limits of unionization, and the distinctiveness (if any) of their collective goals and methods. At the same time it has become increasingly common to question the adequacy of the traditional division of occupations into 'manual' and 'white-collar', and the unity and coherence of the global category of 'non-manual' employment.

As a corollary, the issue has been posed – from a variety of contrasting perspectives – of the relationship between the interests and political orientations of the expanding 'white-collar' strata and the traditional conception of the working class. Most notably, it has been the subject of intense debate whether Marx's classic prediction of class polarization is contradicted by the rise of what many term a 'new middle class'. Conversely, some have argued that most 'non-manual' occupations today represent merely a new *form* of proletarian labour: hence the notion (from which this book derives its title) of a 'new working class'. Such controversies provide the focus of the first part of this reader.

This introductory essay first surveys recent data on occupational trends, pay, and other conditions of employment of 'white-collar' labour in Britain. The central issues discussed in the subsequent readings are then critically reviewed, with particular reference to the theoretical approaches to class of Marx and Weber which continue to inform much contemporary sociological debate.

*   *   *

In their survey of trends in the British labour force during the present century, Bain and his colleagues refer to 'the rapid growth of the white-collar labour force' as the most notable feature.

> Between 1911 and 1966 the number of white-collar workers increased by 176 per cent, while the number of manual workers increased by only 5 per cent, having actually decreased in total since 1931. The disparate growth of these two groups is reflected in the increasing relative importance of the white-collar occupations. The white-collar section of the labour force increased from 18.7 per cent to 38.3 per cent of the total between 1911 and 1966 while the manual share decreased from 74.6 per cent to 58.3 per cent.

Over the period as a whole, they add, the growth of clerical labour has been especially marked; while in more recent years, scientific and technical employees have been the fastest growing group.[5] This analysis has been updated by Price and Bain, on the basis of 1971 data, to provide Table 1.1.

Two familiar propositions concerning salary incomes are reiterated by Bain in his study of white-collar unionism: that 'many, if not most, white-collar workers continue to receive larger incomes than manual workers'; but that conversely, 'the narrowing of the white-collar–manual earnings differential has been one of the most striking changes in pay structure during the twentieth century'.[6] Yet both arguments could be misleading if presented without further qualification. Historical trends in pay relativities

TABLE 1.1   *The occupied population of Great Britain by major occupational groups, 1911–71*

Occupational groups	Numbers of persons in major occupational groups (000s)							Major occupational groups as a percentage of total occupied population						
	1911	*1921*	*1931*	*1951*	*1961*	*1966*	*1971*	*1911*	*1921*	*1931*	*1951*	*1961*	*1966*	*1971*
Employers and proprietors	1 232	1 318	1 407	1 117	1 140	832	622	6·7	6·8	6·7	5·0	4·8	3·4	2·6
All white-collar workers	3 433	4 094	4 841	6 948	8 479	9 461	10 405	18·7	21·2	23·0	30·9	35·9	38·3	42·7
Managers and administrators	631	704	770	1 245	1 270	1 514	2 085	3·4	3·6	3·7	5·5	5·4	6·1	8·6
Higher professionals	184	196	240	435	718	829	928	1·0	1·0	1·1	1·9	3·0	3·4	3·8
Lower professionals and technicians	560	679	728	1 059	1 418	1 604	1 880	3·1	3·5	3·5	4·7	6·0	6·5	7·7
Foremen and inspectors	237	279	323	590	681	736	736	1·3	1·4	1·5	2·6	2·9	3·0	3·0
Clerks	832	1 256	1 404	2 341	2 994	3 262	3 412	4·5	6·5	6·7	10·4	12·7	13·2	14·0
Salesmen and shop assistants	989	980	1 376	1 278	1 398	1 516	1 364	5·4	5·1	6·5	5·7	5·9	6·1	5·6
All manual workers	13 685	13 920	14 776	14 450	14 020	14 393	13 343	74·6	72·0	70·3	64·2	59·3	58·3	54·7
Total occupied population	18 350	19 332	21 024	22 515	23 639	24 686	24 370	100·0	100·0	100·0	100·0	100·0	100·0	100·0

SOURCE: Robert Price and George Sayers Bain, 'Union Growth Revisited: 1948–1974 in Perspective', *British Journal of Industrial Relations*, November 1976, p. 346.

are very difficult to assess, for at least three reasons. There is a lack of reliable data, at least until relatively recently: it was only in 1968 that the comprehensive official earnings survey of 1906 was repeated. Earnings figures alone, even if accurate, fail to indicate the total value of both financial and non-monetary benefits obtained from an employer (a point considered further below). And finally, there has been no even trend in relative pay during the present century. In the first half-century, percentage differences tended to reduce in periods of rising prices and wages, and to increase during years of recession. In the 1914–18 war and the short-lived post-war boom, wages were raised more promptly in response to prices than were salaries. But in the economic collapse of the early 1920s, wage-earners suffered drastic cuts while salaries remained relatively stable. During and for a few years after the 1939–45 war there occurred the most significant narrowing of earnings inequalities, in percentage terms, since the century began. But from the 1950s this trend was partially reversed, though there have been notable fluctuations in recent years.

The uneven pattern of movements in earnings is evident from Routh's detailed study of occupations and pay. Using a modified version of the census categories of 'occupational class' he indicates the relationship in seven different years between the average earnings of men and women in each group and average earnings of all employees (Table 1.2). While caution is necessary in interpreting these figures,[7] they show that the extent of any decline in white-collar income advantages will vary according to the 'base year' adopted. In very general terms, percentage differentials *widened* in the decade before 1922–4, and narrowed slightly in the following decade (perhaps reflecting a delayed pattern of salary reductions as the depression continued). The Second World War, like the first (partly because of rapid inflation) brought a considerable closing of differentials; but from the 1950s the trends have been fluctuating and uneven, with significant shifts within as well as between 'manual' and 'white-collar' incomes.

The variation in the experience of different salaried occupations is clear from Routh's table. Over the period of his study as a whole, male managers and forepersons have largely maintained, and females actually increased, their income advantages over 'manual' workers. Movements in the position of 'professional' groups are difficult to evaluate because of substantial changes in

TABLE 1.2 *Occupational class averages as percentages of the mean for all occupational classes, men and women*

	1913–14	1922–4	1935–6	1955–6	1960	1970	1978
Men							
1. Professional							
A. Higher	405	372	392	290	289	211	209
B. Lower	191	204	190	115	120	136	137
2B. Managers etc.	247	307	272	279	263	245	203
3. Clerks	122	116	119	98	97	97	93
4. Foremen	152	171	169	148	144	121	118
Manual							
5. Skilled	131	115	121	117	113	104	110
6. Semi-skilled	85	80	83	88	83	93	97
7. Unskilled	78	82	80	82	76	83	86
Men's average	116	114	115	119	120	123	121
Women							
1. Professional							
A. Higher	..	..	..	(218)	(217)	178	169
B. Lower	110	137	130	82	86	88	98
2B. Managers etc.	99	102	104	151	142	135	128
3. Clerks	56	68	61	60	61	61	69
4. Forewomen	70	98	96	90	86	73	81
Manual							
5. Skilled	54	56	53	60	56	49	57
6. Semi-skilled	62	63	62	51	48	47	59
7. Unskilled	35	47	45	43	40	44	57
Women's average	62	66	64	60	59	59	68

SOURCE: Guy Routh, *Occupation and Pay in Great Britain 1906–79* (Macmillan, 1980) p. 124.

the occupational composition of this category. The most clear-cut example of declining salary advantage is provided by male clerks, whose earnings were in line with those of skilled 'manual' workers until the Second World War but then fell substantially below. The very different experience of *female* clerks perhaps reflects the extent to which routine clerical employment has become 'women's work' – or merely a starting point for young males before promotion to more elevated status.

The most recent pattern of relative earnings can be obtained from the New Earnings Survey which is conducted annually. Table 1.3 shows the summary date from the 1980 survey. Overall there clearly remains a substantial differential between wage and salary levels, which would be considerably greater but for

TABLE 1.3 *Earnings distributions*

Employees whose pay was not affected by absence	Full-time men aged 21 and over		Full-time women aged 18 and over	
	Manual	Non-manual	Manual	Non-manual
Average gross weekly earnings of which:	£117·7	£141·3	£68·0	£82.7
overtime payments	£15·8	£4·9	£2·5	£1·0
PBR etc payments	£9·8	£3·7	£6·0	£0·7
shift etc premium payments	£3·7	£0·9	£1·4	£0·9
Distribution of gross weekly earnings:				
10 per cent earned less than	£71·8	£80·3	£45·6	£51·4
25 per cent earned less than	£86·3	£100·4	£53·8	£61·0
50 per cent earned less than	£105·0	£127·7	£64·7	£75·7
25 per cent earned more than	£129·0	£163·8	£78·1	£96·6
10 per cent earned more than	£156·7	£215·0	£92·9	£122·3
percentage earning less than £40	0·2	0·2	4·1	1·7
£45	0·4	0·3	9·1	4·0
£50	0·7	0·5	17·2	8·2
£60	2·9	1·8	39·2	23·0
£70	8·5	4·6	61·4	40·5
£80	17·6	9·8	77·5	56·3
£90	30·0	16·5	88·1	68·4
£100	43·3	24·6	93·3	77·5
£110	56·3	33·5	96·2	84·0
£120	67·3	43·1	97·7	89·1
£130	75·8	51·8	98·6	92·5
£150	87·5	67·3	99·3	96·9
£200	97·5	86·9	99·9	99·3
£300	99·7	97·4	100·0	99·9
Average weekly hours	45·4	38·8	39·6	36·7

SOURCE: *New Earnings Survey 1980* (HMSO, 1980) p. A5.

earnings supplements which 'manual' workers obtain from over-time, payment by results (PBR) and shift work. (Given the considerable disparity in hours worked, particularly by male employees, the average hourly earnings exhibit a much greater differential than weekly earnings.) But what is equally obvious is the wide spread of salary levels: the highest-paid 'non-manual' employees earn far more than the highest-paid 'manuals', whereas among the lowest-paid there is very little difference. Hence there is considerable overlap between wages and salaries.

In approximate terms, the higher-paid half of male 'manual' workers earn more than the bottom third of 'non-manuals', while the top third of 'manuals' earn more than the bottom half of the 'white-collar' category; and the same is true for women.

To some extent, similar conclusions may be drawn from comparisons of 'fringe benefits' and other conditions relating to employment. It is a commonplace that 'staff' have traditionally enjoyed advantageous terms and conditions of employment, but that in recent years there has occurred a certain equalization. Wedderburn and Craig indicate, on the basis of a survey conducted in 1968, the general disparity between 'operatives' and 'staff' in terms of occupational sickness and pension schemes; length of holidays and choice of holiday dates; and stringency of controls over time-keeping and attendance.[8] But they also point to evidence of 'differentiation within the non-manual strata. It is small in respect of the traditional fringe benefits, but there is a discernible break in respect of other items like period of notice, choice of holiday time and disciplinary measures.'[9] More recent trends, almost certainly, have further reduced the differentiation between 'manual' and routine 'white-collar' employees, but have probably accentuated the disparities between more and less favoured 'non-manual' groups.

A more detailed picture of of heterogeneity within the general category of 'non-manual' employment may be gained from the occupational breakdown in the New Earnings Survey, presented in Table 1.4. The contrast between the incomes of senior management and the established professions on the one hand, and routine clerical, technical and sales workers on the other, is readily apparent; it would appear even more starkly were the official categories to itemize some of the highest-paid occupations within which total employment is too small to present separately. What is also very clear is the pattern of sexual differentiation within 'white-collar work'. Of the seventy-five men's occupations listed, there are thirty-four in which average earnings are above those for male 'non-manual' workers as a whole; but in only three of these are enough women employed to achieve a separate record.[10] By contrast, women *do* appear for half of the occupational categories for which male salaries are below the average. There are eight occupations for which women but no men are listed (nursing auxiliaries, and seven clerical and related titles); in all cases, pay is below the average for 'non-manual' women.

TABLE 1.4   *Average earnings (£) of full-time 'non-manual' workers whose pay is unaffected by absence*

	Gross weekly earnings	10% earned below	10% earned above		Gross weekly earnings	10% earned below	10% earned above
MEN (21 AND OVER)				**Professional and related in science, engineering, technology and similar fields**	147·5	93·0	213·9
Professional and related supporting management and administration	167·7	98·2	255·1	Scientists and mathematicians	162·4	99·8	233·0
Company secretaries	(178·9)	107·3	264·3	Engineers—civil, structural, municipal	157·4	100·9	218·3
Accountants	157·1	90·6	234·1	Engineers—mechanical	160·1	113·5	225·9
Estimators, valuers, etc.	(139·5)	85·7	201·0	Engineers—electrical/electronic	165·2	108·8	236·2
Finance, insurance, tax, etc. specialists	209·6	116·0	330·4	Engineers—production	147·0	105·0	195·0
Personnel and industrial relations officers and managers	(185·5)	112·8	294·0	Engineers—planning, quality control	147·0	101·1	213·7
Work study, etc. officers	(155·2)	99·4	233·8	Engineers—other	160·0	98·3	229·4
Systems analysts, computer programmers	157·3	97·1	224·3	Metallurgists and other technologists	(150·7)	97·4	206·2
Marketing and sales managers and executives	183·2	112·6	266·5	Engineering and other draughtsmen	128·4	91·1	171·0
Advertising and public relations managers and executives	(171·4)	105·7	260·7	Laboratory technicians (scientific, medical)	112·0	74·7	162·4
Purchasing officers and buyers	(146·5)	91·1	229·7	Engineering technicians, etc.	132·3	96·3	168·3
Public health and other inspectors	150·5	92·4	224·8	Architects and town planners	(166·0)	103·0	242·7
General administrators—local government	(166·8)	117·6	232·3	Planning assistants and building, etc. technicians	122·6	83·9	160·7
				Quantity surveyors	(132·9)	77·4	200·2
Professional and related in education, welfare and health	139·6	86·2	201·0	Building, land and mining surveyors	(137·9)	80·7	200·4
University academic staff	(205·7)	126·7	291·3	Ships' officers	(178·1)	113·0	265·9
Teachers in establishments for further education	154·4	111·5	203·6	**Managerial (excluding general management)**	145·6	82·4	219·2
Secondary teachers	125·3	86·9	159·9	Production and works managers, works foremen	163·3	102·8	240·7
Primary teachers	123·5	87·1	161·0	Engineering maintenance managers	149·6	96·5	217·2
Other teachers	(125·8)	84·8	162·1	Site managers, clerks of works, general foremen (building and civil engineering)	140·0	96·5	199·8
Vocational/industrial trainers	139·4	99·0	185·8	Transport managers	146·2	91·1	209·7
Welfare workers	124·8	77·9	174·2	Warehousing, etc. managers	(128·4)	82·7	176·7
Medical practitioners	(242·2)	135·1	375·7	Office managers	169·1	97·1	251·6
Nurse administrators and executives	(144·0)	107·8	177·5	Managers—wholesale distribution	(140·7)	90·7	204·3
Registered and enrolled nurses, midwives	(97·8)	64·7	138·1	Managers—department store, supermarket, etc.	(121·9)	78·4	180·3
Literary, artistic and sports	148·6	82·7	238·4				
Journalists	(172·5)	105·5	272·0				
Industrial designers	(139·9)	90·4	199·4				

11

TABLE 1.4 – *continued*

	Gross weekly earnings	10% earned below	above		Gross weekly earnings	10% earned below	above
Branch managers of other shops	(112·9)	68·8	164·5	Security officers and detectives	(118·8)	77·3	177·2
Managers of independent shops (employees)	(98·3)	58·6	159·8	Security guards, patrolmen M	115·2	75·4	166·7
Hotel, catering, club or public house managers	98·7	60·1	153·4				
Police inspectors and above, fire service officers	(196·8)	141·1	267·7	**WOMEN (18 AND OVER)**			
				Professional and related supporting management and administration	121·6	73·7	173·4
Clerical and related	103·5	70·2	144·9	**Professional and related in education, welfare and health**	100·0	62·2	138·6
Supervisors of clerks	124·7	93·2	155·4	Teachers in establishments for further education	128·0	88·2	169·5
Costing and accounting clerks	93·1	65·9	123·8	Secondary teachers	109·8	79·4	146·1
Cash handling clerks	97·6	67·8	134·0	Primary teachers	106·7	78·7	134·1
Finance, insurance, etc. clerks	98·4	70·7	128·2	Other teachers	107·9	73·7	142·2
Production and materials controlling clerks	96·6	68·9	127·9	Welfare workers	99·1	59·9	140·8
Shipping and travel clerks	(104·0)	68·8	149·6	Nurse administrators and executives	121·8	95·1	147·9
Records and library clerks	91·2	64·1	126·2	Registered and enrolled nurses, midwives	82·2	58·9	115·8
General clerks and clerks not indicated elsewhere	96·3	69·7	131·0	Nursing auxiliaries and assistants	66.4	50·9	84·8
ADP processing equipment operators	(117·7)	78·5	163·5				
Telephonists	(104·3)	75·8	155·5	**Literary, artistic and sports**	(105·1)	53·3	166·8
Postmen, mail sorters, messengers M	105·5	70·1	157·2	**Professional and related in science, engineering, technology and similar fields**	97·5	63·4	142·8
				Laboratory technicians (scientific, medical)	85·3	61·9	113·5
Selling	113·1	65·7	163·0				
Sales supervisors	(112·2)	69·2	146·3	**Managerial (excluding general management)**	90·9	54·8	148·7
Salesmen, shop assistants, shelf fillers	(90·3)	52·1	137·3	Office managers	(113·9)	69·1	164·2
Roundsmen and van salesmen M	106·2	74·0	140·2	Branch managers of other shops	(77.2)	52·0	115·0
Technical sales representatives	128·8	86·5	181·9	Hotel, catering, club or public house managers	(75·4)	24·5	121·9
Sales representatives (wholesale goods)	109·3	72·4	148·9				
Other sales representatives and agents	(129·7)	75·0	191·8	**Clerical and related**	74·3	50·9	100·8
				Supervisors of clerks	103·0	67·2	135·7
Security and protective service	135·8	89·1	193·7	Costing and accounting clerks	72·2	50·2	97·1
Supervisors (police sergeants, fire fighting, etc.)	172·9	129·9	230·3	Cash handling clerks	71·8	51·4	93·4
Policemen (below sergeant) (public and private)	142·2	103·9	186·5	Finance, insurance, etc. clerks	72·8	48·9	100·1
Firemen (public and private)	118·4	94·2	144·2	Production and materials controlling clerks	69·6	50·8	92·0
Prison officers below principal officer	(191·7)	122·8	263·5				

TABLE 1.4 – *continued*

	Gross weekly earnings	*10% earned:*			*Gross weekly earnings*	*10% earned:*	
		below	*above*			*below*	*above*
Shipping and travel clerks	(76·5)	52·1	107·3	Key punch operators	77·0	56·6	102·8
Records and library clerks	69·9	52·8	88·8	ADP processing equipment operators	74·0	52·4	99·4
General clerks and clerks not identified elsewhere	72·0	50·1	94·8	Other office machine operators	(74·0)	53·9	95·6
Retail shop check-out, etc. operators	56·6	46·2	65·7	Telephonists	70·3	49·7	92·1
Receptionists	58·8	40·9	79·1	**Selling**	59·7	42·7	83·4
Secretaries, shorthand typists	80·2	55·6	107·4	Sales supervisors	72·7	56·1	97·4
Other typists	68·5	48·7	89·8	Saleswomen, shop assistants, shelf fillers	54·7	41·8	68·1
Calculating machine operators	68·0	52·8	86·6	**Security and protective service**	(105·7)	68·1	147·9

M = occupations officially classed as 'manual'.
( ) = data derived from small sample and must be used with caution.
SOURCE: *New Earnings Survey 1980* (HMSO, 1980) pp. A18–22.

The range of internal differentiation in pay and conditions, and the existence of a distinct category of lowly rewarded 'women's work', clearly cast doubt on the adequacy of the general category of 'white-collar employment' as a means of classifying occupations. This occupational heterogeneity sets the context for the reading in the following chapter, in which Bain and Price review attempts to offer a systematic basis for the conventional dichotomy. Echoing Mill's argument, they dismiss definitions which rest on the distinction between mental and manual labour. Not only does all work involve elements of both, but some 'white-collar' jobs (such as those of filing clerk or copy typist) demand less intellectual application than many skilled 'manual' occupations.

Efforts to identify the essence of 'white-collar' employment in functional terms (such as Croner's analysis in terms of administration, design, supervision and commerce) are likewise rejected. For these amorphous categories merely multiply the problems of definition, and can in practice establish the boundary around 'non-manual' work only on the basis of a set of arbitrary judgements. Distinctions in terms of work milieux are seen by some as a more promising basis for differentiation (the wearing of a white collar being seemingly dependent on a clean environment and congenial tasks); but here too the criterion fails to match sufficiently closely the conventional division between occupational types.

Bain and Price offer as their own definition of the essence of 'white-collar' employment the 'possession of, or proximity to, authority'. At the margins, such proximity may be purely symbolic: a cultural survival of work patterns and responsibilities which have long been superseded. Ambiguities in popular definitions of the boundaries of 'manual' and 'non-manual' work – mirrored in some of the official classifications – may themselves reflect the elasticity and imprecision of this criterion.

Emphasis on the ambiguity of specific occupational roles is a theme of many of the subsequent readings; but this in itself suggests a problem. For if many occupations are ambiguously placed in terms of authority, why is difficulty so *rarely* experienced in applying the conventional 'white-collar' label? Doubts arise as soon as the notion of 'proximity to authority' is probed. In what respects is a 'white-collar airline pilot closer to authority than a 'blue-collar' engine driver, a laboratory technician than a garage mechanic, a shop assistant than a factory storekeeper? If cultural lag is to explain such distinctions, one might expect popular usage of the 'non-manual' label to alter more regularly than is actually the case. And in any event, if popular terminology is to be regarded primarily as the residue of historical development, what is required is an explicitly historical focus on occupational categorization: a focus which Bain and Price do not provide.

Their conclusion might well be refined through attention to the sexually differentiated character of 'white-collar' employment. In the case of men, the term has indeed often denoted some involvement in the hierarchy of managerial control or in the exercise of state power. Otherwise it has tended to indicate some form of 'professional' competence,[11] or more modestly the application of specially cultivated intellectual skills (which in an era of restricted general education may have meant little more than simple literacy). In the case of women, by contrast, connotations of authority or intellect have normally been far weaker: a 'genteel' or 'respectable' work environment, sufficiently distinct from the traditional context of female drudgery in factory, farm or household, has provided a sufficient basis for 'white-collar' status.

A comprehensive elucidation of the historically emergent meanings of 'white-collar' would require an understanding of the complex interplay of state and managerial control, material

advantage, the criteria of social esteem and ideological legitimation, and the sexual division of labour. Only through a grasp of the
relevance of *all* these factors – which are discussed in many of the
subsequent readings, though often without sufficient attention to
their interrelationship – can the continuing practical and
ideological importance of the 'manual'/'non-manual' dichotomy
be fully understood.

In popular discourse, the distinction between 'manual' and
'non-manual' labour relates closely to that between working and
'middle' classes. Thus to investigate the coherence of the notion of
'white-collar', and to consider whether the conventional dichotomy rests on fundamental or merely superficial differences
within the labour force, is to confront implicitly the issue of class
structure. Indeed this concern is often explicit: as with Parkin,
who rests his whole analysis of power and inequality in modern
society on the premise of a 'class boundary line between the blue-
collar and white-collar categories'.[12] To stress the material
importance of the division between 'white' and 'blue' collars is
thus normally to insist that the twentieth-century expansion in
clerical, technical and supervisory occupations entails that the
working class as such has declined numerically and continues to
dwindle; and that the 'middle-class' status of roughly half the
working population carries with it a necessary commitment to the
existing social and economic order.

This issue is central to most authors represented in Part I of this
book. Underlying much of their argument are the classic controversies between and within the theories of class derived from
Marx and Weber. An explicit, though necessarily brief consideration of the Marxian and Weberian perspectives must
therefore precede a review of the readings contained in Chapters 3
to 7.

Etymologically, the notion of class is directly linked to that of
classification: classes were the categories within which the ancient
Romans were enumerated for census purposes. Such classification
involved no necessary theory or assumptions concerning the
relationship between those assigned to different categories; and in
this respect, the notions of social class applied by the Registrar
General (as well as many modern sociologists) follow a venerable
tradition. But there is also a significantly different tradition of
class analysis which derives from the industrial revolution. The
rise of capitalist manufacture exerted a profound influence on

both the structure and the language of class. Feudal society had been founded on a relatively stable differentiation between nobility, gentry, freemen and serfs; the industrial revolution was built upon the mutual but unequal interdependence of the new classes of capitalists and propertyless wage-labourers. The stark interrelationship of class, property and power stimulated·a new usage of the terminology of class: at one and the same time a product and a projected explanation of the new and explosive social conflicts.

While an explicit association between class and conflict became a widespread element in the terminology of popular politics,[13] it was Marx who presented class anatagonism as the fundamental principle of social theory. 'The history of all hitherto existing society',·wrote Marx and Engels in the Communist Manifesto, 'is the history of class struggles.'[14] The argument in this famous programmatic statement was that capitalist expansion was increasingly displacing the traditional classes, creating instead a polarization into 'two great hostile camps': the working class or proletariat, and the capitalist class or bourgeoisie. The clearer this fundamental division, the more would workers recognise their common class identity and the systematic opposition between their interests and those of the bourgeoisie, transforming existing intermittent and fragmented social conflicts into a revolutionary class struggle.

In more general and theoretical terms, three propositions are central to Marx's conception of class. The first is that social relations within *production* are the most fundamental determinant of class structure. The second is that classes derive their definition and identity from the *relationships* between them: a class is not a self-contained entity, to be understood in terms of its internal characteristics alone. The third is that the relationship of *antagonism* between classes is the most important motor of social transformation, and the underlying explanation of the structure of social institutions existing at any given point of time. Yet while an emphasis on class pervades the whole of Marx's work, at no point did he elaborate systematically a generalized theory of class; and there are important variations in his approach when confronting different practical and interpretative issues.[15] Though his most familiar argument is that of a dichotomy of classes, he refers elsewhere to the 'three great classes of modern society': wage-labourers, capitalists and landowners;[16] while in his detailed analyses of economic and political struggles he often refers to a multiplicity of classes. This is partly because his model of capitalist production, as a pure socio-economic form, is an abstraction from the far greater complexity of empirical reality; accordingly, there will inevitably exist subsidiary groups or classes, not unambiguously related to either of the 'two great hostile camps', whose role in particular periods of social or political upheaval may exert a critical influence upon events. What is clear, however, is that an approach which defines class primarily in terms of antagonistic production relations cannot make use, except in the loosest of senses, of the notion of 'middle class'.[17]

Significantly, in his references to the emergent growth of 'white-collar' occupations Marx seeks to locate their functions within the dichotomous model of production relations. This is clear from his discussion of the role of clerks within capitalist production. As capitalism expands, he argues, there is a consequential increase in the amount of activity devoted to the *realization* of value rather than its production.[18] Office work, insignificant in the earliest phase of capitalist industry, becomes much more important, necessitating 'the employment of commercial wage-workers who make up the actual office staff'. These employees do not stand in precisely the same relationship to capital as ordinary workers, for they do not produce surplus value. There are nevertheless significant affinities, for the clerk 'adds to the capitalist's income by helping him to reduce the cost of realizing surplus-value'. To the extent that clerks save the capitalist more than the cost of their own salaries they perform unpaid labour even though they do not produce surplus value; and this 'in effect, amounts to the same thing with respect to his capital. It is, therefore, a source of profit to him.'[19]

In considering the level of clerical salaries, Marx points to parallels with the wages of other workers. 'The commercial worker, in the strict sense of the term, belongs to the better-paid class of wage-workers – to those whose labour is classed as skilled and stands above average labour.' As with skill differentials more generally,[20] the 'advance of the capitalist mode of production' would inevitably undermine such advantages. On the one hand, employers would subdivide and simplify office tasks in order to reduce the skill content; on the other, the spread of public education undermined the scarcity value of literacy.[21] Hence the differences in income and job content which gave clerks the appearance of a separate class were the transitory effects of a temporary phase of capitalist development: in the long term, their fate involved assimilation within the working class.

In the case of supervisory staff, Marx's analysis points to an opposite tendency. Any large-scale productive operation involving the co-operation of numerous workers, Marx suggests, requires some 'directing authority': 'a single violin player is his own conductor; an orchestra requires a separate one'.[22] But under capitalism this function of co-ordinating collective effort assumes a coercive character; for the employer's pressure to extract the maximum surplus from the workforce provokes resistance which can be contained only by an elaborate system of discipline and control. Thus a hierarchy of management arises: 'an industrial army of workers under the command of a capitalist requires, like a real army, officers (managers) and N.C.O.s (foremen, overseers), who command during the labour process in the name of capital. The work of supervision becomes their established and exclusive function.'[23] With the diffusion of share ownership in the modern limited company, Marx noted later, the salaried manager who administered the capital owned by others became the 'actually functioning capitalist'.[24] For Marx, then, the 'special kind of wage-labourer' charged with controlling the labours of others was only in a purely formal sense a worker; in reality he was part of the capitalist class.

Actual developments since Marx wrote have of course proved far more problematic than the simple polarization thesis implies. Within the 'manual' labour force the trend in skill composition is a contentious question: for while many traditional crafts have disappeared or have lost much of their technical complexity (and hence have become relatively lower paid), new skills have also arisen. Though many of the arguments which posit an overall 'upskilling' of the labour force seem highly exaggerated, it could be suggested that the fairly stark dichotomy of craftsmen and labourers which existed a century ago has given way to a much more differentiated hierarchy of skill levels and wage relationships. Meanwhile the growth of 'white-collar' employment has increased the complexities; for while the salary data presented earlier show that many 'non-manuals' are in income terms no better placed than 'average labour', the majority retain significant advantages. It is no less clear that even small distinctions in the material position of different occupational groups can exert substantial influence on subjective perceptions of identity and interests, leading to conflict and division rather than class unity.

Such factors have encouraged sociological attempts to interpret class in much more differentiated terms than Marx; and to emphasize the processes whereby 'objective' class position may be overlaid by less tangible social definitions. Both of these considerations were central to the theses on class and status set out by Weber.[25] In his view, class was definable by 'the typical probability of 1. procuring goods 2. gaining a position in life and 3. finding inner satisfactions, a probability which derives from the relative control over goods and skills and from their income-producing uses within a given economic order'.[26] Like Marx he pointed to a basic division between the propertied and the propertyless, but he also stressed the importance of differences *within* each group. Life chances – and hence class situation – would vary according to the different types of property that owners possessed, and also according to the different kinds of services which those without property could offer on the labour market. Thus class structure was not a simple dichotomy but rather was highly differentiated.

Weber went on to argue that class position provided no *necessary* basis for collective action: whether or not members of a class recognized common interests and acted upon these was 'linked to general cultural conditions, especially to those of an intellectual sort'.[27] More universally the source of conscious common identity was 'status groups', defined in terms of 'a specific, positive or negative, social estimation of *honour*' and associated with 'a specific *style of life*'.[28]

Weberian categories and arguments have proved a valuable resource for sociologists whose central focus has been the complexity of modern class relations: not least because the brevity of Weber's own discussion allows considerable scope for interpretation; and also because, in the political climate in which academic sociology expanded, Weber represented a more respectable intellectual authority than Marx. In fact in would be misleading to regard Weber's analysis as wholly contrary to that of Marx. Despite the importance of status as against class in Weber's general analysis, he comments – in a phrase which calls to mind Marx's diagnosis of the dynamism of capitalist accumulation – that 'every technological repercussion and economic transformation threatens stratification by status and pushes the class situation into the foreground'.[29] And again, while denying any universal connection between class and social conflict, he identified the 'class situation of the modern "proletariat"' as characteristic of circumstances in which the transparent connection between life chances and the existing economic order engendered class consciousness and action. There are thus close parallels between Weber's *specific* remarks on the role of class within capitalist society, and Marx's view of the development of class struggle.

Yet while both stress the importance of economic-based class relations within capitalism, there are crucial divergences in their conceptions of class formation. As Crompton and Gubbay put it: 'Weberian theory focuses on the way in which societal rewards are *acquired*, and the manner in which patterns of acquisition are determined by the market. Marx's theory focuses on the manner in which new values are *created*, and the social relationships arising out of and sustaining this process.'[30] For Weber, conflicts of interest arose, not within production but in the labour market: capitalism had directed collective action 'toward price wars on the labor market . . . . Today the central issue is the determination of the price of labour.'[31] For Marx by contrast, the wages struggle, while important, was only a subsidiary manifestation of the antagonism between labour and capital and would assume a diminishing significance with the maturation of class conflict. It is moreover noteworthy that Marx himself identified the fundamental weakness of any definition of class on purely market criteria: because of the 'infinite fragmentation of interest and rank into which the division of social labour splits labourers as well as capitalists and landlords', any attempt to relate class to the 'identity of revenues and sources of revenues' would imply the existence of an infinity of classes.[32]

This was a problem to which Weber could offer no theoretically coherent solution. He recognized that, given an equation of class and market situation, 'a *uniform* class situation prevails only when completely unskilled and propertyless persons are dependent upon irregular employment'.[33] But to impose some order on the multiplicity of skills, qualifications, experience and aptitudes which most employees brought to the labour market he was forced to rely on the conventional categories of everyday discourse. Thus ordinary labourers are differentiated in the familiar terms of skilled, semi-skilled and unskilled; more generally Weber writes that 'social classes are a) the working class as a whole – the more so, the more automated the work process becomes, b) the petty bourgeoisie, c) the propertyless intelligentsia and specialists (technicians, various kinds of white-collar employees, civil servants – possibly with considerable social differences depending on the cost of their training), d) the classes privileged through property and education'.[34] 'White-collar employees' are thus explicitly excluded from the working class; but Weber offers no serious explanation of this definition of class boundaries.[35]

Ironically, then, while Weberian analysis is commonly presented as more refined and sophisticated than that of Marx,[36] the reduction of class to market relations is crude and theoretically sterile by comparison with an approach which encompasses production relations. Some more recent writers have accordingly sought to sharpen the analytical focus by incorporating other elements of Weberian sociology. Thus Dahrendorf presents a dichotomous schema of class formation in which the key determinant is possession of or subjection to authority; in this model, which again excludes *production* relations from the analysis, 'salaried employees who occupy positions that are part of a bureaucratic hierarchy' are all part of the ruling class, while all others are part of the working class.[37] Other writers have sought to emphasize the continuing importance of status as against class in contemporary social relations. Paradoxically, too, some aspiring defenders of Marxist orthodoxy have in practice fallen victim to the limitations of the Weberian approach: accepting the definition of class in terms essentially of market relations, but arguing that on the evidence of the reward structure many of those classed as 'white-collar' should be viewed as tendentially members of the working class.

There are perhaps elements of this tendency in Klingender's classic analysis of clerical labour in Britain, extracts from which introduce Chapter 3. Writing in the context of the world economic crisis of the 1930s, and the rise of fascist parties whose support was commonly believed to derive disproportionately from the ranks of 'white-collar' employees, his arguments were designed to inform the political strategy of the labour movement. The basic thesis, outlined in the book's introduction, was that changes in the material situation of the 'intermediate strata' of employment had eroded many of their objective differentiations from the traditional working class; but that this 'proletarianization', at least in the short term, was a source of volatility in their social and political identity.

Starting from the remarks in Marx's *Capital* on 'commercial labour' which have already been cited, Klingender points to the 1870 Education Act as undermining the scarcity value of the literary skills on which high clerical salaries formerly rested. By the end of the century, he argues, clerks earned roughly the same as skilled 'manual' workers. Concurrently there took place a second key development: the rapid expansion in the size of the clerical labour force and the radical alteration in its structure. Women were rapidly recruited into what was traditionally a male preserve, and among both sexes employment became heavily weighted towards the younger age groups. These changes signified an important dilution of skills: the rise of large modern offices allowed the subdivision and simplification of tasks, while the typewriter was of central importance in the feminization of clerical work.[38] Finally the inter-war economic crisis brought a further relative decline in clerical salaries,[39] while at the same time destroying the security of employment traditionally enjoyed by 'white-collar' staff. This objective proletarianization attracted some to the disparate politics of right-wing reaction, but also offered a rational basis for common action with the traditional working class.

The theme of proletarianization has figured prominently in much of the subsequent literature, with neo-Weberian analysts typically disputing Klingender's conclusion. Lockwood's study is in many respects the most systematic of such challenges. His book is subtitled 'a study in class consciousness', and its central concern is to elucidate 'why there should be a divergence in the class awareness of clerks and manual workers'. The starting point is the proposition that clerical workers *do* exhibit distinctive attitudes towards their employers, trade unions, and political affairs; and an explanation for this specificity is sought in objective differences in their socio-economic circumstances.

Lockwood's discussion (of which the extract in this reader forms the conclusions) is organized around a distinction between market, work and status situations. In his discussion of the labour market, Lockwood insists that the income advantages of clerical workers are far from wholly eroded, and points to a range of 'fringe benefits' as reinforcing their economic privileges. But he suggests that even more important differentiations derive from the organization of work itself. Clerks traditionally worked in small units and in close contact with their employers, who typically offered salary and career advancement as rewards for individual initiative and 'loyalty'. Though large-scale, bureaucratically administered modern offices have adversely affected work autonomy and career opportunities, Lockwood stresses that most clerical functions remain physically segregated from production activities, and argues that their work milieu and consequential social relations inhibit clerks from identifying their position and interests with those of manual labour. Thus real differences in class position interact with the traditional differentiation of status associated with popular notions of 'white-collar' employment. Even if changes in the nature of clerical work have attenuated some of the former claims to social prestige, the longstanding status distinction remains far from obsolete.

Lockwood claims to synthesize the theoretical insights of Marx and Weber, suggesting that the dual categories of market and work situation subsume 'what Marx essentially understood as "class position"'. This is, to say the least, debatable. As suggested above, the key focus on *market* relations as a determinant of class derives from Weber rather than Marx; and in his discussion of 'work situation', Lockwood is concerned with a range of discrete elements in work conditions rather than with the nature and dynamics of the *capitalist labour process* – the theme of many of the subsequent writers in this book. It is significant that the notion of 'bureaucratization', which carries much analytical weight in Lockwood's account of changes in the nature of clerical work, is a concept crucial for Weber's theory of modern social development which is in no way located within an analysis of the dynamics of the capitalist enterprise and of contemporary production relations.[40] And indeed Lockwood's very usage of the term 'class situation' is significant; for fundamental to Marx's approach in all his writings is the view that class is not an attribute intrinsic to the 'position' of any given group, but is rather a concomitant of the *relationship between social groups*.

There are interesting parallels between Lockwood's *Blackcoated Worker* and the slightly earlier study by C. Wright Mills, whose assessment of changes in American occupational structure also sought to combine the approaches of Marx and Weber. Mills notes that the proportion of the nineteenth-century labour force represented by industrial wage-earners was much smaller in the

United States than in Britain, and that conversely there were far more farmers, self-employed and small entrepreneurs: the 'old middle class'. In the present century this latter group has declined substantially, while there has been a particularly rapid growth of salaried occupations and of employment in 'service' industries: what Mills terms the 'new middle class'.

Unlike the old, the new 'middle class' is formed of essentially propertyless employees; in this one respect there is no difference from 'manual' labour. But applying the Weberian notion of market-derived life chances, Mills insists that the class position of the two categories is significantly different – even though the differences may recently have narrowed somewhat. He goes on to argue that many 'white-collar' employees are distinguished by the power over others which they exercise in the course of their work. (Mills is careful to emphasize the need to differentiate in this respect *within* the loose category of 'white-collar' labour; in particular he stresses that *female* 'non-manuals' are almost invariably in a position of subordination.)

Like Lockwood, Mills adds that status considerations reinforce 'objective' differences between occupational groups; but in a later section of his book he argues that 'every basis on which the prestige claims of the bulk of the white-collar employees have traditionally rested has been declining in firmness and stability'. In a passage which recalls Klingender's notion of the volatility of 'proletarianized' clerks, Mills coins the expression 'status panic' to indicate the contradictory responses to the loss of many of the traditional accoutrements of social superiority.

These early studies sought to establish how far the traditional distinctiveness of 'white-collar' (and especially clerical) employment had been eliminated by changes in the first part of the present century. But if Klingender's view of the clerk as proletarian was premature, what conclusions should be drawn from the more recent trends in those developments to which he pointed: feminization, mechanization, subdivision of tasks and the closure of promotion opportunities? And looking to the future, what will be the consequences of the 'new technology' for these occupations? The study by Counter Information Services summarizes some of the implications for office work of recent advances in microelectronics. The vision of the automated office has been so frequently, but misleadingly depicted by modern writers[41] that today the notion of rapid and radical transformation invites a certain scepticism. Yet there are at least three reasons for suspending disbelief. The first is that a *combination* of technical advances in the areas of computerization, word-processing and telecommunications offers scope for a degree of 'rationalization' of 'white-collar' labour which none of these developments alone would entail. Secondly, the miniaturization of electronic components has increased the capacity and reduced the cost of automated systems to an extent which offers employers considerable economies through the displacement of labour. And thirdly, a climate of financial crisis induces both private corporations and public agencies to adopt drastic strategies to reverse the expansion in the size and cost of 'white-collar' labour.[42]

American experience is commonly regarded as a pointer for other western capitalist economies, and post-war trends in office work in the United States may thus prove prototypical. The collective study *Work in America*, commissioned by the Secretary of Health, Education and Welfare in the Nixon administration, offers a popularly oriented account which is clearly influenced by the vogue for discussion of the 'quality of working life'. It points to a continuing decline in the relative pay, status, security and job satisfaction of routine 'non-manual' employees, arguing that in many respects their position is inferior to that of factory workers, with whose work their own tasks bear increasing resemblance.

It is significant that Braverman, in his exposition of the theme that capitalism tends constantly to degrade and de-skill occupations requiring special expertise or experience, devotes a separate chapter to clerical workers. New techniques and organizational structures, he argues, have polarized office employment. Some new positions of skill and authority have been established (at least temporarily) for a privileged minority; but the large majority now represents 'an immense mass of *wage-workers* [which] has lost all former superiorities over workers in industry'. Hence 'the traditional distinctions between "manual" and "white-collar" labor, which are so thoughtlessly and widely used in the literature on this subject, represent echoes of a past situation which has virtually ceased to have meaning in the modern world of work'.[43]

Some objections to this thesis are raised by Giddens in the extract discussed below. More generally, it should be noted that Braverman's whole study abdicates analysis of the relationship between workers' material location within capitalist production, and their subjective consciousness of identity and interests. He is thus unable to confront the Weberian argument that 'class' and 'status' hierarchies function independently, and that subjective considerations of prestige may therefore exert a persistent influence on the social orientations of those conventionally classified as 'white-collar'.

If recent capitalist development has indeed been notable for generating new differentiations *within* 'non-manual' employment, the role of technically qualified staff in science-based production exemplifies this tendency admirably; and discussions around this theme provide the content of Chapter 5. A useful introduction is Galbraith's famous stress on the *collective* character of technically informed decision-making in modern large-scale organizations. The range and complexity of modern science and technology, the need for long-term planning, and the sheer quantity of information to be assimilated, all require the articulation of a complex network of communication, discussion and decision. This network, for which Galbraith suggests the name 'techno-structure', is in his view of paramount importance for the functioning of modern capitalism.

Galbraith's argument, with its emphasis on the power of corporate decision-makers to manipulate the market and evade the control of shareholders, is in some respects reminiscent of the thesis of the 'managerial revolution' popular some decades earlier.[44] But in other respects it anticipates a more recent argument: that knowledge itself, rather than human labour, has become the main productive force; and hence that 'the new dominant class is defined by knowledge and a certain level of education'.[45] As is the case with many popular expositions of the thesis of 'post-industrialism', Galbraith's treatment of relations of *production* is somewhat elusive: his focus is on decisions *about* production rather than production itself. But it if is to be plausibly argued that economic relations have been radically transformed, two types of issue require detailed analysis. On the one hand, what are the various *labour processes* engendered within technically advanced economies, and what distinctive identities and interests adhere to those who perform them? And on the other, in what ways is technical knowledge objectified in the means of production, and how do the dynamics of capital accumulation influence the *applications* of advanced technology and shape the policy decisions of modern corporate management?[46]

Such questions are central to Mallet's famous study, from which the present reader draws its title. In what is in essence a combination of discursive analysis and individual case studies, Mallet's principal argument is that technically qualified labour – whose work often straddles the conventional 'manual'/'white-collar' division – represents a 'new working class' with a radical potential to fulfil the historic role assigned by Marx to the factory proletariat.

Unlike the authors considered previously, Mallet treats relations of production as central to his whole argument. The development of modern industry has in his view rendered obsolete conventional notions of what constitutes the working class; today the only acceptable criterion is whether an occupation 'performs a productive function' while being separated from the actual direction of the production process. In these terms, there is no serious difference between process operators in automated industries (officially classified as manual labour) and 'white-collar' technicians in large, factory-like research units. Both are potentially revolutionary groups, insists Mallet: not in the traditional sense of overturning the whole existing social order, but because the degree of their engagement with and understanding of the modern production system leads them to question the irrational dynamic of profit and the hierarchical powers of management. Their consequent pressure for collective control by producers themselves challenges capital at its most vulnerable point.

Much subsequent writing has involved a critical engagement with Mallet's theses. Some writers are concerned primarily with the empirical basis of his conclusions; others with the meaning and application of his criteria of class. How does one differentiate between productive and unproductive labour (a focal issue in many of the readings which follow)? And how determine whether, or which, members of the technically qualified strata perform directive functions?

Gorz takes up this latter theme, stressing the ambiguous role of technical experts and suggesting three main reasons for responding cautiously to Mallet's argument. First, technical expertise may be a subsidiary and legitimizing aspect of occupational roles characterized primarily by control over subordinates. Secondly, the value of specialized competence is itself a product of a hierarchically divided social and educational system, and 'scientific experts' thus have a vested interest in perpetuating their privileged knowledge. Thirdly, scientific education and training involve a socializing process which leads technicians to view themselves as superior to ordinary workers. Hence the collective struggles of such groups are 'profoundly ambiguous'. Often reacting against the erosion of their privileges, 'they rebel not *as* proletarians, but against being *treated* as proletarians'.

The second brief extract from *Work in America* reinforces this point. Discontent is increasingly apparent even at senior levels of modern corporate management. It would be extravagant, however, to interpret insecurity, unease, or even the pursuit of collective protection against corporate rationalization[47] as evidence of the spread of 'proletarianization' up the management hierarchy. Yet how *are* such phenomena to be interpreted? The Special Task Force does not attempt to explain, while Gorz fails to draw out the implications of his own analysis. Is it always clear in which circumstances scientific and technical staff 'supervise, organize, control and command' other workers? Is their 'superiority' within the organization primarily a reflection of subjective values and identities, or of real differences in their relationship to capital? And if collective action by such staff seeks to preserve their own advantage rather than to abolish capitalist relations of production, are they acting very differently from skilled 'manual' workers who strike to protect traditional wage differentials and defend their job autonomy?

Mandel approaches this problem by discussing the development of capitalist production itself, arguing that 'the immediate needs of late capitalist technology' entail the direct involvement of scientific labour within the production process. The expansion of scientific education and research would be viewed as a direct response to trends within the sphere of production. Those specialized staff who are integrated into the production process are indeed subject to proletarianizing tendencies: reduction of income advantages, subdivision and simplification of functions, loss of job autonomy. But when 'intellectually qualified labour' is involved in the hierarchy of capitalist control, or the oppressive apparatus of the state, it is less subject to such tendencies and occupies a different class position. Unfortunately, Mandel too offers no clear criteria to distinguish groups performing productive functions from those sustaining capitalist control. And he appears to make the rash assumption that there are few occupations which perform *both* functions (or neither) and hence whose class position is ambiguous.

The whole argument that technical staff whose functions accord with the criteria of Mallet or Mandel will *act* as a new working class is challenged in Mann's review of the debate. Much of the literature which asserts the potentially vanguard role of these occupational groups focuses on the experience of the struggles in France in May 1968. But Mann questions whether the 'radical' demands and actions of these groups possessed genuine revolutionary or anti-capitalist connotations; in general they reflected a technocratic viewpoint. Mann suggests that the militancy of technicians and '*cadres*' owed much to the specific rigidity of the French managerial structure (and hence the lack of promotion opportunities), rather than to the general characteristics of their productive status.

Whatever view is taken of this controversy, it should be stressed that scientifically trained production staff remain a very small (even if fast growing) proportion of the modern labour force. Numerically far more significant has been the growth of what is commonly termed the 'tertiary' sector of employment. Throughout the advanced economies, the 'primary' sector of agriculture and extractive industries has declined dramatically during the past century and continues to shrink. More recently there has occurred a fall in the relative (and in some countries absolute) numbers employed in manufacturing industries. The modern growth sector, by contrast, involves what are conventionally, but often misleadingly, termed 'service' industries and occupations.[48]

Braverman analyses this expansion as the absorption within capitalist production of a wide variety of activities traditionally performed outside the sphere of market relations. Such functions as cleaning, cooking and child care, which were once almost invariably carried out as unpaid household labour (or else by hired domestic servants), have increasingly become transformed into commodities, provided at a price by capitalist organizations.[49] Yet in the process, *service* has ceased to be the dominant motive for these activities: workers are hired to perform 'services' primarily because capital can derive profit from their labour. For this very reason, the conventional distinction between the production of goods and services is of little significance; and indeed the demarcation is often virtually impossible to draw in practice. Far from 'service' workers constituting a new and more emancipated category of labour, their subordination to the priorities of capital exactly parallels that of traditional employees. Indeed a particularly high proportion of such occupations involve low wages, uncongenial working conditions, and little or no recognized skill. The notion of 'service' provides an ideological gloss to positions whose inferior social status is indicated by predominantly female employment.

Mandel seeks to explore more systematically the different types of 'service' activities. In particular he examines services produced for capitalist enterprises rather than private consumers: for example, much of the activity of transport and commercial undertakings. The rapid expansion of such employment reflects in his view a fundamental contradiction between the increase in useful production made possible by modern science and technology, and the constraints imposed by a capitalist economic structure. Two developments receive emphasis: the search by capital for new commodities to produce for profit; and the elaboration of intermediate processes to help realize the surplus from what is produced. These two developments have become so intertwined that it is often difficult, in Mandel's view, to determine which activities are productive or unproductive in the Marxist sense (a problem discussed further below).

The readings considered so far have in the main comprised short extracts with a focus on particular occupational groups. Many of the items in Chapter 7 are longer, and wider ranging in their interpretative aspirations. The issues set out in the previous discussion of Marx and Weber form a constant point of reference for these authors.

Giddens offers a partial synthesis of the two classic approaches, while proposing a number of concepts and theses of his own. He stresses the difficulty of constructing any *general* theory of 'white-collar' labour; from a Weberian perspective, the market position of professional, technical or managerial groups is very different from that of routine clerical or sales workers. Challenging notions of a general tendency to 'white-collar proletarianization', he argues that the erosion of economic advantages has primarily affected these latter occupational groups – who are mainly female. But most male 'white-collar' employees are part of a privileged managerial hierarchy, and are so regarded by most 'manual' workers.

In broad outline, much of Giddens's analysis follows the largely

Weberian approach of Lockwood in his study of clerks. But he refines the latter's notion of 'work situation' through an examination of the division of labour within production, and in particular what he terms 'paratechnical' relations (those relationships among workers generated by a given technical organization of work activities). Taking such factors into account reveals important differentiations between groups which are similarly placed in labour market terms, thus accentuating the difficulty of identifying the class position of any 'white-collar' occupation.[50]

The second extract from Braverman's *Labor and Monopoly Capital* examines what he terms the 'middle layers' of employment: the technical, professional and lower managerial staff who together account for almost one in five of the American labour force. The fact that they are 'propertyless' wage-earners does not in itself make them part of the working class: otherwise top corporate management – whose employee status is merely the modern guise of traditional capitalist functions – would be working class too. The problem stems from the existence of a 'range of intermediate categories, sharing the characteristics of worker on the one side and manager on the other in varying degrees'. Quoting E. P. Thompson's eloquent thesis that 'class is a relationship, and not a thing',[51] he concludes that it is neither possible nor necessary to offer a precise or fixed definition of the class position of such employees.

A clear corollary of this argument is that the 'middle layers' do not constitute a distinct class, but are located ambivalently between the two main class groupings in capitalist society. Thus Braverman employs the term 'middle class' only in quotation marks. The four following writers, despite major differences of approach, all insist by contrast that these intermediate occupations (or certain of them) *should* be regarded as a distinctive class. Urry is perhaps the most cautious of the four. Marxist analysis, he argues, identifies two and only two functions within capitalist production: those of capital and of labour. But individuals and groups need not be unambiguously involved in the performance of one function alone. The managerial occupations whose rise reflects the dissociation within modern capitalism between legal ownership of the means of production and direction of the production process constitute a substantial intermediate class, *partially* involved in performing the capitalist function. It is unclear from Urry's analysis why this group should be regarded as a distinctive class, rather than one component of an internally differentiated capitalist class.

Most Marxist writing considered so far gives only cursory attention to occupations outside the sphere of capitalist production itself. Such employment is central to the notion of a professional-managerial class proposed by the Ehrenreichs. Class, they argue, must be defined in terms both of a common relationship to the process of social production, and of a common experience in private life. The persistence of capitalism depends not only on the accumulation of surplus value within productive industry, but also on the 'reproduction of capitalist culture and capitalist class relations' within everyday life. This in turn depends on a network of agencies and institutions, employing administrators and professionals whose function is necessarily repressive. Since they do not directly control the exploitation of workers' labour power they do not form part of the ruling class; nevertheless the interests of this expanding group of employees are 'objectively antagonistic' to those of workers.

The Ehrenreichs note the internal diversity of this group: no clear boundaries divide it from the working or ruling classes. It is possible to ask – as with Urry's analysis – whether the authors satisfactorily demonstrate how and why the occupations discussed constitute, on their own definition, a separate class. In what is admittedly an exploratory essay, they do little to clarify the imprecise notions of 'professional' and 'managerial' employment, and hence to elucidate the concept of a professional-managerial class. It is unclear whether the diagnosis of an antagonism of interests to the working class rests primarily on the *function of institutions* within which professionals and managers are employed, or on the specific role which they perform *within* these institutions. If the former, then even the most routine and subordinate employees of these institutions fall within the boundaries of the professional-managerial class: a conclusion which the authors surely do not intend. But if the latter, an explicit analysis is required of the 'relations of production' within schools, newspapers, advertising agencies, television companies, police forces, social work departments and so on; whereas there is a notable absence of discussion of the division of labour within these institutions and of the labour processes of different occupational groups. Moreover, the argument seems to rest on an unproblematic conception of ideology and culture: do all books, poems, theories, newspapers or lectures merely and necessarily consolidate bourgeois class relations? And the functional integration of institutions within capitalist society is likewise assumed to be uncontradictory: is it not possible that educational or welfare institutions may in part encourage working-class assertiveness? To admit the possibility that 'radical social work', for example, can be more than an illusion would seem to challenge the theoretical foundations of the notion of a professional-managerial class.[52]

The two following readings are both cast within the 'structuralist' approach to Marxist analysis associated particularly with the work of Althusser (though both writers differ in significant respects from his theoretical position). While this is not the place to pursue broad controversies concerning the nature and validity of Althusserian analysis,[53] some comments may help to introduce what would otherwise appear as obscurities in the texts. A crucial premise is the relative autonomy of what such writers term 'theoretical practice': intellectual analysis cannot proceed by means of a direct and unmediated relationship with empirical reality, but must be framed within a body of concepts and assumptions. An argument or theory always reflects a distinctive analytical structure, or 'problematic': a specific focus on reality which poses certain issues for consideration and not others, and entails that the answers to the questions which *are* posed will assume a given form and character. A 'social formation' – the overall social structure at a given historical moment – can be examined at a variety of different levels (or 'instances'): economic, political, ideological; and the categories and propositions appropriate for analysis at one level are not necessarily applicable at another.

This methodological premise encourages a preoccupation with elaborating and defining concepts and their theoretical inter-relationships, often with minimal concern for the evidence of the 'real world'. Thus many critics accuse 'structuralists' of a sterile and jargon-ridden scholasticism. The latter typically respond that such criticism betrays a failure to differentiate between empirical description and theoretical analysis. Thus Poulantzas, in a famous debate with Miliband, has insisted that such categories as class, capitalism or surplus value cannot be simply derived from or reduced to the evidence of patterns of interpersonal relations within society. He insists on the necessity of 'comprehending social classes and the State as *objective structures*, and their relations as an *objective system of regular connections*, a structure and system whose agents, "men", are in the words of Marx, "bearers" of it'.[54] An analysis of 'positions' within this objective structure involves very different issues (a distinctive 'problematic'), in particular as regards susceptibility to empirical validation, from an analysis of the actual behaviour of 'agents' who occupy these positions. This distinction (which raises a host of complex methodological and epistemological issues) is of crucial importance for the discussion by both Poulantzas and Carchedi of the class position of various 'white-collar' groups.

Poulantzas writes with an explicit political purpose: as he states in his Foreword, 'today it is more than ever the case that an essential component of revolutionary strategy consists in knowing the enemy well, and in being able to establish correct alliances'. Highly critical of what he regards as the opportunism of the French Communist Party, he insists that a detailed analysis of the function and interests of 'the so-called "new middle strata"' must precede any principled decision on the nature and limits of an alliance between the workers' movement and such groups.

Like many of the previous authors, Poulantzas begins by insisting that ownership/non-ownership of the means of production is an insufficient criterion for class analysis;[55] it is essential in addition to establish whether a position involves performing productive labour. At first sight, this provides a definition of the working class which coincides with that of Mallet: 'performing a productive function and being excluded from the ownership or direction of the instruments of production'. But as Mandel indicates, while the notion of productive labour is of key importance in Marxist economic theory its meaning is ambiguous and has attracted intense controversy. For Mallet, the term should be construed broadly, for modern capitalist development has extended the boundaries of productive activity. Poulantzas however insists on an extremely circumscribed (and idiosyncratic) definition. His approach would seem to exclude from the working class not only salaried employees but also most 'manual' workers: for those who work for the state or in private 'service' industries, while possibly exploited, are not *both* producers of surplus value *and* 'directly involved in material production'.

Not all who fail this rigorous test are assumed to possess the same relation to the working class proper. Managers and supervisors are directly engaged in the exercise of command over the working class; most employees of state apparatuses[56] participate in maintaining capitalist domination. But clerical workers in industrial enterprises are typically in a subordinate position and do not exercise control over production workers; their interests may thus objectively converge with the latter – even though, Poulantzas asserts on somewhat impressionistic grounds, they normally identify subjectively with management.

Poulantzas goes on to consider evidence of a polarization within the group which he terms the 'new petty bourgeoisie': there is occurring a 'reproduction of the mental/manual worker division actually within mental labour' (an argument closely related, though not in terminology, to that of Braverman). He suggests that there are three main sectors in which objective affinities with the working class have become most marked, though in very different ways. The first two are routine employees in the commercial and 'service' sectors, and subordinate office workers in state and private bureaucracies; in both cases the largely female employment is evidence of subordination. The third group are technical and engineering staff directly involved in the production process in manufacturing industry, who are relatively advantaged yet come close to the definition of productive labour. It could be argued that Poulantzas's discussion here, while often insightful, rests on superficial points of reference which contrast strikingly with the rigour of his prior formulation of class criteria; seemingly he is obliged to ignore his initial definitions of class (bourgeoisie, proletariat, new petty bourgeoisie) for the purposes of practical analysis, in favour of a classification of occupational groups which lacks substantial theoretical foundation.

Carchedi endeavours to overcome some of the difficulties which beset Poulantzas, by focusing more centrally upon the labour process within contemporary capitalist production.[57] Marx himself noted two key features of capitalist development. Early capitalist manufacture was based largely on the disciplined co-ordination of the discrete contributions of individual producers; in the later stages of capitalism, work tasks became so interdependent that the productive contribution of any individual could no longer be isolated.[58] And secondly, as was seen previously, Marx stressed that the legal ownership of capital became divorced from 'the work of direct and constant supervision of the individual workers and groups of workers'.[59]

Carchedi follows Marx in arguing that the functions originally performed by the individual capitalist have thus become collectivized – the 'global function of capital' – and that the essence of this function is the control and surveillance of productive labour.[60] But those he terms the 'new middle class' also undertake the work of 'co-ordination and unity' which would be necessary even in a non-exploitive economy; to this extent they also form part of the 'collective worker'. Variations in the balance between these two contradictory functions are reflected in the salary levels of different agents; though Carchedi admits his inability to explain why the rewards for performing the capitalist function (the 'revenue element') are of any given amount. This analysis, Carchedi suggests, helps clarify the notion of proletarianization by indicating two distinct applications of the concept. The first (susceptible to analysis in either Marxist or Weberian terms) involves the erosion of the material basis of skills attracting higher than average returns in the labour market. But the second, and more complex sense involves the reduction of the capitalist element in the functions of particular 'new middle class' positions. Empirically, the two processes may be interrelated; as an occupation loses its capitalist functions, its skilled status may also become displaced or undermined.

Johnson's discussion of the work of Poulantzas and Carchedi (of which only a brief extract is included here) helps set their arguments in context. Their emphasis on the structural determination of class reflects the influence both of the Althusserian approach and of the practical debates within the French and Italian left. While sympathetic to their aims, he nevertheless presents a number of potent objections to their respective approaches. In the case of Carchedi there are three basic criticisms. First, the notion of an 'economic identification' of class abstracted from a general analysis and definition is confused and mechanical. Secondly, the theoretical distinction between capitalist and worker functions cannot be applied as a simple dichotomy for the purposes of detailed analysis; in practice, argues Johnson, Carchedi's arguments are akin to those of conventional sociologists such as Dahrendorf. And thirdly, whatever the value of his work for the analysis of occupations directly involved within the sphere of production, Carchedi provides only the most diffuse guide to understanding those outside.

One of the merits of Poulantzas is that he *does* seek to relate the 'economic' to the 'political' and 'ideological' levels; whereas Carchedi seems to reduce capitalist domination to control over the labour process, Poulantzas stresses the central importance of political and ideological domination in sustaining class relations in modern capitalism. Nevertheless, here too Johnson points to major weaknesses. There is a logical slide in Poulantzas's analysis: after his lengthy elaboration of the determinant significance of productive labour, his subsequent diagnosis of class identity is based effectively on a loose distinction between 'mental' and 'manual' labour; the whole edifice is thus flawed by 'conceptual ambiguity, if not downright mushiness'.

Olin Wright subjects Poulantzas to an even more rigorous critique; since his arguments are clearly presented they can largely be allowed to speak for themselves. In brief, Poulantzas offers a definition of productive labour which is arbitrary and un-Marxist, and fails to show how this criterion can establish divergences of interest sufficient to constitute a class division. His treatment of the relative importance of economic, and political/ ideological criteria in determining class position is perverse and confusing. And most fundamentally, his whole approach pre-supposes that all positions within modern capitalism must fall within one or other of his three basic categories.

Wright himself suggests that any theory of class must incorporate the existence of objectively contradictory locations; and indicates three such locations, mediating between bourgeoisie, petty bourgeoisie and working class. Thus the managerial hierarchy is ambiguously placed between working and ruling classes. Foremen and supervisors in large corporations possess such limited power that they are not substantially different from those they supervise; conversely, senior corporate management differ from the capitalist class only through the formal absence of legal ownership of the capital they direct. But middle manage-ment and technical specialists cannot be even approximately assimilated with any of the main class groupings. Wright rejects the notion that they represent a new petty bourgeoisie; though he does suggest that some occupations (such as semi-autonomous professional employees) are contradictorily located between working class and petty bourgeoisie.

In the final reading of Part I, Crompton and Gubbay suggest a theory of class formation based on a prior analysis of the political economy of modern capitalism. Following Carchedi, a primary point of reference is the dichotomy between control and co-ordinated labour, but they introduce further differentiations, and go on to distinguish class interests from subjective consciousness and action. Where Wright talks of 'contradictory location' they employ the term 'structural ambiguity', emphasizing the absence of coherent interests among those whom Carchedi identifies as 'new middle class'. In consequence, they argue, subjective perceptions and strategies are often 'inconsistent and vacillating'. Crompton and Gubbay distinguish between positions of control in 'capitals', 'non-capitals' and 'quasi-capitals';[61] and suggest also that the difference between these three contexts can engender significant divisions within the working class (defined in terms of subordinate labour).

As against Wright, they question whether variations in the range or degree of control attached to a particular occupation necessarily provide a criterion of structural ambiguity. The fact that a foreman may himself be subject to bureaucratic direction does not alter his function as an agent of capitalist control. While the growth of hierarchical and functional differentiation within management may complicate or qualify the relations between supervisors and their subordinates, it does not contradict their basic antagonism of interests.

This argument is however open to the same criticism that Johnson directs against Carchedi: it assumes that a clear-cut division can be made between positions involving control on behalf of capital, and those involving pure subordination. For hierarchy commonly exists *within the collective labourer*, particularly where clear craft demarcations exist. A bricklayer or a main-tenance fitter traditionally exerts control (at times overtly and coercively) over his labourer; does this entail that he is an 'agent of the global function of capital'? Are gang-leaders or chargehands (who may sometimes be chosen by gang members themselves) the bottom rung of the management hierarchy, or merely subordinate workers to whom certain functions of co-ordination have been delegated? How should it be determined whether foremen perform the work of control and surveillance rather than that of control and unity?[62] Ultimately, the boundary between the two functions is both empirically and conceptually more imprecise than Carchedi, or Crompton and Gubbay, can admit.

A second basic criticism of Crompton and Gubbay must be their failure to include any reference to the sexual division of labour within their analysis of class. A number of the authors surveyed here have recognized, at least in passing, the significance of 'feminization' as a feature of the changing role of certain 'white-collar' occupations. The fact that female labour power is seemingly of lower average value than that of men,[63] and that women's general social subordination is typically reproduced within relations of production in the capitalist enterprise, must be integrated within any analysis of the functions of global capital and the collective worker. In other words a 'unisex' theory of capital flows is an insufficient basis for a political economy of class.

The notion of structural ambiguity thus needs to be extended. Within contemporary capitalism, the boundaries of the collective worker are imprecise and perhaps indeterminate; while the capital relation itself extends far beyond the labour process within individual capitals. But how far? Is the sexual division of labour merely a secondary complication of a primary differentiation based on ownership/non-ownership or control/subordination; or a fundamental axis of differentiation in its own right? Are state activities unproblematically an adjunct to the global function of capital; or in part a contradictory (even 'non-capitalist'?) outcome of working-class pressure? An adequate theoretical assessment of the role of many of the occupations within the 'new working class' is scarcely possible in the absence of adequate and integrated answers to such questions.

This conclusion serves as an important preliminary to the second part of this book. If a wide range of 'white-collar' positions involve major structural ambiguities, then many individuals and groups possess considerable scope for selective emphasis among the various contradictory aspects of their own situation and of their relations with other groups. Relatively peripheral factors may (as Crompton and Gubbay argue) decisively influence perceptions of interests and the individual or collective strategies through which these are pursued. Responses to *changes* in their situation (perhaps elements of 'proletarianization') may reflect similar influences: relatively minor contingencies may determine whether 'status panic' inhibits any form of collective strategy; whether union organization is embraced as a means to defend or retain former authority and advantage; or whether alliances are sought with groups whose interests were previously regarded as divergent. Ambiguities in the changing class position of 'white-collar' occupational groups will thus become refracted and even amplified in the collective organizations and actions which they create.

NOTES AND REFERENCES

1. John Stuart Mill, *Principles of Political Economy* (Longmans Green, 1865 edn) p. 26.
2. For details of legal differentiations based on this distinction see Chapter 2 by Bain and Price; and also Hilda R. Kahn, *Salaries in the Public Services in England and Wales* (Allen and Unwin, 1962).
3. The distinction between 'manual' and 'non-manual' occupations (the latter term being used in common discourse interchangeably with 'white-collar') has been employed in official statistics since the last century, and since 1911 has formed the basis of an officially defined hierarchy of 'social class' for the presentation of certain census and demographic data. The seventeen 'socio-economic groups' introduced by the Registrar General in 1951 also differentiate rigidly between the two categories, as do the earnings data published by the Department of Employment. While the definitions employed by the two agencies are in general the same, there are a few confusing divergencies: see Kahn, *Salaries in the Public Services*, pp. 303–4; there have also been some changes in classification over time. For the Department's current grouping of 'non-manual' occupations see Table 1.4.
4. Kahn, *Salaries in the Public Services*, discusses this distinction, concluding (p. 315) that 'though there are a fair number of differences between wages and salaries, none of these can be applied as strict criteria on the basis of which the two groups can be isolated with any very fine degree of precision'.
5. George Sayers Bain, Robert Bacon and John Pimlott, 'The Labour Force' in A. H. Halsey, *Trends in British Society Since 1900* (Macmillan, 1972) pp. 97–8.
6. George Sayers Bain, *The Growth of White-Collar Unionism* (Oxford University Press, 1970) pp. 53–4.
7. Some of the reasons have just been noted. In addition, much of Routh's evidence is based on income tax returns, accentuating the problems of coverage and reliability. In interpreting his results it is necessary to take account of the industrial distribution of employment within occupational categories. Thus the curious fact that male semi-skilled workers on average earned less than unskilled workers in 1922, is probably explained by the fact that workers formally classified as semi-skilled were heavily concentrated in those manufacturing sectors severely affected by recession and wage reductions. Similarly, women formally classed as skilled were to be found largely in textiles, which was particularly depressed in the 1930s; hence the fact that average wages were less than those of semi-skilled women in 1935–6.
8. Dorothy Wedderburn and Christine Craig, 'Relative Deprivation in Work', in Dorothy Wedderburn, *Poverty, Inequality and Class Structure* (Cambridge University Press, 1974) pp. 143–5.
9. Ibid., p. 145.
10. The three occupations are further education teachers, nurse administrators

and office managers (of whom very few are women).

11. It is a sociological commonplace that the concept of a profession is itself imprecise and contains strong ideological connotations. In exploring the 'white-collar' status of professional and associated occupations, the notion of 'proximity to authority' is not directly applicable; though arguably, in a more diffuse sense a privileged access to social (and especially state) power represents a crucial foundation of professional advantage. See Terence J. Johnson, *Professions and Power* (Macmillan, 1972).

12. Frank Parkin, *Class Inequality and Political Order* (McGibbon and Kee, 1971) p. 26.

13. See Asa Briggs, 'The Language of "Class" in Early Nineteenth-Century England', in Asa Briggs and John Saville, *Essays in Labour History* (Macmillan, 1960).

14. Karl Marx and Frederick Engels, 'Manifesto of the Communist Party', in *Collected Works*, vol. 6 (Lawrence and Wishart, 1976) p. 482.

15. For a valuable survey of the development of Marx's approach to class see Stuart Hall, 'The "Political" and the "Economic" in Marx's Theory of Classes', in Alan Hunt, *Class and Class Structure* (Lawrence and Wishart, 1977).

16. Notably in the famous, unfinished last chapter of *Capital*, vol. 3 (Lawrence and Wishart, 1959) p. 862.

17. Certainly the term 'middle class' can be found in Marx's writings, but as a conventional label without serious theoretical content. There are three main senses in which he uses the term: an emergent class, notably the rising bourgeoisie before it has overcome the social and political dominance of the aristocracy; the remnants of a previous system of production, such as independent traders and producers and other 'petty bourgeois' groups; and groups outside the sphere of production altogether. It is in this latter sense that Marx, in notes on Malthus and Ricardo which have attracted recent attention, refers to 'the constantly growing number of the middle classes': *Theories of Surplus Value*, pt. 2 (Lawrence and Wishart, 1969) p. 573. His concern is with such groups as servants, criminals and idlers who are detached from the process of capitalist production, and *not* with what is normally regarded as 'white-collar' labour.

18. The following points are crucial for an understanding of Marx's analysis of capitalist production. An object or service produced for sale on the market is a commodity, and its exchange value is roughly determined by the amount of labour required for its production. Within capitalist production, the worker's ability to work – what Marx terms *labour-power* – is itself a marketable commodity; thus *its* value – the worker's wages – reflects the amount of labour needed to produce labour-power, in other words to provide subsistence for the worker and his/her dependants. The capitalist is able to derive profits because workers' wages – the value of their labour-power – amount to less than the value of what they produce: part of their work, in other words, is unpaid or surplus labour, and provides the capitalist with surplus product. This surplus product is transformed into *surplus value* through being exchanged on the market: this realization process does not create new value, but merely alters the form of what has already been produced so as to allow the capitalist to consume or invest the surplus.

19. *Capital*, vol. 3, pp. 288, 293–4.
20. Marx devoted little systematic attention to skill differentials, and possible sectional strategies to preserve these. He attributed the higher pay of 'skilled labour' in part to the greater costs of training, etc., in part to the force of convention after the real basis for differentiation had disappeared. In either case he assumed that in the longer term advantaged groups would be reduced to the position of 'average labour' (apart perhaps from a small minority assimilated within the ranks of capitalist management), thus increasing the polarization of classes.
21. Ibid., pp. 294–5.
21. *Capital*, vol. 1 (Penguin, 1976) pp. 448–9. It is a familiar point that the possibilities of 'democratic management' within a non-capitalist system of production were not systematically considered by Marx and Engels.
23. Ibid., p. 450.
24. *Capital*, vol. 3, p. 863.
25. Like Marx, Weber never provided a finished systematic discussion of class: his most important general analysis was published posthumously.
26. Max Weber, *Economy and Society* (Bedminister Press, 1968) p. 302.
27. Ibid., p. 929.
28. Ibid., p. 932.
29. Ibid., p. 938.
30. Rosemary Crompton and Jon Gubbay, *Economy and Class Structure* (Macmillan, 1977) p. 16.
31. *Economy and Society*, p. 931.
32. *Capital*, vol. 3, p. 863.
33. *Economy and Society*, p. 302.
34. Ibid., pp. 304–5.
35. This arbitrary demarcation is applied uncritically, and even more crudely, by Frank Parkin in *Class Inequality and Political Order*. As already noted, he regards modern societies as simple dichotomies of two classes, blue- and white-collar, differentiated by a 'line of cleavage . . . in the reward position' (p. 25). This dichotomy holds good, he insists, despite the internal differentiations within each group and the considerable overlap in reward position.
36. Thus H. H. Gerth and C. Wright Mills, *From Max Weber* (Routledge and Kegan Paul, 1948) comment (p. 47) that 'Weber does not squarely oppose historical materialism as altogether wrong; he merely takes exception to its claim of establishing a single and universal causal sequence'.
37. Ralf Dahrendorf, *Class and Class Conflict in Industrial Society* (Routledge and Kegan Paul, 1959) p. 55. While Dahrendorf insists that authority relations are necessarily dichotomous – and hence that the notion of a 'middle class' is vacuous – he denies that social class as such is polarized in modern societies. For (in a highly formalistic application of Weberian categories) he argues that authority relations occur not at a general societal level but within 'imperatively co-ordinated associations', and that the possibility of dominance in some social contexts and subordination in others creates a complex and differentiated social structure.
38. An important analysis of the feminization of office work in the United States is by Margery Davies, 'Woman's Place is at the Typewriter', *Radical America*,

8 (July–August 1974).

39. Routh suggests (*Occupation and Pay*, p. 80) that Klingender misinterprets the available earnings data in his discussion of inter-war salary movements.

40. For more detailed discussion of this point see Crompton and Gubbay, *Economy and Class Structure*, pp. 20–3.

41 .A more balanced assessment of early post-war trends can be found in W. H. Scott, *Office Automation* (OECD, 1965).

42. For a more speculative assessment of the consequences of the 'micro-processor revolution' see Clive Jenkins and Barrie Sherman, *The Collapse of Work* (Eyre Methuen, 1979).

43. Harry Braverman, *Labor and Monopoly Capital* (Monthly Review, 1974) pp. 325–6, 355.

44. The classic statement of this theme, first published in 1941, is James Burnham, *The Managerial Revolution* (Penguin, 1962). For a critique see Theo Nichols, *Ownership Control and Ideology* (Allen and Unwin, 1969).

45. Alain Touraine, *The Post-Industrial Society* (Wildwood House, 1974) p. 51. A very similar theme is developed by Daniel Bell, *The Coming of Post-Industrial Society* (Heinemann, 1974). A critique of such approaches is offered by Krishan Kumar, *Prophecy and Progress* (Pelican, 1978).

46. In contrast to the view that scientific expertise provides the basis for effective influence on corporate decision-making, it could more plausibly be argued that the *accountant* rather than the engineer plays the dominant role in policy formulation. See, for example, Theo Nichols and Huw Beynon, *Living with Capitalism* (Routledge and Kegan Paul, 1977) and Huw Beynon and Hilary Wainwright, *The Workers' Report on Vickers* (Pluto Press, 1979).

47. The spread of union membership among middle managers has been a notable development in Britain in recent years.

48. Despite the grandiose theories sometimes associated with the notion of the 'service economy', the reality of the changing industrial structure is more prosaic. As the readings in Chapter 6 indicate, the 'tertiary' or 'service' sector includes a diversity of activities (indeed the term itself is very much a residual category), for the most part concerned tenuously if at all with the provision of pubic service. For a discussion of this point see Richard Hyman, 'Occupational Structure, Collective Organisation and Industrial Militancy' in Colin Crouch and Alessandro Pizzorno, *The Resurgence of Class Conflict in Western Europe*, vol. 2 (Macmillan, 1978).

49. Or else by various agencies of the state. The significance of the growth of such public employment, and in particular of the 'welfare state', is discussed further below.

50. While Giddens does go further than most Weberians in considering production relations, his central analytical focus involves the distribution of life chances. Curiously enough, his discussion of Marx seems to conflate production and distribution relationships, suggesting that any groups who are not productive should, in Marxist terms, be regarded as exploiters. For a critical discussion of his treatment of this question see Crompton and Gubbay, *Economy and Class Structure*, pp. 29–34.

51. E. P. Thompson, *The Making of the English Working Class* (Pelican, 1968) p. 11. Thompson's insistence (p. 13) that 'class is a cultural as much as an economic formation' is however difficult to square with the pervading

argument of Braverman's book.

52. A selection of critical assessments of the Ehrenreichs's analysis is compiled in Pat Walker, *Between Labour and Capital* (Harvester, 1979).

53. Alex Callinicos, *Althusser's Marxism* (Pluto Press, 1976) offers a review of some of the main issues while maintaining a detachment from the more partisan approaches on either side of the debate.

54. Nicos Poulantzas, 'The Problem of the Capitalist State', in Robin Blackburn, *Ideology in Social Science* (Fontana, 1972) p. 242.

53. Both Poulantzas and Carchedi employ two terms – confusing to the uninitiated – to denote forms of control exercised by managers without formal property rights in the means of production. 'Economic ownership' denotes the ability to make long-term strategic decisions over the disposition of capital; 'possession', the more limited day-to-day control over its application.

56. Poulantzas adopts and elaborates Althusser's conception of the state as an almost all-pervasive feature of capitalist society, manifest in two distinct forms: the 'repressive state apparatus' (police, judiciary, armed forces), and also the 'ideological state apparatuses' which include churches, schools, mass media, the family, trade unions and political parties. Not only does this approach conflate the state and bourgeois society, but it is open to the same objection as raised above in respect of the Ehrenreichs: the possibility of a *contradictory* relationship between specific institutions and the stability of capitalist class relations is excluded by definition.

57. Adopting the premise of the theoretical distinctiveness of different levels of analysis, Carchedi describes his objective as merely the *economic identification* of specific occupational groups on the basis of their role in capitalist production relations; a complete definition of their class position would need to incorporate the political and ideological 'instances'. Hence he follows Poulantzas in assuming that clerks are proletarian in terms of production relations, but petty bourgeois in political and ideological terms.

58. 'The product is transformed from the direct product of the individual producer into a social product, the joint product of a collective labourer, i.e. a combination of workers . . . . With the progressive accentuation of the co-operative character of the labour process, there necessarily occurs a progressive extension of the concept of productive labour . . . . In order to work productively, it is no longer necessary for the individual himself to put his hand to the object; it is sufficient for him to be an organ of the collective labourer, and to perform any one of its subordinate functions' (*Capital*, vol. 1, pp. 643–4). It is difficult, to say the least, to square Marx's argument with Poulantzas's usage of the notion of productive labour.

59. Ibid., p. 450.

60. Carchedi suggests that an analogous function is performed by those in control of 'unproductive' sectors of employment, where subordinate workers though not exploited are 'economically oppressed'. In sharp contrast to Poulantzas, class identity in his view is not primarily affected by whether or not subordinate employees perform productive labour.

61. Non-capitals are defined as 'enterprises which do not accumulate capital themselves but whose purpose is to foster the growth and stability of the overall process of capital accumulation'; while this accords with the

perspective on state activity adopted by Poulantzas and the Ehrenreichs, it is unclear how this definition applies to those 'private non-capitals' which Crompton and Gubbay mention in the extract in Chapter 7. Quasi-capitals are defined primarily as state enterprises which parallel at least some of the functions of private capital.

62. Kahn (*Salaries in the Public Services*, pp. 303–4) has noted the uncertainty within official statistics about how to classify foremen. 'The foreman,' she quips, 'so long as he only talks to, preaches at, or swears at his men ought, strictly speaking, to be classed as salaried; to the extent that he rolls up his shirt sleeves and gives them a hand, he is a wage-earner.' To complicate matters further, Stephen Hill (*The Dockers: Class and Tradition in London* (Heinemann, 1976) pp. 39–40) reports that dock foremen, while involved primarily in 'non-manual, administrative tasks' are concerned mainly in controlling the flow of work rather than in supervising dockers' efforts.

63. See Veronica Beechey, 'Some Notes on Female Wage Labour in Capitalist Production', *Capital and Class*, 3 (Autumn 1977).

2 The Problem of Definition

Who is a White-Collar Employee?

George Sayers Bain and Robert Price

British Journal of Industrial Relations, vol. x, no. 3 (November 1972) pp. 325–38

'White-collar employee' is a vague term. Its meaning differs between countries, and even within a single country it often means one thing to one person and something else to another. Indicative of the confusion surrounding the term is the large number of synonyms which it has acquired : 'salaried employee', 'office worker', 'non-manual worker', and 'blackcoated worker'. . . .

Historically, the most popular type of definition has been the one characterized here as the brain–brawn approach. The notion of a 'white-collar employee' first crystallized around clerical employment at a time when access to the minimum educational qualifications required for such work was restricted and when manual work work typically involved a high level of direct physical exertion. In such conditions, the notion of an intellectual–manual dichotomy in the labour force was perhaps a not unreasonable approximation to reality, and it became fixed both in the popular consciousness and in legal and administrative regulations.

The first major examination of the 'white-collar phenomenon' to tackle explicitly the problem of definition was that of the German sociologist, Emil Lederer. He was fully aware of the heterogeneity of the types of occupation that had conventionally been classified as white-collar, and he thus considered it impossible to define a white-collar worker in terms of a set of 'positive' criteria. Nevertheless, he was prepared to define white-collar employment in a negative sense as 'all those employees who do not work . . . in purely manual occupations'.[1] In Lederer's view, white-collar work was fundamentally characterized by its intellectual and non-manual character. . . .

The major criticism which can be levelled at the brain–brawn approach is that it merely shifts the definitional problem from the terms 'white-collar' and 'blue-collar' to two different but equally problematic adjectives – 'intellectual' and 'manual'. Hence if this approach is to yield a satisfactory definition, it is necessary to define these two terms independently. Even in the unlikely event that these terms could be satisfactorily defined, it is improbable that this approach would yield an adequate definition of a 'white-collar employee'. For it would have to show that work of an intellectual nature is either exclusively performed by white-collar employees, or, at least, that white-collar employment involves significantly greater intellectual effort than manual work.

This would be an extremely difficult, if not impossible, task. There can hardly be any white-collar employment so intellectual in nature that it requires no physical labour; conversely, there can hardly be any manual work that requires no intellectual effort. Since virtually every job contains some elements of both intellectual and manual work, the problem becomes one of distinguishing between 'predominantly intellectual' and 'predominantly manual' labour.

In deciding that a lithographic artist was not engaged in manual labour, a . . . judge reasoned that in the course of his work the artist

> . . . necessarily uses his hands, but the use to which he puts them is not labour, because it involves no strenuous exercise of the muscles of his hand or his arm. The real labour involved is labour of the brain and intelligence.[2]

Perhaps not surprisingly, this involved reasoning produced several questionable judgments. It is debatable whether a tramcar driver, a hairdresser, a guard of a goods train, a stoker employed in a hospital, and a professional clown are white-collar employees as the courts held. Just to add to the confusion, a conductor and a professional football player were held to be manual workers by some jurists and to be non-manual workers by other jurists. The occupational structure is more heterogeneous now than at the time when these judgments were made, and hence it would be even more difficult to apply the intellectual–manual distinction to contemporary job descriptions. By almost all definitions of the term, a filing clerk and a copy typist would be classified as white-collar employees, while a highly skilled electrician and a compositor in the printing industry would be classified as manual employees. It is extremely doubtful whether the work performed by the first two occupations involves greater intellectual effort than the work performed by the latter two. . . .

The functional approach provides a very different and, in many ways, a more satisfactory definition of a 'white-collar employee'. The major exponent of this approach is Fritz Croner. . . . He rejects definitions of white-collar work that rest on notions such as 'intellectual', 'educated', 'higher status', and so on, because of their more or less subjective quality. He turns instead to 'objective' aspects of job content as the basis of his analysis.

White-collar employees are defined as those who perform the following functions: administration . . . ; design, analysis and planning . . . ; supervisory/managerial . . . ; commercial . . . .[3] Croner argues that these four functions are the distinguishing mark of white-collar employment because they were once performed by the employer. In the early stages of capitalist development, the employer had personally to perform a large number of functions besides the typical entrepreneurial functions of innovating and risk-bearing. These were mainly concerned with the organization and management of the business and included the clerical, accounting and controlling, buying and selling, supervisory, and planning and technical tasks. Croner suggests that these various aspects of the employer's general responsibility can be summarized by the four broad functions he designates as characterizing white-collar employment.

As a firm grow in size and complexity, the employer must increase the scope and intensity of performance of these functions in order to maintain control over the operation of his expanding enterprise . . . The larger the enterprise grows, the further the process of sub-division and delegation is carried, the longer becomes the line of authority, and the greater becomes the social distance between the employer and the lowest grades of his staff. But regardless of how elementary and routine the work of these lowest grades, in Croner's view it is still white-collar employment because it is part of the work previously performed by the employer. . . .

The major defect of the functional approach, as with the brain–brawn approach, is that it merely shifts the definitional argument. . . . For the terms 'supervisory and managerial'; 'design, analysis, and planning'; 'administrative'; and 'commercial' are as flexible or as rigid as the wit and ingenuity of the person using them. For example, Croner's category 'design, analysis, and planning' includes an area described as 'the production of goods' which covers such occupational groups as designers and draughtsmen who 'produce, shape or form items for production'. This category is specified in such a way that it obviously could be interpreted to include the pattern-maker, the welder, and the turner, not to mention the potter and the women of the clothing trade. . . .

The Swiss sociologist, Roger Girod, has adopted a more eclectic approach to the definition of a 'white-collar employee'.[4] After surveying several possible criteria for distinguishing white-collar from manual employees, he offers two which in his view have some validity. These are: the nature of the work milieu, and the object and function of the work itself.

Girod distinguishes between two major types of work milieu in terms of purely physical conditions: for manual workers the work environment is 'mechanical', for white-collar workers it is 'bureaucratic' or 'non-mechanical'. . . . The main difficulty with this criterion, as with the two earlier approaches, is that it merely shifts the definitional problem. The task now becomes to define clearly the difference between a 'mechanical' and a 'non-mechanical' environment, and this is particularly difficult to do. Is the laboratory technician or the draughtsman working in a mechanical or a bureaucratic environment? The use of mechanical apparatus might appear to qualify them for the former, while their office-type of environment might place them in the latter. Similarly, do typists and telephonists qualify as 'bureaucrats', or are they to be considered as 'mechanical' personnel?

The second and more elaborate criterion offered by Girod is based on the 'objects' and 'functions' of occupations. The first term refers to the nature of the objects upon which the worker operates, while the second term refers to the function that is performed by the worker operating upon these objects. Thus Girod implies two things in describing a job as 'manual': first, that the job is concerned with material objects, and second, that the function of the workers' contact with these objects is to make them 'usable'. Non-manual work, on the other hand, involves acting upon other people; its function is to organize, shape, or 'inform' human conduct . . .

But many occupations do not fall neatly into one or the other of these categories. There are a large number of cases in which the line between 'material-oriented' and 'people-oriented' activities is blurred. . . . An even more damaging objection to this criterion lies in the nature of the occupational division that it would create. Occupations that are generally considered to be typically white-collar, such as mechanical engineers, air-line pilots, medical auxiliaries, and laboratory technicians, would logically have to be classified as 'material' oriented and hence blue-collar. Similarly, occupations which are generally considered to be manual, such as ticket-collectors, bus conductors, and doormen, would have to be regarded as 'person-oriented' and hence white-collar. . . .

The notion that there is a clear distinction between white- and blue-collar employees still persists in the popular consciousness, and the theories discussed here indirectly give an indication of what the source of this consciousness may be. The features which they propose for distinguishing the essence of white-collar employment – type of dress, the nature of the work environment, and the function performed – can be regarded as different external symbols of a more fundamental common feature, the possession of, or proximity to, authority. The 'non-manual' nature of white-collar work, as well as the content of the duties performed, tend to produce a functional proximity to authority; the nature of the work environment and the type of dress tend to create an environmental proximity to authority. In other words, although a majority of white-collar employees occupy a subordinate position at work in the same way as do blue-collar employees, the possession of these readily identifiable symbols may link them in the popular consciousness 'with that part of the productive process where authority is exercised and decisions taken'.[5] Even in non-industrial sectors of the economy, such as the distributive trades and national and local government, the white-collar worker is the person who takes your money in shops and gives your orders in offices; in Lockwood's words, the person 'on the other side of the desk who is somehow associated with authority'.[6]

A process of what can be called 'assimilation by association' would seem to be at work. A group whose work possesses characteristics which have become symbolically associated with the possession of, or proximity to, authority may become assimilated to the white-collar group by its association with those symbols. In many cases, social and industrial change has robbed these symbols of their content, and they may indicate in reality neither functional nor environmental proximity to authority; nevertheless, jobs which possess the symbols are still commonly classified as white-collar. . . .

An empirical examination of consciousness and self-consciousness in regard to occupational universes is likely to illuminate important aspects of the stratification patterns of industrial societies by directing attention to individuals' and groups' perceptions of white-collar work and the forces which create and sustain those perceptions. But it is unlikely that such an examination would yield a universal and clear-cut classification of the labour force into white-collar and manual categories. For even if perceptions of authority are the fundamental factor determining popular conceptions of who is a white-collar employee, people's evaluations of which groups are associated with authority are likely to vary.

NOTES AND REFERENCES

1. Emil Lederer, *Die Privatangestellten in der modernen Wirtschaftsentwicklung* (J. C. B. Mohr/P. Siebeck, 1912) pp. 23–4.
2. J. Warrington, *In re Lithographic Artists*, 1913.
3. F. Croner, *Soziologie der Angestellten* (Kiepenheuer und Witsch, Cologne, 1962).
4. Roger Girod, *Études Sociologiques sur les Couches Salariees: Ouvriers et Employés* (Marcel Rivière, 1961).
5. W. G. Runciman, *Relative Deprivation and Social Justice* (Routledge and Kegan Paul, 1966) p. 47.
6. David Lockwood, *The Blackcoated Worker* (Allen and Unwin, 1958) p. 132.

3 Clerical Labour: Some Early Arguments

Clerks as Proletarians

F. D. Klingender

The Condition of Clerical Labour in Britain (London: Martin Lawrence, 1935) pp. xi–xii, 17–19, 58, 61–3, 98–9

The differentiation of social classes remains as clear to-day as it was in the days when Marx and Engels made their famous social diagnosis on a class basis, though the structure of society has naturally undergone many changes. Thus the capitalist or bourgeois class remains clearly distinguishable by its ownership of the means of production; the elements within that class to-day are more homogeneous than when Marx wrote, since the owners of land and of industrial capital and the financiers no longer represent separate sections but are one and the same group.

The essential mark of the proletariat remains the fact that it owns no capital and depends for its livelihood on the sale of its labour power, having no control over the disposal of the product of its labour.

The social strata which lie between the capitalists and the proletariat do not constitute a class in the true sense of the term, for they perform as a group, no specific economic function. These intermediate strata partake of the characteristics of each of the main classes. Some are small capitalists; some are persons possessing no capital and distinguished from the proletariat only by the relatively high price at which they dispose of their labour power; while others get their living partly by ownership and partly be selling their labour power. . . .

The middle class has undergone large changes in its structure since the middle of last century when Marx wrote. The peasantry, the independent handicraftsmen, and the small shopkeepers have declined in numbers, but they have been replaced by a 'new middle class' of salary-earners directly dependent upon capitalist employers. Small owners of businesses and the lesser dealers have now become the employees and agents of large concerns, while the ranks of the intermediate strata have been swollen by a host of clerks, salesmen and other non-manual subordinates of capitalist undertakings.

The change in the structure of the middle class has not basically altered its political character. To-day, as when Marx wrote, it tends to pass from one political camp to another, in periods of prosperity joining in the forward movement of the proletariat and seeking to improve its economic position by raising salaries, and when the slump sets, retreating in fear for the security of its employment to the respectable ranks of supporters of capitalism. It is this vacillating tendency which gives the social stratum we are here discussing its special interest. . . .

The rapid expansion of capitalist production and trade during the nineteenth century brought in its train the spectacular growth of a new clerical working class. At the same time it shattered the patriarchal relations between masters and men which previously had been especially marked in this type of employment. The tendency to reduce the remuneration of clerical labour to the minimum, in view of the monopoly of education which excluded the bulk of the working class throughout the greater parts of the century, had on the whole achieved the assimilation of clerical wages to those of the skilled workers by the end of the period.

Socially, however, the clerks were throughout this era a section of the middle classes, and as gentlemen they pleaded in vain to the gentlemanly instincts of their employers to grant them the remuneration that alone would enable them to 'fill the place in society to which their rank entitled them'. Only in rare instances did any of them recognize that only the fighting methods of the class to which they were being economically reduced could bring about an improvement in their position. . . .

After the relative stagnation of the eighteen-nineties, British trade again made a great spurt during the first 15 years of the present century. . . . The total number of clerks still continued to rise, but the rate of that rise was no longer increasing after 1900; during the decades 1881–91, 1891–1901, and 1901–11 the percentage growth was 30·2, 48·1 and 37·5 respectively. Moreover, an important structural change now becomes clearly noticeable – the higher rate of increase in the number of women. . . . Whereas the number of women had been less than one-twentieth of the number of men in 1881, the proportion almost reached one-quarter in 1911. . . .

Throughout this period the clerical group increased much faster than the total occupied population . . . but even as late as 1911 it was only 4·6 per cent. of that total (5·2 per cent. for the males, 3·1 per cent. for the females).

A further very interesting fact . . . is the very high proportion of young clerks. More than one-half of the males were under 25 years in 1881, by 1911 the proportion was still 46·6 per cent.; the corresponding figures for the total male occupied population in those years were 32·6 per cent. and 28·8 per cent. The preponderance of young women is still more striking: two-thirds of them were under 25 in 1911, as compared with about one-half for all occupied women. These developments necessarily reacted profoundly on the economic position of the clerical class as a whole. . . .

The growth in the number of clerks in the decade after 1921 only slightly exceeded that of the general occupied population . . . and the most important factor is the pronounced decline in the rate of increase for women. . . .

It is necessary at this point to indicate two important changes in the conditions of clerical work itself which greatly affected the status, remuneration, and chances of employment for clerks. I refer to the twin processes of office rationalization – large-scale amalgamations and the introduction of machines. The former process is characteristic of the whole imperialist period, although in the sphere of merchant and finance-capital large-scale monopolies are found at a very much earlier date. . . .

The amalgamation process created the monster office in which vast numbers of clerks are herded together for their daily work, just as the concentration of capital in industry herded the former craftsmen or cottage workers in the factory. By the resulting specialization of clerical functions it increased the productivity of clerical labour and was thus destined to have a decisive long-term reaction on the demand for that labour. But this reaction is infinitely intensified by the second process to be discussed, that of office mechanization. It is this process which completes the technical proletarianization of clerical labour. Just as in industry the former craftsmen were first brought together in the large-scale 'factories' of the manufacturing period, before the nature of their work was revolutionized by the advent of modern machinery and they themselves transformed into proletarians in the modern sense, so it is the advent of the office machine, after the establishment of the office-factory, which vitally transforms the work of the clerks and finally destroys the former craft basis of their trade.[1] Even before the full development of the process now under discussion, the first step towards proletarianization was the process by which the relations between employers and employed were depersonalized. A small fraction of the craftsmen or clerks, as foremen, chief clerks, etc., escaped the process of depersonalization for a time, and their existence in the clerical sphere gave rise to the myth of a specific difference in the economic principles regulating the remuneration of clerks and other workers.

Like technical rationalization in industry, the mechanization of office work began on a large scale much later in this country than in its younger imperialist rivals, especially the U.S.A. and Germany. Moreover the accountancy and statistical side of clerical labour, the mechanization of which appears to us to-day as practically co-extensive with the conception of office rationalization, was affected by this tendency very much later than the essential clerical process of writing. The typewriter is to-day such an everyday thing that we should hesitate to call an office mechanized in which this was the only machine. Yet the introduction of this machine at the end of the nineteenth century had the most revolutionary effect on the nature of clerical work. John Stuart Mill . . . could justly speak of the 'mechanical labour of copying' as the most characteristic aspect of clerical work – performed at that time exclusively by men – and the same fact is illustrated by the early census classification which up to 1871 grouped all clerks engaged in book-keeping tasks not with clerks, but with accountants. The introduction of the typewriter eliminated the whole class of male writers and copyists, i.e., the class from which the very name of 'clerk' derives. Typewriting became a female occupation almost from the start, and I can scarcely be wrong in regarding this fact as an important cause for the spectacular entry of women into clerical occupations prior to the war.

The second phase of mechanization, affecting book-keeping

began as a serious factor before the war, though it did not assume wide importance until later; it became general mainly during the stabilization period, with which we are concerned in the present chapter. Nevertheless, in this country at least it is by no means complete even to-day. A continuous and rapid process of change and technical improvement is still revolutionizing this branch of office machinery. The change is twofold: on the one hand certain machines, mainly of the largest and most costly type, are extended to ever wider fields of office work, until to-day practically every branch of book-keeping, invoicing, and statistical work can be performed by some models; on the other hand certain other machines are evolved for the performance of the most highly specialized and intricate tasks. Nor is mechanization confined to the accountancy type of operations. It has vitally transformed and rationalized all methods of recording, filing, and indexing; in addition there are in practically all large offices to-day elaborate inter-office communication systems, time-recording systems, machines for printing circulars, show-cards, catalogues, and other advertising material; the envelope is mechanically addressed, sealed and stamped, and even the process of dictation has been mechanized with the result that the skill of shorthand-writing may become superfluous. . . .

The most important reaction of the world crisis on the standards of clerks was the removal of the final barrier against their complete economic proletarianization: that of security of employment. For the great majority of clerks this is to-day a thing of the past, and they have therefore acquired the last decisive characteristic of the wage worker, that of uncertainty with regard to the future. This fact cannot be removed by any revival of trade; it is firmly implanted on clerical occupations through the rationalization processes that reaped their first fruits during the crisis. It is often argued that office mechanization does not cause unemployment, and the great increase in the number of clerks long after the introduction of the typewriter is cited as a proof of this contention. All such abstract arguments are, however, entirely beside the point. When the typewriter was introduced, capitalism was just about to enter its imperialist phase and the vast expansion of international trade and of the scale of business units generally more than counteracted any tendency towards a fall in the number of clerks due to the new machines. The second great mechanization move is taking place under entirely different conditions. Capitalism has entered a stage of general crisis; after stagnating during the post-war period, world trade has fallen catastrophically, and in the state of tariff and economic war at present prevailing there is not the slightest probability that it will again rise to its pre-crisis level before the outbreak of the next 'round of wars and revolutions'.

The economic status of the great mass of clerks has thus finally and irrevocably been identified with that of the manual working class. The same factors determine the living standards of both; working class methods of struggle alone can bring about an improvement in the economic position of the clerks, they alone can protect them against further degradation.

NOTES AND REFERENCES

1. One of the most striking symbols of the completed proletarianization of the clerks – one, moreover, which is vehemently resented by the clerks themselves – is the time recording clock.

Clerks and the Ambiguities of Class

David Lockwood

The Blackcoated Worker: a Study in Class Consciousness (London: Unwin University Books, 1958) pp. 202–11

The charge of 'false' class consciousness which has been frequently levelled at the blackcoated worker is grounded in the assumption that manual workers and clerks share the same basic market situation: that is, they are both propertyless, contractual labour. The clerk, really a proletarian in a white collar, was, according to this point of view, blinded to the true facts of his class position by an obdurate snobbery, by an incurable pretentiousness. . . .

The initial difficulty of such an argument lies in the weight it attaches to the sheer fact of 'propertylessness' as a criterion of class division. In general terms, of course, there are good grounds to agree with Weber, echoing Marx, that, ' "property" and "lack of property" are the basic categories of all class situations'. . . . [But] all those who fall into the category of propertyless and contractual labour do not necessarily share an identical market

57

situation.

As a consequence, any empirical study of class consciousness must begin by taking into account actual differences in the market situations of propertyless groups. To define such differences out of existence at the very beginning as being irrelevant to the long-run development of class alignments and class consciousness is nothing less than an abdication from sociological understanding. Variations in class identification have to be related to actual variations in class situations and not attributed to some kind of ideological aberration or self-deception.

Nowhere is this conclusion more relevant than in the case of blackcoated 'false' class consciousness. The outstanding fact which all but the most biased observers of the class system must recognize is that, although he shares the propertyless status of the manual worker, the clerk has never been strictly 'proletarian' in terms of income, job security and occupational mobility. . . . In the first place, clerks have had a relatively high income throughout the greater part of the period with which we have been concerned. . . . Their privileged economic position was also buttressed by the small part which their remuneration plays in the total costs of the enterprise relative to wages, as well as by the interests of employers in securing the loyalty and commitment of their office staffs. . . . Secondly, and more important than sheer differences in income, blackcoated workers traditionally enjoyed a much greater degree of job-security than manual workers. Though this condition was never absolute and uniform throughout the clerical field, job-security was something on which the clerk could generally count. . . . Thirdly, clerks, and particularly male clerks, have had superior chances of rising to managerial and supervisory positions. Finally, in addition to the official and unofficial rights to pensions on retirement which many clerks have enjoyed, must be added the non-pecuniary advantages of office work – its cleanliness, comfort, tempo, hours, holidays – all of which should be included in a calculus of relative rewards. . . .

Both in the factory and in the labour market, the outstanding features of the work situation of modern wage-labour are, on the one hand, the physical separation and social estrangement of management and workers, and, on the other, the physical concentration and social identification of the workers themselves. . . . This type of work situation is one that clearly maximizes a sense of class separation and antagonism. Insofar as the work situation of the modern wage-earner approximated such a pattern of relationships, it took on the character of a 'proletarian' class situation. When, however, this type of 'proletarian' work situation is compared with that of the blackcoated worker, it is evident that in this respect, too, the behaviour of the clerk has been influenced by an administrative division of labour which, over great areas of clerical employment, entailed radically different relationships. . . . The older, paternalistic work environment of the counting house was . . . inimical to the development of any sense of common identity among clerks. At the same time, any feeling of class identification with the manual worker was absolutely precluded by the relations of production. Physically, clerks were scattered among a large number of small offices, working in close contact with employers, and divorced from the factory workmen. Their working relationships were largely determined by personal and particular ties, which meant that there was little uniformity in standards of work and remuneration, and that individualistic aspirations to advancement were strongly encouraged.

In the period of the modern office it is necessary to distinguish between those fields of clerical employment where paternalistic influences are still operative, and those where bureaucratic forms of administration have been established. In the former, the relatively small size of the office, the internal social fragmentation of the office staff through occupational, departmental and informal status distinctions, and the absence of any institutionalized blockage of mobility, have continued to militate against the growth of collective action among clerks. In addition, the lack of any widespread, systematic criteria of job grading and remuneration – reflecting the particularism characteristic of an inchoate labour market – has, for the greater part of the period, proved a further obstacle to the development of occupational consciousness. In those bureaucracies, on the other hand, where larger office units, strict classification and grading, blocked upward mobility and unhindered horizontal mobility were the rule, there have been reproduced impersonal and standardized working relationships comparable with those created by the factory and labour market. It is here that the work situation of the clerk has been most favourable to the emergence of that feeling of collective interdependence among employees which is prerequisite to their concerted action. But even where working conditions have fostered group action by clerks, the continuing physical and social

59

division between clerks and manual workers has generally remained a barrier to the mutual identification of the two groups. The sense of social distance between manual and non-manual worker may, in turn, be traced primarily to their relative proximity to administrative authority. Bound up as it is with the general organization of discipline and authority, the relationship between clerk and manual worker lends itself readily to hostility and resentment on both sides. . . .

Class focuses on the divisions which result from the brute facts of economic organization. Status relates to the more subtle distinctions which stem from the values that men set on each other's activities. . . . Status distinctions can aggravate or mollify class-conscious feeling. The clearest instance of the first process is to be seen in the effect which the rigid status division between manual and non-manual work has had on working-class consciousness in European countries. . . . Because the distinction between manual and non-manual work provided a clearly identifiable dividing line across which many other differences – in income, security, promotion possibilities, authority, education – could also be contrasted, it was readily seized on as a line of status demarcation. The consequences of this social gulf for the mutual orientation of blackcoated and manual workers were no less significant than those stemming from economic position and working environment. Indeed, the chief result was to accentuate those other differences and invest them with a more general relevance. When differences in advantage are overlaid by differences in social worth, mutual identification is precluded; especially when superiority is asserted on the one side as vigorously as it is denied on the other. For the middle-class status of the clerk was not unequivocally recognized, particularly by the working man. It is precisely this ambiguity in the status of the clerk, deriving largely from the lack of consistency and consensus entailed by the inclusion in the middle class of all but those who work with their hands, that provides the major clue to the 'snobbishness' of the clerk. . . . The exaggerated status consciousness of the blackcoated worker was produced by his marginal social position, and by the vicious circle of clerical 'snobbishness' and working-class 'contempt' to which it gave rise. A self-perpetuating 'status' barrier between clerk and manual worker was thus brought into existence.

The lowered social status of blackcoated work at the present time is the outcome of a long and complex process of change whereby many of the former bases of the clerk's prestige have been undermined, making the line between the middle and working classes less distinct. As a group, clerical workers are now more heterogeneous and the sheer fact of 'brain work' is less and less the hallmark of middle-class status. Under these conditions the class consciousness of the blackcoated worker exhibits greater diversity. Because of his increased marginality there is perhaps a greater tendency for the class identification of the clerk to be either extreme working class or extreme middle class, though this question obviously requires much more research. What does seem tolerably clear is that the traditional superiority of non-manual work has not been entirely eradicated by the changes of the last half-century, even though it has been more frequently questioned. This is best stated by saying that the loss of middle-class status by the clerk is not tantamount to the acquisition of working-class status, either from the point of view of the clerk or the manual worker. The differences between the two groups that lend themselves most readily to status usurpation by the clerk are at the same time those which are most firmly entrenched in the hierarchy of authority of modern industry and administration. In short, differences in class situation, and especially in work situation, continue to incite status rivalry between clerk and manual worker, and status rivalry in turn weakens their consciousness of class identity.

The New Middle Class in America

C. Wright Mills

White Collar: the American Middle Classes (London: Oxford University Press, 1951) pp. 70–5

Occupations, in terms of which we circumscribe the new middle class, involve several ways of ranking people. As specific activities, they entail various types and levels of *skill*, and their exercise fulfils certain *functions* within an industrial division of labor. These are the skills and functions we have been examining statistically. As sources of income, occupations are connected with *class* position;

and since they normally carrry an expected quota of prestige, on and off the job, they are relevant to *status* position. They also involve certain degrees of *power* over other people, directly in terms of the job, and indirectly in other social areas. Occupations are thus tied to class, status, and power as well as to skill and function; to understand the occupations composing the new middle class, we must consider them in terms of each of these dimensions.

'Class situation' in its simplest objective sense has to do with the amount and source of income. Today, occupation rather than property is the source of income for most of those who receive any direct income: the possibilities of selling their services in the labor market, rather than of profitably buying and selling their property and its yields, now determine the life-chances of most of the middle class. All things money can buy and many that men dream about are theirs by virtue of occupational income. In new middle-class occupations men work for someone else on someone else's property. This is the clue to many differences between the old and new middle classes, as well as to the contrast between the older world of the small propertied entrepreneur and the occupational structure of the new society. If the old middle class once fought big property structures in the name of small, free properties, the new middle class, like the wage-workers in latter-day capitalism, has been, from the beginning, dependent upon large properties for job security.

Wage-workers in the factory and on the farm are on the propertyless bottom of the occupational structure, depending upon the equipment owned by others, earning wages for the time they spend at work. In terms of property, the white-collar people are *not* 'in between Capital and Labor'; they are in exactly the same property-class position as the wage-workers. They have no direct financial tie to the means of production, no prime claim upon the proceeds from property. Like factory workers – and day laborers, for that matter – they work for those who do own such means of livelihood.

Yet if bookkeepers and coal miners, insurance agents and farm laborers, doctors in a clinic and crane operators in an open pit have this condition in common, certainly their class situations are not the same. To understand their class positions, we must go beyond the common fact of source of income and consider as well the amount of income.

In 1890, the average income of white-collar occupational groups was about double that of wage-workers. Before World War I, salaries were not so adversely affected by slumps as wages were but, on the contrary, they rather steadily advanced. Since World War I, however, salaries have been reacting to turns in the economic cycles more and more like wages, although still to a lesser extent. If wars help wages more because of the greater flexibility of wages, slumps help salaries because of their greater inflexibility. Yet after each war era, salaries have never regained their previous advantage over wages. Each phase of the cycle, as well as the progressive rise of all income groups, has resulted in a narrowing of the income gap between wage-workers and white-collar employees.

In the middle 'thirties the three urban strata, entrepreneurs, white-collar, and wage-workers, formed a distinct scale with respect to median family income: the white-collar employees had a median income of $1896; the entrepreneurs, $1464; the urban wage-workers, $1175. Although the median income of white-collar workers was higher than that of the entrepreneurs, larger proportions of the entrepreneurs received both high-level and low-level incomes. The distribution of their income was spread more than that of the white collar.

The wartime boom in incomes, in fact, spread the incomes of all occupational groups, but not evenly. The spread occurred mainly among urban entrepreneurs. As an income level, the old middle class in the city is becoming less an evenly graded income group, and more a collection of different strata, with a large proportion of lumpen-bourgeoisie who receive very low incomes, and a small, prosperous bourgeoisie with very high incomes.

In the late 'forties (1948, median family income) the income of all white-collar workers was $4000, that of all urban wage-workers, $3300. These averages, however, should not obscure the overlap of specific groups within each stratum: the lower white-collar people – sales-employees and office workers – earned almost the same as skilled workers and foremen, but more than semi-skilled urban wage-workers.

In terms of property, white-collar people are in the same position as wage-workers; in terms of occupational income, they are 'somewhere in the middle'. Once they were considerably above the wage-workers; they have become less so; in the middle of the century they still have an edge but the over-all rise in incomes is making the new middle class a more homogeneous income group.

As with income, so with prestige: white-collar groups are differentiated socially, perhaps more decisively than wage-workers and entrepreneurs. Wage earners certainly do form an income pyramid and a prestige gradation, as do entrepreneurs and rentiers; but the new middle class, in terms of income and prestige, is a superimposed pyramid, reaching from almost the bottom of the first to almost the top of the second.

People in white-collar occupations claim higher prestige than wage-workers, and, as a general rule, can cash in their claims with wage-workers as well as with the anonymous public. This fact has been seized upon, with much justification, as the defining characteristic of the white-collar strata, and although there are definite indications in the United States of a decline in their prestige, still, on a nation-wide basis, the majority of even the lower white-collar employees – office workers and salespeople – enjoy a middling prestige.

The historic bases of the white-collar employees' prestige, apart from superior income, have included the similarity of their place and type of work to those of the old middle-classes' which has permitted them to borrow prestige. As their relations with entrepreneur and with esteemed customer have become more impersonal, they have borrowed prestige from the firm itself. The stylization of their appearance, in particular the fact that most white-collar jobs have permitted the wearing of street clothes on the job, has also figured in their prestige claims, as have the skills required in most white-collar jobs, and in many of them the variety of operations performed and the degree of autonomy exercised in deciding work procedures. Furthermore, the time taken to learn these skills and the way in which they have been acquired by formal education and by close contact with the higher-ups in charge has been important. White-collar employees have monopolized high school education – even in 1940 they had completed 12 grades to the 8 grades for wage-workers and entrepreneurs. They have also enjoyed status by descent: in terms of race, Negro white-collar employees exist only in isolated instances – and, more importantly, in terms of nativity, in 1930 only about 9 per cent of white-collar workers, but 16 per cent of free enterprisers and 21 per cent of wage-workers, were foreign born. Finally, as an underlying fact, the limited size of the white-collar group, compared to wage-workers, has led to successful claims to greater prestige.

The power position of groups and of individuals typically depends upon factors of class, status, and occupation, often in intricate interrelation. Given occupations involve specific powers over other people in the actual course of work; but also outside the job area, by virtue of their relations to institutions of property as well as the typical income they afford, occupations lend power. Some white-collar occupations require the direct exercise of supervision over other white-collar and wage-workers, and many more are closely attached to this managerial cadre. White-collar employees are the assistants of authority; the power they exercise is a derived power, but they do exercise it.

Moreover, within the white-collar pyramids there is a characterisitc pattern of authority involving age and sex. The white-collar ranks contain a good many women: some 41 per cent of all white-collar employees, as compared with 10 per cent of free enterprisers, and 21 per cent of wage-workers, are women. As with sex, so with age: free enterprisers average (median) about 45 years of age, white-collar and wage-workers, about 34; but among free enterprisers and wage-workers, men are about 2 or 3 years older than women; among white-collar workers, there is a 6- or 7-year difference. In the white-collar pyramids, authority is roughly graded by age and sex: younger women tend to be sub-ordinated to older men.

4 Clerical Labour and the New Technology

Automation and the Clerk

Counter Information Services

The New Technology (London: CIS, 1979) pp. 8–12

The most widespread application of new technology, and the area where the largest number of jobs is immediately at risk, is within the office. Factory workers are already familiar with the drive for greater productivity: the breaking down of each job into its simplest component parts; the meticulous measurement of each worker's performance: the removal of all individual initiative; the pacing of work by machine rather than by the operator; the necessity to spend every second of the day at the machine; the constant drive to speed-up; and the perpetual attempt to cut jobs. Now these techniques are within the reach of the office manager as well as the plant manager. The effect on job opportunity, particularly for women, will be drastic.

There are now more women in paid employment than ever before. In the UK there are 9·1 million women workers compared to 13·1 million men – they form 41 per cent of the workforce. . . .

The increase in the number of employed women has not been matched by a decline in the traditional distinctions between men's and women's work. Women are still concentrated in certain industries and in particular, predominantly low paid, occupations. Over 70 per cent of women are employed in the service industries, as compared to only 40 per cent of men. No less than 40 per cent, two out of five, of all women workers are in clerical occupations: clerks, typists, secretaries, office machine operators, telephonists and similar jobs. There are three million women office workers. The importance of clerical and office work to the female workforce cannot be overstated.

The number of office workers has been growing steadily – office wage costs are increasingly eating into company profits. . . . The cost of running offices, mainly wages, accounts for half of the total operating costs of all US corporations. In government and service industries such as banks and insurance firms, the office wage bill is a full three-quarters of total costs. In the UK, wages now account for nearly 80 per cent of all office costs. While costs have doubled over the last decade, office productivity has remained almost stagnant. US estimates reckon that it has increased by only 4 per cent while, in the same ten years, industrial productivity nearly doubled. This is not surprising given that whereas there is some $25 000 of investment behind every production worker, there is only $2000 worth for each office worker.

As office employment and wage costs have soared, the price of office automation equipment had been falling by about 10 per cent per year. Rationalisation of the office has become a real and economic possibility. . . .

Silicon technology, initially developed in the field of computers, has not only spread into the areas of office equipment and tele-communications, it has converged the three areas. The combination, known as 'information technology', opens the door for the automated office from which paper, as the medium for handling information, has practically disappeared. Office work is largely concerned with acquiring, storing, transforming, presenting and sending information. While clerical workers transform, store and transmit information, executive level office workers assimilate existing information, manipulate it and generate new information.

Information originates as speech, typed or handwritten text and accounts, diagrams or photographs. The new technology can deal with all these forms: word processors deal with text; data processors with accounts; electronic telephone systems with speech; and facsimile transmitters with images. The computer services all of them. . . .

Both the word processor and the accounting machine are now based on very similar technology, utilising the microcomputer or a larger, centralised computer. Although we will deal here mainly with word processors, as a new phenomenon dramatically affecting office employment, probably just as many jobs will be lost in the immediate future to increasingly available electronic calculating techniques. As a recent advertisement for Philips Data Systems puts it, 'for £44 a week, Philips' new computers will take over all the routines and give you more time to get down to business. That's less than the cost of a clerk, yet Philips' computers handle the work of three . . . All your payroll, ledgers, invoicing, stock records and VAT take minutes instead of hours – with accuracy guaranteed. At £44 a week, Philips' computers pay for themselves over and over again'.

The word processor enables a typist to produce the work of two or three, while reducing the skill she needs. The typist types into the machine's memory, and what she types appears on a visual display unit (like a TV screen). Only when the display shows that the memory holds the text in the correct form will she instruct the machine to print it out. This is done by a separate printer which is many times faster than the speediest typist.

There is no need for time consuming erasure when correcting errors on the word processor. Until now, the number of errors and the need to go back, white them out and retype has been the limiting factor on a typist's speed. Now errors can be retyped at the touch of a key and less skilled typists can work at the same speed as more accurate ones (this advantage of word processors is much vaunted by advertisers).

The word processor automatically centres, indents and justifies margins as instructed. The skill required to produce a neat well laid out document is eliminated. It will produce any number of error free copies of an original text once it is in the memory. The operator can automatically interrupt standard material to insert text specific to each letter, such as a name and address and account number. Complex editing, including re-ordering of paragraphs, inserts and revision of lay-out is possible. This eliminates the need for retyping the entire text as documents are edited prior to the final draft. Automatic sorting enables input typed into the memory to be sorted into alphabetic order after being typed in random order. Qualified selection enables items to be selected from the memory by specified criteria, e.g. all subscribers in London. . . .

Once the word processor is connected to the data processing power of a large computer, and . . . to the telecommunications networks of the world, then the ingredients of total automation of office work are there. Letters need no longer be posted: they can be transmitted from one work station to another – or indeed to many hundreds of others at once – while a copy is safely stored in the originating processor's memory, to be recalled at the touch of a key.

The Post Office estimates that, for an organisation sending 2000 pages of A4 a month an average of 100km, by 1986 the cost of sending each page will be 11p by first class post; 2·5p by word processor on a store and forward overnight basis; 5·4p by facsimile transmission; and 37p by telex. But these savings are small compared to those to be made in labour costs in the preparation of the documents. In 1976, in the UK, one A4 page cost an estimated £2.75 to prepare and 8½p to transmit. Productivity in text preparation will be dramatically raised by the word processor.

There are already over 9000 word processors installed in the UK, and the market is expected to double by 1981. Word processing is with us now. What are the effects of its introduction?

The main effect is increased productivity. And that means fewer jobs. Word processor suppliers claim that the average typist or secretary spends only 30 to 35 per cent of her time at the typewriter, and a high proportion of this time is spent retyping corrected drafts, standard letters and forms. Many processor suppliers claim cost savings of 50–100 per cent. Logica, distributor of the UNICOM system, claims productivity increases of 150–400 per cent, or one typist doing the work of 2½ to 5 typists on conventional equipment.

One large employer estimated that a typist spent her day like this:

	Conventional typewriter	Stand alone word processor
Typing text	27%	55%
Telex	6%	6%
Retyping	17%	5%
Correcting errors	11%	5%
Paper handling	10%	—
Waiting time	5%	5%
Rest allowance	24%	24%

The time spent by the typist on typing doubles with the shift to word processing. In this case the employer expected that the installation of 4 word processing units would reduce the central typing pool from 14 typists and 1 supervisor to 11 typists and 1 supervisor, while simultaneously increasing the workload, and the workspeed.

Bradford Council reduced its staff in one section from 44 to 22 with the introduction of 9 word processors, resulting in an increased productivity of 19 per cent and an estimated annual saving of £59 000. The authority now wishes to introduce word processing across the whole education department, with a possible loss of 200 jobs. . . . The Provident Financial Group installed three IBM memory typewriters into a central typing pool. They reduced their full time typing staff from 27 to 17, their part time staff from 13 to 3, and increased the workload. The jobs were cut through natural wastage. Productivity is being monitored. The Halifax Building Society progressed from automatic typewriters which they had used for 10 years to a system of 16 IBM word processors. The workforce has not been reduced, but the workload has almost trebled. The typists are at the machines all day apart from two minute breaks and a lunch break. . . .

There are many other examples showing the same characteristics. The pattern so far has been that a large number of jobs *have* been lost, but only small numbers at any one time. Because of the high turnover of labour in offices, managements have usually been able to reduce their staffs by 'natural wastage', i.e. not replacing workers who leave of their own accord, are invalided out, or reach retirement age: rather than by forcing redundancy. What this means is that job opportunities are lost. In local government, the pattern has been one of 'redeployment' to another section – again this means an overall loss in job prospects. Companies whose business has been expanding have not reduced their staffing levels – but nor have they expanded them while output has risen many times over.

The introduction of word processors has had other results besides job loss. For those who operate them, the intensity of work is increased, and those aspects of office work that make it less unpleasant than factory work are systematically removed. Monotype claims in its advertisements: 'Costly and energy-wasting procedures are abolished: the walking, waiting, filing, correcting, updating and supervision go, and are replaced by a system that does what you want it to do'.

What this looks like in practice is described in a report on the experience in Bradford's word processor installation: 'the machines are in constant operation and are programmed by the rate material comes in. The workers have one ten minute break in the morning and afternoon, and otherwise have no contact with other workers during office time. All new work comes in through a special anti-static glass box, and no non-section workers enter the room.'

A word processor operator in a Leeds manufacturing company describes her work: 'We work a 7½ hour day with half an hour for lunch. We have a ten minute break in the morning and another ten minutes in the afternoon, but the afternoon isn't official. We've been on flexitime for two years but now it looks as if they're trying to get rid of it. All the word processing machines are switched on and off at the same time, and they want us to make a record of all the work we do, so they can monitor how many orders each person is dealing with'.

There is growing concern at the potential health hazards involved in sitting in front of a Visual Display Unit (VDU) screen all day. Eyestrain which produces headaches, fatigue, focusing inabilities, nausea, and even psychological reactions can result from long hours reading data on the VDU's cathode ray tube. . . .

An additional feature of word processing is the change it brings about in office hours. Pressure to get maximum possible use of the new machinery moves managements to try and move away from flexitime, and, if possible, even introduce shift working. The trend is likely to spread, particularly with the use of telephone lines to transmit text and data, which is cheaper in the evenings. Logica, the office systems company, has had an additional 6pm to 10pm shift for well over a year.

Another benefit to management is the ability to monitor its office staff more closely than ever before. Built-in supervision is a major selling point. . . .

Those who favour the use of new technology make much of the notion that it relieves people from boring, repetitive jobs. In the case of word processors the opposite is true. From being a member of a social office, responsible for all stages of document preparation bar its origination, office workers become little more than skilled machine minders. And those skills that the typist once needed are lessened. . . .

Office automation will provide the employer with huge productivity gains over the next decade, at little real capital cost. Just as important for the employer though, those gains will be accompanied by a major reassertion of control of the employers over the office work process. A word processor or accounting machine not only increases the productivity of the operator: it also divests the operator of control over his or her own labour.

White-Collar Woes

Special Task Force to the Secretary of Health, Education and Welfare

Work in America (Cambridge, Mass.: MIT Press, 1973) pp. 38–40

The auto industry is the *locus classicus* of dissatisfying work; the assembly-line, its quintessential embodiment. But what is striking is the extent to which the dissatisfaction of the assembly-line and blue-collar worker is mirrored in white-collar and even managerial positions. The office today, where work is segmented and authoritarian, is often a factory. For a growing number of jobs, there is little to distinguish them but the color of the worker's collar: computer keypunch operations and typing pools share much in common with the automobile assembly-line.

Secretaries, clerks, and bureaucrats were once grateful for having been spared the dehumanization of the factory. White-collar jobs were rare; they had higher status than blue-collar jobs. But today the clerk, and not the operative on the assembly-line, is the typical American worker, and such positions offer little in the way of prestige. Furthermore, the size of the organizations that employ the bulk of office workers has grown, imparting to the clerical worker the same impersonality that the blue-collar worker experiences in the factory. The organization acknowledges the presence of the worker only when he makes a mistake or fails to follow a rule, whether in factory or bureaucracy, whether under public or private control. . . .

Traditionally, lower-level white-collar jobs in both government and industry were held by high school graduates. Today, an increasing number of these jobs go to those who have attended college. But the demand for higher academic credentials has not increased the prestige, status, pay, or difficulty of the job. For example, the average weekly pay for clerical workers in 1969 was

$105.00 per week, while blue-collar production workers were taking home an average of $130.00 per week. It is not surprising, then, that the Survey of Working Conditions found much of the greatest work dissatisfaction in the country among young, well-educated workers who were in low-paying, dull, routine, and fractionated clerical positions. Other signs of discontent among this group include turnover rates as high as 30 per cent annually and a 46 per cent increase in white-collar union membership between 1958 and 1968. A 1969 study of 25 000 white-collar employees in eighty-eight major companies showed a decline in the percentage of positive responses concerning several key factors of job satisfaction since 1965. For example, there was a 34 per cent decline in the belief that their company would act to do something about their individual problems. These changing attitudes (and the failure of employers to react constructively to them) may be affecting the productivity of these workers: a survey conducted by a group of management consultants of a cross section of office employees found that they were producing at only 55 per cent of their potential. Among the reasons cited for this was boredom with repetitive jobs.

Loyalty to employer was once high among this group of workers who felt that they shared much in common with their bosses – collar color, tasks, place of work. Today, many white-collar workers have lost personal touch with decision makers, and, consequently, they feel estranged from the goals of the organizations in which they work. Management has exacerbated this problem by viewing white-collar workers as expendable: because their productivity is hard to measure and their functions often non-essential, they are seen as the easiest place to 'cut fat' during low points in the business cycle. Today, low-level white-collar workers are more likely to be sacrificed for the sake of short-term profitability than are blue-collar workers.

5 Technicians in Modern Capitalism

The Technostructure

J. K. Galbraith

The New Industrial State, (London: Pelican, 1969) pp. 70–2, 74, 79–80

The need to draw on, and appraise, the information of numerous individuals in modern industrial decision-making has three principal points of origin. It derives, first, from the technological requirements of modern industry . . . . The real accomplishment of modern science and technology consists in taking ordinary men, informing them narrowly and deeply and then, through appropriate organization, arranging to have their knowledge combined with that of other specialized but equally ordinary men. This dispenses with the need for genius. The resulting performance, though less inspiring, is far more predictable.

The second factor requiring the combination of specialized talent derives from advanced technology, the associated use of capital, and the resulting need for planning with its accompanying control of environment. . . .

Finally, following from the need for this variety of specialized talent, is the need for its coordination. Talent must be brought to bear on the common purpose. More specifically, on large and small matters, information must be extracted from the various specialists, tested for its reliability and relevance, and made to yield a decision. . . .

Decision in the modern business enterprise is the product not of individuals but of groups. The groups are numerous, as often informal as formal, and subject to constant change in composition. Each contains the men possessed of the information, or with access to the information, that bears on the particular decision together with those whose skill consists in extracting and testing this information and obtaining a conclusion. This is how men act successfully on matters where no single one, however exalted or intelligent, has more than a fraction of the necessary knowledge. It is what makes modern business possible, and in other contexts it is what makes modern government possible. . . .

In the past, leadership in business organization was identified with the entrepreneur – the individual who united ownership or control of capital with capacity for organizing the other factors of production and, in most contexts, with a further capacity for innovation. With the rise of the modern corporation. . . . the entrepreneur no longer exists as an individual person in the mature industrial enterprise. Everyday discourse, except in the economics textbooks, recognizes this change. It replaces the entrepreneur, as the directing force of the enterprise, with management. This is a collective and imperfectly defined entity. . . . It includes, however, only a small proportion of those who, as participants, contribute information to group decisions. This latter group is very large; it extends from the most senior officials of the corporation to where it meets, at the outer perimeter, the white and blue collar workers whose function is to conform more or less mechanically to instruction or routine. It embraces all who bring specialized knowledge, talent or experience to group decision-making. This, not the management, is the guiding intelligence – the brain – of the enterprise. There is no name for all who participate in group decision-making or the organization which they form. I propose to call this organization the Technostructure.

The New Working Class

Serge Mallet

La nouvelle classe ouvrière (translation by Richard Hyman) (Paris: Éditions du Seuil, 1963) pp. 10–15 and *The New Working Class* (Nottingham: Spokesman Books, 1975) pp. 66–8, 28–30

Outside the factory gates, the worker appears absorbed within a vast urban community in which differences in standards of living seem merely quantitative: an inadequate basis for a theory of social stratification. Within production itself, by contrast, the basic features distinguishing the working class from other sections of the population seem unchanged.

Some writers consider that the growing uniformity of social conditions renders questionable the very notion of 'working class'. My own position is simply that during the evolution of the working class certain extraneous factors – tied to the worker's role as consumer rather than as producer – have been wrongly treated as distinctive features of class composition, and that these must be purged from the concept of class.

In the same way, empirical observation has led certain technical factors to be treated as criteria of membership of the working class, and changes in this area have been invoked as evidence of the 'withering away of the working class'. Working-class employment has been identified with manual labour, distinguished from the work of the artisan only in being performed collectively. But this identification has long lost its objective basis: the skilled labour of the setter, or the tracer in an aircraft factory, has from the outset involved strictly intellectual operations.

As long however as working-class labour has involved a significant application of physical energy, even if other elements are involved; as long as it has taken place in a traditional factory where men operate machines, the confusion between working-class and manual labour has been perpetuated. A clear line of division thus separates those in the factory who are subjected to the discipline of the machines from those whose activities have no immediate and visible link with the rhythm of production. 'White-collar' employees – technicians, minor engineers, draughtsmen, staff in research units – bear only the most remote affinity to the traditional worker. Should one therefore regard them as external to the working class? Should one conclude that their growing importance is a corollary of a reduction in *its* numerical importance? Should one place them in the same category as unproductive staff in financial institutions?

In practice the social consciousness of these staff is far more determined by technical relations than by their mere status as salaried employees. Relations between management and manual workers, for example, differ considerably according to the type of factory. In general one can say that in highly mechanised factories, where the mass of workers are mere machine-minders tied to the production line, managers act primarily as overseers... and often appear as the workers' principal enemy. These are the foremen who try to force up production; while the efficiency engineers, committed to planned productivity rather than disruptive bursts of effort, attempt to cool their ardours. In general, management in a mechanised factory has acquired a sergeant-major mentality, and its harshness is an almost direct function of the degree of exploitation. . . .

But as methods of production evolve, this type of management tends to lose its utility. With the development of automated processes, the manual labour alters: young workers with a technical training take the place of unskilled machine-minders. This generates a new kind of conflict between workers and management. A recent study in an electronics factory in the Paris area, where modern equipment and methods had been introduced, showed that while the old workers accepted readily enough the prerogatives of management, the young ones – recruited from technical college and adapted to modern manufacturing techniques – were critical of its incompetence, its old-fashioned routines, its slave-driving methods. Their views converged with those of the methods engineers who, in most modern factories, consider the old ranks of management . . . as an obstacle both to the improvement in labour productivity and to the spirit of 'co-operation' which they seek to establish with the workers . . . . The modern factory has seen the emergence of a section of highly trained technicians who exercise managerial functions . . . .

Thus the very definition of the working class has become more difficult. It is clear that criteria drawn from everyday life (housing, leisure activities, clothes, food, etc.) are an insufficient basis for classification . . . . Modern housing has become standardised. Modern consumer goods are distributed among all social strata. Holidays – even winter holidays – are no longer the special privileges of an elite. Of course while the key elements of today's standard of living are spread across numerous social groups, their distribution nationally is still unequal. The existence of regional disparities, the coexistence of areas with a modern standard of living and archaic areas, is an essential feature of our society. But it does not form the basis of class differentiation . . . .

Distinctions based on various technical criteria are also quite arbitrary. The research technician, integrated within the programme of his research laboratory, is as much a 'proletarian' as the worker monitoring a control panel in an automated workplace. While some categories of worker still perform their jobs in harsh physical conditions – in chemicals, mining, construction, sectors of modern industry with assembly-line operations – these conditions are in no way different from those of certain occupations within the public services . . . .

Finally, traditional legal criteria – monthly as against hourly payment – are less and less significant. Manual workers in the state sector, and in many areas of private industry, are today 'monthly staff'. The gradual elimination of individual payment by results has involved this development in almost every important industry.

After eliminating the sociological, technical and administrative criteria which used to define the working class, we are left with only one condition common to numerous categories of salaried worker: that of performing a productive function and being excluded from the ownership or direction of the instruments of production which they service. A single, and to my mind sufficient, criterion.

Of course the limits of production itself have become increasingly extended. Today one is forced to include within productive activities the services and units which create the preconditions of production strictly defined. Research units and planning departments have the same claim as the workshops to be contributing to new values, to the creation of surplus product. The sales and marketing departments, whose economic function is dominant, create none. It might be said that this distinction is wholly theoretical; that staff in the sales or publicity departments of a large firm, if questioned, would certainly not consider themselves different from their colleagues in adjacent offices which are linked to industrial production; and that by contrast the storekeeper, whose function contributes nothing to the creation of value, considers himself as much a worker as the machine operator whom he serves. But the 'decisive moments' which unfortunately often escape the notice of sociologists give us a different picture: in periods of social conflict it is always the productive sectors which lead the way. It is their action which inspires the movement . . . .

Workers employed in automated industries (or industries in the process of automation) have been called the 'new working-class'. In fact, this term covers two different types of wage earners, both born of new technical developments and both involved in this process of 'integration in the firms'.

a) The new factory uses two types of workers who are still classified as manual workers. These are the foremen, loaders, operators, and preparers, who are assigned to automated production units; and the maintenance workers, who are in charge of repairing and keeping watch over the machinery. The type of qualification required of them is quite different. The first, who in practice do not manipulate objects, are selected because of their faculties of attention, visual facility, and initiative. They are the human checkers of possible mechanical faults. Their job demands quite a comprehensive knowledge of the synthetic production process in which they become inserted. The latter's qualification is of a more traditional nature; mechanics, electricians, watchmakers etc. Yet they too are in touch with all the production posts, and have a total view of the production process, in which they exert rather more responsibility. While automation on the one hand totally eliminates the contact between man and object, on the other hand it destroys the fragmentation of work and recreates the synthetic vision of a complex task at the level of the team, or even of the whole work force. Production units become smaller and human contacts between groups of workers are more frequent, less anonymous than those in a Taylorised factory.

Such workers who are integrated in the firm – that is to say in a *stable production unit* – are also integrated in their own group. In the same way, the corollary of the change in the functions of work is a closer relation between workers and *cadres* (junior management). Engineers who control a distillation unit in a refinery and may have been promoted out of the rank-and-file, are linked to the few white-overalled worker-technicians under their command through a hierarchy defined within the same social group. This is not at all comparable to the position of exploitation engineers (pit managers in the coal industry for example) giving orders to an army of anonymous unskilled workers from whom they are separated by a class barrier. In any case, modern industry favours gradations, and as a result, the separation between workers, technicians and junior management tends to become less marked.

b) The other group, numerically greater, is not exclusively born of automation, but is partly due to the trend in modern industry to devote much time and effort to operations anterior to the classical production process (studies and research) and beyond it (commercialisation, market research etc.). They are the technicians in research units. Standing apart, often some distance away from the place of production, they no longer have much contact with the workers, and the feeling of superiority with which traditionally the white-collar workers looked down on the blue-collar workers disappears with this loss of physical contact due to distance. The enormous development of research units has, on the other hand, created real intellectual production units, in which working conditions grow increasingly similar to those of a modern workshop, but devoid of physical strain, dirt and stink – though with the same planned timing and mechanisation of office work.

The similarity between the industrial diseases – mostly nervous and psychical – which can be observed in both groups confirms this growing homogeneity between office and factory work. . . .

Is the new working class revolutionary? If one means by this question a revolutionary consciousness in the traditional sense of the term, finding its expression in the determination firstly to seize political power by any means and at any price, and only then to go on to the next phase of organising society in a new way, then the working class is without question not revolutionary. It is not revolutionary because it imposes two conditions preliminary to the transformation of existing structures. The first is that the transformation of the economic, social and political structures cannot be had at the price of the destruction of the existing means of production, or even of its serious weakening – 'the machine is too valuable to smash'. Secondly, it has taken note of the negative consequences of the achievement of political power which is not immediately accompanied by the transformation of the structures of the social hierarchy. Furthermore, it does not consider itself capable of conquering here and now the elements needed for the realisation of these new social relations. It therefore has a tendency to place before the cry 'we must take power' the question 'What shall we do with it?'

But if one understands by 'revolutionary' the wish to modify the existing social relations fundamentally, then the objective conditions within which the new working class acts and works makes it the perfect avant-garde of the revolutionary socialist movement. In fact, the more important research, invention and quality control become, the more human work becomes concentrated in the preparation and the organisation of production, the more the sense of initiative and responsibility increase; to put it briefly, the more the modern worker reconquers *on the collective level* the professional autonomy which he had lost during the period of the mechanisation of work, and the more will demands for control develop. Today's conditions of production offer objective possibilities for the development of generalised self-management of production and the economy by those who carry the weight. But these possibilities are confronted simultaneously by the capitalist structures of the relations of production, its criteria of profitability based on the short-term profit of the owners, and the technocratic structure of the firms which seem more to inhibit the harmonious development of their own productive possibilities. The recent social conflicts, which have developed during the last few years in the West, and the strike of May 1968 which crowned this series of movements, have shown that the advanced sectors of the working class are no longer content to make wage demands. Instead they challenged the techo-bureaucratic centres which direct the economy, to such an extent that they no longer seemed to be justified by developing technical and economic needs. On the contrary they appeared to be a survival from the past, protecting the privileged status of the existing hierarchies.

The evolution of the trade union movement in Western Europe reflects the new characteristics of this growing consciousness: just about everywhere it is the evolution of industrial sectors where the new working class predominates which tends to shift union organisations which have until now been characterised by purely reformist actions, towards a fundamental questioning of the system of capitalist production. . . .

Precisely because it is placed in the centre of the most complex mechanisms of organisational capitalism, the new working class is brought to realise more quickly than the other sectors the contradictions inherent in the system. Precisely because its elementary demands are largely satisfied, the new working class is led to ask itself other questions whose solutions cannot be found in the sphere of consumption. Its objective situation places it in the position of seeing the deficiencies in modern capitalist organisation, and to arrive at a consciousness of a new way of organising productive relationships, as the only way of satisfying the human needs which cannot be expressed within the present structures. Its action tends to be fundamentally challenging not simply of capitalism but, what is more, of all technocratic ways of controlling the economy. It is the hierarchical status of industry which is called into question each time there is a demand for some sort of control.

Technicians and the Class Struggle

André Gorz

'Technology, Technicians and Class Struggle'
(originally published in 1971) in André Gorz (ed.) *The Division of Labour: the Labour Process and Class-Struggle in Modern Capitalism* (Brighton: Harvester, 1976) pp. 167–9, 171–9

Even though it seems legitimate to consider that industrial scientific and technical workers belong to the category of productive, exploited and alienated workers, it does not seem correct to consider them to be purely and simply an integral part of the working class. . . .

It is . . . not adequate, in characterizing the position of scientific and technical workers in the production process, to examine it solely from the point of view of the relationship between capital and labour. It is just as important to consider it from the point of view of their relationship to other workers, and this will have an important bearing on the way in which scientific and technical workers consider their own class membership; it thus has an effect on their class-consciousness. We therefore need to distinguish:

1) situations where technical workers supervise, organize, control and command groups of production workers who, whatever their skills, have an inferior position in the industrial hierarchy and are subordinated to the former;
2) situations where the process is predominantly carried out by technical workers doing routine or repetitive work, with no authority or hierarchical privilege over other workers in the same production unit. . . .

Until recently it has been generally assumed that the division, specialization and separation of jobs in industrial production was not a prerequisite of the *capitalist* division of labour but was necessitated by the *technical* imperatives of large-scale mechanized production. It has been assumed that minutely fragmented and repetitive jobs are a consequence of the rationalization of the technical division of labour. It has moreover seemed that this unskilled and repetitive labour needed to be co-ordinated, supervised, planned and timed by technical experts responsible for overseeing all or part of the complex final product, for all or part of the overall work process. These experts, it seemed, needed to have both superior technical skills and intellectual and hierarchical authority.

But if we look into it more closely, we must ask: why must labour be minutely fragmented? Why must the narrowly specialized jobs be performed separately by different workers? . . . In fact it was not the development of the technical basis of production that caused the fragmentation of work. It was quite the other way round. From the very beginning what the capitalist bosses were after was to maximize their power and control over wage labour. The work process was organized with this aim in mind, and this was effective in determining the forms of production technology. . . .

These brief remarks should be enough to make it clear that the infinitesimal fragmentation of jobs is not the consequence of a technology that has developed according to its own laws, independently of the social and political context, but of a technology that is designed to function as a weapon in the class-struggle and to enable the amount of labour demanded from each worker to be 'scientifically' determined to prevent the worker from 'stealing' from the boss the time to smoke a cigarette, to read a newspaper or to put his feet up for a while. Work has not been made idiotic because the workers are idiots, or because you can increase the efficient expenditure of a given amount of human energy by turning them into idiots. Work has been made idiotic *because the workers cannot be trusted.* As long as they retain any control over their own work they are liable to use this against their exploiters. 'Scientific' work organization is above all the scientific destruction of any possibility of workers' control. . . .

Domination is necessary to maximize exploitation, to maximize the extent to which work serves the interests of capital and not those of the workers. The aim of capital is accumulation, and the pursuit of this aim involves the separation of the producers from the product of their labour, from the means of production and from work itself, which must be imposed on them from outside as a predetermined quantity, fixed by the inhuman necessities of the labour process. Hence there is a vicious circle:

1) since the purpose of production is not the satisfaction of the producers' needs, but the extortion of surplus labour, capitalist production cannot rely upon the workers' willingness to work;
2) the less capitalist management wishes to rely upon the willingness of the workers to work, the more extraneous, regimented and idiotic work has to become;
3) the more extraneous, regimented and idiotic work becomes, the less capitalist management can rely upon the workers' willingness. . . .

That is why all those whose job it is, because of their technical qualifications, to supervise the smooth running of production in fact work to reproduce the hierarchical division of labour and capitalist relations in production. This applies just as much to the lower-ranking technicians (time-and-motion men, quality-control inspectors and so on) as to the engineers and higher-grade technical workers, and others who perform the functions of authority and supervision. . . . They have a monopoly of the technical and intellectual skills required by the production process and they *deny* these skills to the workers. Their role is to dequalify workers and to reduce work to manual work pure and simple. They represent the skill and knowledge of which workers have been robbed, the separation between intellectual and manual work, between conception and execution. They enjoy significant financial, social and cultural privileges. They are the workers' most immediate enemy. In a machine-tool shop every technician hired may turn ten or twenty hitherto skilled workers into unskilled underdogs (providing, of course, that semi-automatic machines are installed at the same time).

As an illustration . . . I give here an extract from a conversation I had with a young technician . . . in a machine-tool factory. He had done three years of technical studies and was very proud of his knowledge. He earned twice as much as the workers he was supervising. When I asked him what he knew that the workers did not he replied: 'I have studied calculus and mechanics, and I'm a very good industrial draughtsman.'

'Do you ever use calculus in your work?'

'No. But I'm glad I've learned it. It's a good training for the mind.'

'What about the draughtsmanship? Is that very useful?'

'Of course. You can't possibly make anything unless you can read a blueprint, It's like the ABC.'

'Well then, if all the workers in your workshop know how to read a blueprint what do you know that they don't, apart from calculus?'

'I've got a more comprehensive insight into what it's all about.' . . .

This technician had been to a technical college for three years. You will have noticed that it was his knowledge of calculus that, more than anything else, gave him a sense of superiority. His hierarchical and social privileges were based on this 'mental training'. But the calculus was of no use to him at all in his work. . . . His hierarchical superiority stemmed from superiority of *useless* knowledge. He had not been trained in calculus to become more *efficient* (more productive) than untrained workers, but to become *superior* to them. And the workers had not failed to learn calculus because they were too stupid to learn it, but because they were intended to remain culturally, and therefore hierarchically, inferior, whatever their skill.

But . . . these socio-cultural differences between the directly productive workers and the low-ranking technical cadres are not *class* differences . . . . Although they are in a hierarchically oppressive position with respect to the workers they are themselves oppressed, exploited and alienated in their own work. Their position in relation to those above them in the hierarchy and to the representatives of capital is just the same as that of the workers in relation to them. But this objective class position must be understood correctly: these low-ranking technical cadres are not *bound* to owe allegiance to any other than the working class; they *can* feel themselves to be an integral part of this class, for that is what they are objectively. If Marxist analysis in terms of classes is to have any meaning they cannot be excluded *a priori* from the working class. But equally, they cannot be included in it without qualification, because while it is true that they belong objectively to no other class, it is also true that they are conditioned by their technical training to think of themselves as *not* belonging to the working class. We could say that they are workers who have been mystified, and that their hierarchical privileges sustain this mystification.

But mystification can be overcome. In situations of acute conflict an ideological breakthrough is possible. This can happen in periods of revolutionary crisis, or during a mass factory occupation or 'work-in' and so on. When, during a bitter struggle, the workers attack the capitalist division of labour and demand or set up a different way of doing things, without hierarchies and with equal pay for all (or demand some non-hierarchical system of pay increases), they may sometimes win over technical staff to their way of thinking. In the infectious atmosphere of a strike some of these technicians may even be found in the forefront of the struggle. Cases of this were to be seen in France in May 1968 and in the long 'hot autumn' of 1969 in Italy.

But the fact that this kind of ideological conversion is possible does not mean that it is inevitable. And it certainly does not mean that technical workers are destined to form the vanguard. The nature of their role in production does not prepare them for class confrontations, let alone for assuming positions of leadership. How they behave in a period of confrontation will depend mostly on their previous political and ideological education; and they don't get education like this in technical college. They get it from the politically radicalized workers in the course of the struggle when they come to understand that they stand to win more than they would lose by the abolition of the hierarchical division of labour . . . .

It might seem at first sight that the hierarchical and social privileges discussed above are not possessed by the growing stratum of technical and scientific personnel who work in big engineering firms, in the 'scientific' industries and research centres, and are themselves subjected to the capitalist division of labour. In recent years we have seen mass-rebellions and strikes by draughtsmen and engineering, technical and research staff in the scientific industries, computer firms and research institutes. In many cases such rebellion was motivated by the frustration and humiliation that these workers experienced when they were subjected to the same job-evaluation, fragmentation and hier-archical control of work as manual workers. When intellectual workers cease to exercise hierarchical authority over manual workers, and are themselves reduced to being producers of immaterial commodities – projects, programmes, systems, in-formation – or to being supervisors of automated processes, they

86

in their turn can come to seem proletarianized and alienated from the stupefying specialization of their work.

But we must be careful not to jump to the conclusion that their rebellion is the sign of a leap to proletarian class-consciousness ... More often than not the rebellion of intellectual workers is profoundly ambiguous: they rebel not *as* proletarians, but *against* being *treated* as proletarians. They rebel against the hierarchical organization, fragmentation and meaninglessness of their work, and against the loss of all or part of their social privileges.... Their struggle against hierarchy and authority is usually part and parcel of their demand for the reinstatement of the privileges they once enjoyed as members of the professional 'middle class'. They refuse proletarianization for themselves (but only for themselves), and assume that they can avoid it because they think of themselves as distinct from the workers. Hence the ambiguity of their struggles, which are in fact anti-monopolist rather than anti-capitalist in character.

Managerial Discontent

Special Task Force

Work in America, pp. 40–2

One finds evidence of increasing dissatisfaction with jobs even among such traditionally privileged groups as the nation's 4½ million middle managers. For example, where this group once represented a bulwark of company loyalty, today one out of three middle managers indicates some willingness to join a union. Another striking indicator of discontent is the apparently increasing number of middle-aged middle managers who are seeking a mid-career change.

Why should there be job dissatisfaction among people who earn twenty thousand dollars a year? Some trained observers say that the new values of the counter-culture have had a noticeable effect even on these workers who clearly espouse mainstream views. As evidence, it is claimed that where it used to be considered a sign of dedication and admirable ambition for a manager to be seen carrying home a full attaché case, today it is seen only as compulsive behavior or evidence of 'workaholism'.

Instead of pointing to such cultural explanations, management scientists point to the inherent qualities of the jobs of middle managers as the prime source of their dissatisfaction. Characteristically, middle managers perceive that they lack influence on organization decision making, yet they must implement company policy – and often without sufficient authority or resources to effectively carry it out. They must then compete to gain the attention of top management for support for their particular projects or functions. This leads to tension, conflict, and unproductive and frustrating in-fighting in that spectrum on the organization chart with responsibility for planning, integrating, and controlling the entire managerial system. The manager's discontent thus spreads throughout the organization. For example, managers without power often establish a style that consists of applying inflexible rules and procedures – thus, they bureaucratize an institution and frustrate change down the line.

Frustration often causes managers to lose their commitments to their jobs and the companies they work for. A Gallup Poll in 1972 asked whether the respondents thought 'they could produce more each day if they tried'. While 57% of the total public responded that they could, the figure for professionals and businessmen was 70%, only slightly behind the 72% of 18–29-year-olds who felt themselves to be least extended on the job.

A general feeling of obsolescence appears to overtake middle managers when they reach their late 30's. Their careers appear to have reached a plateau, and they realize that life from here on will be along an inevitable decline. There is a marked increase in the death rate between the ages of 35 and 40 for employed men, apparently as result of this so-called 'mid-life crisis'. The causes of these feelings are often related to questions of technical competence, but much obsolescence is cultural or interpersonal: some older managers cannot cope with the values of younger subordinates; some cannot adjust their sights to radically new organizational goals; and some have become so identified with a faction in the organization that has lost favor over time that they become ineffective.

The dollar costs of managerial obsolescence are hidden in poor or poorly timed decisions, in a lack of innovation or creativity, and in negative effects on the productivity of others. Businesses seem to reflect this lower productivity of older managers in the salaries they pay them: for each additional year of service with a firm, middle managers typically receive smaller annual increases.

The social costs of managerial obsolescence can be seen in Tayloristic or other outmoded philosophies that these managers instill throughout their companies. Their styles of management lead to tension and, often, to subsequent physical and mental health costs for their subordinates. The personal costs of managerial obsolescence relate to the ways they must compensate for their feelings of inadequacy: such coping mechanisms as alcohol and extramarital affairs are frequently used.

If we use only extrinsic measures of satisfaction – pay, prestige, fringe benefits – managers appear not to have work problems. But the social, industrial, and personal costs related to their intrinsic dissatisfactions make proposals to facilitate mid-career change through portable pensions and retraining seem highly desirable.

Scientific Intellectual Labour

Ernest Mandel

Late Capitalism (London: NLB, 1975) pp. 259–65

The growth of research and development by leaps and bounds has created a vast increase in the demand for highly-skilled intellectual labour-power. Hence the 'university explosion'; which in turn is accompanied by a vast supply of candidates (apprentices) for intellectually trained labour-power, which can be explained by the higher standard of living and individual social promotion associated with it. Already at the end of the 50's, 32.2% of the 20–24 age group were enrolled in higher education in the USA, 16.2% in New Zealand, 13.1% in Australia and the Netherlands and 10% in Argentina; since then these percentages have increased rapidly. At the beginning of the 60's over 75% of 15–19 year olds completed a secondary education in the USA, Australia, New Zealand, Japan, Great Britain, Holland and Belgium.

The most arresting result of the social transformation caused by this 'university explosion' is that at least in the USA, and probably also in several other capitalist countries, the number of academically-educated workers, if not also of students, exceeds that of farmers or peasants today.

The hallmark of this growth of scientific intellectual labour – elicited by the cumulative growth of scientific knowledge, research and development, and ultimately determined by accelerated technological innovation – is the massive reunification of intellectual and productive activity, and the entry of intellectual labour into the sphere of production. Since this reintroduction of intellectual labour into the process of production corresponds to the immediate needs of late capitalist technology, the education of intellectual workers must likewise be strictly subordinated to these needs. . . .

What capital needs is not a large number of highly-qualified intellectual workers. It needs an increasing but limited quantity of intellectual producers equipped with specific qualifications and with specific tasks to fulfil in the process of production or circulation. The greater the cumulative growth of science and the faster the acceleration of research and development, the more the specifically capitalist processes of increasing division of labour, rationalization and specialization in the interests of private profit – in other words, a constant fragmentation of labour – penetrates the spheres of intellectual labour and scientific instruction. . . . A new and acute social contradiction therefore develops between – on one hand, the cumulative growth of science, the social need to appropriate and disseminate it to the maximum, the increasing individual need for fluency in contemporary science and technology – and on the other hand, the inherent tendency of late capitalism to make science a captive of its profit transactions and profit calculations.

This conflict is essentially a new and specific form of the general contradiction characteristic of the capitalist mode of production: the contradiction between expanding social wealth and increasingly alienated and impoverished labour, so long as this social wealth is imprisoned by private appropriation. In late capitalism, this contradiction acquires a new dimension. The more higher education becomes a qualification for specific labour processes, the more intellectual labour becomes proletarianized, in other words transformed into a commodity, and the more the commodity of intellectual labour-power is sold on a specific 'labour market for intellectual and scientific qualifications', and the more the price of this commodity tends to be forced down to its conditions of reproduction, oscillating about its value in response to supply and demand at any given moment. The further this process of proletarianization advances, the deeper the division of labour becomes entrenched within the sciences, accompanied inevitably by increasing overspecialization and 'expert idiocy', and the more students become prisoners of a blinkered education strictly subordinated to the conditions of the valorization of capital. . . .

There are significant differences between the social position occupied by intellectually qualified labour incorporated into the process of production and by intellectually qualified labour integrated into administrative and superstructural institutions. These cannot be reduced to the distinction between those individuals or groups whose material existence is based on the creation of surplus-value and those who receive income from surplus-value, although this dividing line does undoubtedly play a role in determining the social interest of each specific section of the intellectually qualified work-force. The decisive distinction, however, is rather the structural effect which the specific position of each specialized group in the sphere of production, administration or superstructure has on the formation of its consciousness.

The social position of all those groups that occupationally participate in supervising the extraction of surplus-value from the commodity of labour-power or the preservation of constant capital by labour-power, typically induces a general identification of their function with the class interests of the entrepreneurial bourgeoisie. It might even be said that such identification is a precondition of the performance of their specific function in factory or society. Time-and-motion experts who systematically sympathize and solidarize with the workers are no good at their job in a capitalist mode of production; they are not qualified to measure time or motion and will quickly find themselves out of work; in other words, they have to change either their attitude or their occupation. Officers of the law who assist political prisoners to escape have little chance of a career and will likewise lose their job. The same applies in the long run to factory doctors, factory sociologists and psychologists, the administrative personnel of the means of communication, commanders of the bourgeois police and all the senior functionaries of the state apparatus. By contrast, intellectually qualified workers engaged in the immediate process of production or reproduction, or those whose social function does not necessarily come into collision with the class interest of wage-earners – for example, health-insurance doctors or social workers employed by a local authority – are much less liable to identify subjectively with the class interests of capital, and are more likely to align themselves with the class interests of the proletariat.

A Sceptical View of the New Working Class
Michael Mann

Consciousness and Action among the Western Working Class (London: Macmillan, 1973) p. 67

I have cast a fairly sceptical eye over the theory of the new working class. Despite its attractions, two main reservations must be made. Firstly, . . . if the French new workers are relatively class-conscious, this is largely due to the 'archaism' of France, to the reinforcing effects of traditional and idiosyncratic contradictions. Without this reinforcement it is doubtful whether the conflict between 'new workers' and their employers can be elevated to the status of a major 'contradiction'. Why should it be a more important source of instability than differences of age, sex, religion or other sources of tension in modern society? Here we surely move to a multi-factor explanation of social conflict – and not to an expectation of revolution. Secondly, even in France, the new workers' sense of *opposition* and *identity* is relatively weak despite apparent concern with a restructuring of the total society. This is precisely the opposite revolutionary failing of the traditional working class, strong on identity and opposition, weak on totality and alternatives. Yet it gives the new working class the same quality of utopianism, the same failure to translate a mixed consciousness into a consistent series of radical actions.

6 Two Views of 'Service' Labour

The Rise of 'Service' Occupations – I

Harry Braverman

Labor and Monopoly Capital: the Degradation of Work in the Twentieth Century (New York, Monthly Review, 1974) pp. 362–3, 372–3

Beds were made, floors were scrubbed, food prepared and served, children minded, the sick tended long before people were hired to do any of these things. And even after the hiring of servants to do them had begun, these activities were of no interest to the capitalist except in terms of his comfort and household expenses. They became of interest to him *as a capitalist* when he began to hire people to do services as a profitable activity, a part of his business, a form of the capitalist mode of production. And this began on a large scale only with the era of monopoly capitalism which created the universal marketplace and transformed into a commodity every form of the activity of humankind including what had heretofore been the many things that people did for themselves or for each other. . . .

As a quick glance at the list of service occupations will make apparent, the bulk of the work is concentrated in two areas: cleaning and building care, and kitchen work and food service. Female workers outnumber male, as in retail sales work. Training prerequisites for most of these occupations are minimal, a job ladder leading upward is virtually nonexistent, and unemployment rates are higher than average.

The Rise of 'Service' Occupations – II

Ernest Mandel

Late Capitalism, pp. 383–4, 401–3

Under conditions of increasing objective socialization of labour, yet generalized commodity production, a growing division of labour can only be realized if tendencies towards centralization prevail over tendencies towards atomization. In capitalism, this process of centralization is two-fold in character: it is both technical and economic. *Technically*, a growing division of labour can only be combined with growing objective socialization of the labour process by an extension of *intermediate functions:* hence the unprecedented expansion of the sectors of commerce, transport and services generally.[1] *Economically* the process of centralization can only find expression in a growing centralization of capital, among other things, in the form of vertical integration of big companies, multinational firms and conglomerates.

The separation of previously unified productive activities makes the extension of intermediate functions indispensable. If handicrafts become separate from agriculture, peasants must be guaranteed the mediation of work-tools and consumer goods which they previously made by hand, and artisans must be assured of the mediation of previously self-produced foodstuffs through trade. The extension of these intermediate functions tends to result in their *growing independence*. The separation of agriculture and handicrafts leads ultimately to the insertion of independent trade between the two. The more generalized the production of commodities and the more advanced division of labour becomes, the more do these intermediate functions have to be systematized and rationalized in order to ensure continuous production and continuous sales. The tendency towards a reduced turnover-time of capital, inherent in the capitalist mode of production, can only become a reality if capital (commercial- and money-capital) increasingly gains mastery of these intermediate functions. . . .

The apparently homogeneous notion of the expansion of the services sector, that is typical of late capitalism, must therefore be reduced to its contradictory constitutive elements. This expansion involves:

1. The tendency towards a general extension of intermediate functions, as a result of the counterposition of a growing division of labour with a growing objective socialization of labour. Part of this expansion is technically determined, and will therefore outlive the capitalist mode of production itself (extension of the transport and distribution network, the maintenance and repair facilities for machines at the disposal of the consumer, and so on).

2. The tendency towards an enormous expansion both of selling costs (advertising, marketing, to some extent expensive packaging and similar unproductive expenses) and of consumer credit. This aspect of the expansion of the services sector is for the most part socially, and not technically determined; it stems from the growing difficulties of realization and will disappear along with the capitalist mode of production or generalized commodity production.

3. The possibilities for developing the cultural and civilizing needs of the working population (education, health care, recreational activity), as distinct from the pure consumption of commodities, created by the growing productivity of labour and the corresponding limitation of necessary labour time (with growing differentiation of consumption). The services which correspond to these needs are not exclusively tied to the specific form of capitalist production and exchange, and will not in fact be able to develop fully before the capitalist mode of production has been overthrown. Admittedly, both the commercial nature of these services, which are geared to make a private profit, and their content, will undergo a fundamental change: instead of manipulating and alienating real human needs, they will be subordinated to them. In accordance with this tendency, the independent performance of these 'services' will wither away in socialist society as all men and women themselves gradually become capable of performing them. Forms of individual specialization will remain, but society will no longer be divided into 'productive' performers and passive consumers of cultural and civilizing services.

4. The extension of *commodity* production which is not a part of the so-called 'services sector, at all, but is a result of the growing centralization of certain forms of production which were previously largely private. Electricity, gas, water, ready-made meals and electrical household appliances are material goods and their production is commodity production in the real sense and in no way sale of services.

5. The growth in the number of unproductively employed wage-earners, since the massive penetration of capital into the sphere of circulation and services affords capitals which can no longer be invested productively the opportunity of receiving at least the average profit of the non-monopolized sectors instead of obtaining only the average interest. This growth is consequently a result of the tendency towards over-capitalization in late capitalism.

The expansion of the capitalist services sector which typifies late capitalism thus in its own way sums up all the principal contradictions of the capitalist mode of production. It reflects the enormous expansion of social-technical and scientific forces of production and the corresponding growth in the cultural needs of the producers, just as it reflects the antagonistic form in which this expansion is realized under capitalism: for it is accompanied by increasing over-capitalization (difficulties of valorization of capital), growing difficulties of realization, increasing wastage of material values, and growing alienation and deformation of workers in their productive activity and their sphere of consumption.

Is the capital invested in the services sector productive or not? Is the labour performed by wage-earners in this sector productive or unproductive? As long as capital investment in services was marginal in character, the answer to these questions was of only secondary importance for an analysis of the movement of the capitalist mode of production as a whole. However, once the services sector of late capitalism expands to such an extent that it absorbs a considerable part of aggregate social capital, a correct definition of the precise limits of productive capital assumes the greatest importance. The formula 'in capitalism productive labour is labour which creates surplus-value' is inadequate for such a definition. Although it is correct in itself, it remains a tautology. It does not answer the question of the boundaries of productive labour but merely recasts it in another form. The difficulty exists in Marx's own writings . . . .

NOTES AND REFERENCES

1. We analyze further below the great variations in the economic structure of the so-called services sector. The function of middle men, which expands in the course of the growing social division of labour and which can be ascribed in capitalism to enterprises dealing with trade, transport, storage, credit, banks

and insurance, only constitutes a part of this sector, which sociologists and bourgeois political economists make into a pot-pourri of the most various activities, stretching from pure commodity producers (gas, water and power production) to pure parasites and crooks.

7 The Search for Theory: Synthesis or Dissonance?

The Growth of the 'New Middle Class'

Anthony Giddens

The Class Structure of the Advanced Societies (London: Hutchinson, 1973) pp. 179–81, 186–7, 192–6

It is misleading in itself to treat 'white-collar labour' as an undifferentiated category, and the overall expansion of the white-collar sector in the capitalist societies conceals differential rates of growth in various occupational sub-categories. Whereas the relatively early enlargement of the white-collar sector mainly concerned the growth of clerical and sales occupations, in neo-capitalism those occupations usually grouped by census statisticians as 'professional and technical' labour show the highest recent rates of development – although these nowhere comprise any more than a fairly small minority of white-collar workers as a whole. . . .

The significant changes which have occurred, now well-documented, concern, first, a relative diminution of the income of clerical workers within the white-collar sector, and, secondly, the development of some degree of 'overlap' at the margins between non-manual and manual labour. But out of these changes in the gross income statistics an enormous mythology has been built, in much of the technical literature on class as well as in the lay press. The apparent merging in the economic returns accruing to manual as compared to non-manual labour looks very different if the facts of the matter are inspected more closely. In the first place, the traditional superiority of the white-collar worker in terms of job security has by no means disappeared: in general terms, non-manual workers continue to enjoy a greater measure of security, even if . . . there is some cause to suppose that certain categories of manual workers will increasingly enjoy more favourable contractual conditions in the future. Secondly, typical patterns of overall career earnings are quite different in the two categories. . . . Thirdly, a considerably larger proportion of those in non-manual occupations are in receipt of fringe benefits of various kinds, such as pension and sick-pay schemes: in most countries these workers also gain disproportionately from tax remissions as a result of participation in such schemes. . . .

If we consider the totality of economic returns available to manual and non-manual workers, the idea that any kind of overall 'merging' of the two groupings is taking place may be unequivocally rejected. The overlap is confined to segments of skilled manual occupations on the one hand, and of clerical and sales occupations on the other. But the major characteristic of these latter occupations is that they are everywhere increasingly monopolised by women – a fact of great importance in considering the nature of the boundary between the working and middle classes . . . .

We may distinguish two major sources of differentiation within the middle class as a whole: that having its origin in differences in market capacity, and that deriving from variations in the division of labour. The most significant type of difference in market capacity is undoubtedly between the capacity to offer marketable technical knowledge, recognised and specialised symbolic skills, and the offering of general symbolic competence. The marketability of specialised symbolic skills has normally been protected or enhanced by the systematic enforcement of controlled 'closure' of occupational entry, a particular characteristic of professional occupations. The growth of professional occupations has been particularly marked in neo-capitalist society . . . .

Although there certainly are controversial problems of sociological analysis posed by the existence of the professions, professionalisation does not offer major difficulties for class theory. The same cannot be said, however, of other sources of differentiation within the middle class, which have caused many authors to doubt the applicability of any such generic term as the 'middle class' altogether. The term appears to have a definite usefulness in relation to white-collar workers within organisations, where these workers are part of a definite 'office', and consequently of a bureaucratic hierarchy of authority. But what of workers whose tasks are not primarily 'manual', but who are not so clearly involved in any such clearly identifiable hierarchy, and who, while they may often be connected with the professions, are not of them? As C. Wright Mills puts it: 'The old professions of medicine and law are still at the top of the professional world, but now all around them are men and women of new skills. There are a dozen kinds of social engineers and mechanical technicians, a multitude of Girl Fridays, laboratory assistants, registered and unregistered nurses, draftsmen, statisticians, social workers. In the salesrooms, which sometimes seem to coincide with the new society as a whole, are the stationary salesgirls in the department store, the mobile salesmen of insurance, the absentee salesmen – the ad-men helping others sell from a distance.'[1] What, if anything, do such a bewildering variety of occupations share in common with each other, let alone with the white-collar office worker? . . .

Since the turn of the century, when the rate of relative increase in the white-collar sector first became apparent, the idea has been advanced – particularly, of course, by Marxist authors – that this 'new middle class' will become split into two: because it is not really a class at all, since its position, and the outlook and attitudes of its members, cannot be interpreted in terms of property relations. Hence, so the argument runs, the majority of white-collar workers will become 'proletarianised', as befits their condition of propertylessness, while a small minority will move into the dominant class. Today, some seventy years later, the facts continue to belie such expectations. . . .

It is misleading to suppose, as Marxist authors commonly do, that the effect of the mechanisation of office work, the beginnings of which can be traced to the last two decades of the nineteenth century, has been progressively to eliminate the differences between office and shop-floor. Mechanisation, as involved in factory labour, tends to define the total character of the labour task, often reducing the role of the worker to 'machine-minding'. But this has generally not been the case with mechanisation in the office, where typewriters, adding machines, dictating machines, etc., appear as adjuncts to clerical labour, rather than as transforming it altogether. Women, who compose a category within the labour force which is systematically discriminated against in terms of level of income and career opportunities, largely monopolise those occupations which are wholly routinised (e.g., typist, stenographer) . . . . The recent trend towards automating office tasks, by the use of computers in white-collar occupations, does tend to effect a more total reorganisation of office work. But . . . computerised methods . . . far from serving to promote the 'proletarianisation' of clerical employees, . . . normally have the consequence of producing a diminished demand for routine workers, increasing the need for more highly-educated and qualified personnel. . . .

Some of the more original Marxist writers, and others influenced by them. . . . have sought to replace the traditional idea of 'proletarianisation' with a conception of a 'new working class', led by technically qualified workers whose conditions of labour would seem at first sight to separate them quite decisively from the bulk of manual workers. . . . As Touraine expresses the notion:

> We are not thinking here of the new 'proletarians', of white-collar workers who must carry out tasks as repetitive, monotonous and constraining as those of workers on the assembly-line, but rather of relatively high-grade categories: technical workers, designers, higher level white-collar employees, technical assistants, who do not take part in the bureaucratic game, but who are more directly exposed to its consequences than workers of the traditional type . . . .[2]

The necessarily autonomous process of the creation of ('universally valid') technical knowledge clashes with the subordination of such knowledge to the economic aims of the productive enterprise.

Whatever its deficiencies, the theory appears to fit the contemporary trend in the white-collar sector within the capitalist societies, which in some degree has been towards the specific growth of technically specialised occupations. However, it is open to a number of objections. In the first place, one of the premises upon which it rests, the supposition that, in neo-capitalism, knowledge has supplanted technology as the principal productive force, is highly questionable. . . . Even if this were acceptable in the form in which it is put forward, there would be some reason to doubt the overall claims which have been made for the theory, because it tends to exaggerate considerably the degree to which 'scientific and technical' workers have penetrated even those industries making use of highly advanced technique. More important, however, the sense in which the 'new working class' is a 'class' is ill-defined and ambiguous.

NOTES AND REFERENCES

1. C. Wright Mills, *White Collar*, p. x.
2. Alain Touraine, La société post-industrielle (Paris, 1969) pp. 82–3.

The 'Middle Layers' of Employment
Harry Braverman

Labor and Monopoly Capital, pp. 404–6

The complexities of the class structure of pre-monopoly capitalism arose from the fact that so large a proportion of the working population, being neither employed by capital nor itself employing labor to any significant extent, fell outside the capital-labor polarity. The complexity of the class structure of modern monopoly capitalism arises from the very opposite consideration: namely, that *almost all of the population has been transformed into employees of capital.* . . . . [But] the fact that the operating executives of a giant corporation are employed by that corporation, and in that capacity do not own its plants and bank accounts, is merely the form given to capitalist rule in modern society. These operating executives . . . are the rulers of industry, act 'professionally' for capital, and are themselves part of the class that personifies capital and employs labor. Their formal attribute of being part of the same payroll as the production workers, clerks, and porters of the corporation no more robs them of the powers of decision and command over the others in the enterprise than does the fact that the general, like the private, wears the military uniform . . . . The form of hired employment gives expression to two totally different realities . . . .

But between these two extremes there is a range of intermediate categories, sharing the characteristics of worker on the one side and manager on the other in varying degrees. The gradations of position in the line of management may be seen chiefly in terms of authority, while gradations in staff positions are indicated by the levels of technical expertise. Since the authority and expertise of the middle ranks in the capitalist corporation represent an unavoidable delegation of responsibility, the position of such functionaries may best be judged by their relation to the power and wealth that commands them from above, and to the mass of labor beneath them which they in turn help to control, command, and organize. Their pay level is significant because beyond a certain point it, like the pay of the commanders of the corporation, clearly represents not just the exchange of their labor power for money – a commodity exchange – but a *share in the surplus* produced in the corporation.

A Highly Significant Intermediate Class

John Urry

'Towards a Structural Theory of the Middle Class', *Acta Sociologica*, vol. 16, no. 3 (1973) pp. 180–3, 185

There are four different positions that can be identified regarding the class situation of the new middle class. In the first position it is held that since most middle class occupations have been structurally differentiated from what were previously ruling class occupations, and since the middle class is structurally dependent on the authority of the ruling class, so the new middle class is merely an extension of the existent capitalist ruling class. In the second position it is held that the middle class is really much closer to the working class because both groups do not own the means of production. Any identification that members of the middle class may exhibit towards the ruling class is merely false consciousness which will disappear when the middle class come to realise that their class interests are coincidental with those of the working class. A third position is that there is no such thing as *the* middle class but that there are two different groupings with opposed class interests, bureaucrats with ruling class authority, and white collar workers with a proletarian class situation. Finally, there is that position where it is maintained that the middle class is in a structurally ambivalent situation. Lockwood, for example, argues that the blackcoated worker has a more or less proletarian market situation, but a bourgeois work situation. Middle class identifications with the ruling class is explained by the clerks' work-situation, and not *mere* false consciousness.

I shall attempt to defend a position which incorporates aspects of all of these arguments, but especially of the latter two. Let us initially generalise Lockwood's solution. What we can say is that there are large sectors of the middle class who, although they do not own productive property and perhaps only marginally more domestic property than the manual worker, are placed in either powerful or status-favoured positions within the work situation, or within what we might term the work structure. . . .

Marx argues that the nature of capitalism is such that there are two sets of functions: that of capital accumulation and that of producing value or surplus value, and that the one is dependent upon the other. The former is the capitalist function, the latter the function of labour. What though is important is the degree of variation possible in the *bearers* of these functions in different actual capitalist societies. . . .

The first stage in my argument requires that I consider these two functions rather more closely than I have done so far. These functions give rise to two dichotomies: ownership/non-ownership of the means of production; production/non-production of value. If we relate these two dichotomies together we find two uncontroversial classes that emerge, that class which owns the means of production and does not produce value; and that class which is non-owning but value-producing. However, there are two other groupings which we can consider: those who are owners and value-producers; and those who are non-owners and non-producers. The former grouping includes the self-employed and small capitalists employing a few workers. It excludes shopkeepers but apart from them, this grouping includes all those whom we would think of as the petit bourgeoisie. I shall not spend any time in discussing their relative numerical decline in developed capitalist society, nor their likely class allegiance.

The grouping that I want to concentrate upon is that which neither owns productive property nor produces value. This includes shopowners, managers, professionals, technologists, and subordinate commercial employees such as clerks, foremen and shop assistants. Shopowners we can clearly see as part of the petit bourgeoisie so we will concentrate here upon the *new* middle class . . . .

We can firstly point out that the members of all these groupings do not own the means of production, they all work, and they all have a powerful or high-status-situation in the workplace. Secondly, we can distinguish between managers and the remaining groupings in two ways. Managers both are responsible for the hiring of labour and as a group control the day-to-day operations within the workplace. Furthermore, together with the owners of enterprises they are responsible for bearing or performing the function of capital accumulation. Professional workers (traditional professional and technological professional), on the other hand, are not principally responsible for hiring, or for general managerial control over capitalist enterprises. Their function is to maintain the material and human capital necessary for capital accumulation. They are responsible in general for ensuring the persistence of the superstructure, this being a necessary condition of continued capitalist activity. Such a function is exercised in general not within large capitalist enterprises, but rather in other types of organizations in which the professionals are relatively powerful and have fairly high status. Foremen . . . are no different from workers except they have a certain amount of power over such workers within specific contexts. Clerks, likewise, as Lockwood showed, are very much the workers *except* that the nature of the work structure has created a situation in which they enjoy a favoured workplace position and consequent middle class identification. It is of course well-known that this situation may be changing and that there may be some case for arguing that there will be increasing overlap between such blackcoated workers and skilled manual workers . . . .

Why should capitalism give rise to groupings generally located between the capitalists and the proletariat, and . . . the more developed the capitalism, the greater the size and diversity of such groupings?

The best way in which we can answer this question is to consider the nature of early capitalism. What generally we can say is that in each capitalist enterprise there were a very small number of capitalists and these were in dominant market and work situations; and there were a large number of workers in subordinate market and work situations. Furthermore, if we . . . talk about the general market and work structures we can say two things. Firstly, there were two structures within the areas of essentially capitalist production, the market and work structures, and both of these were dichotomised. Secondly, there was an overlap between these two structures such that there were no major social groupings in a position intermediate between those super and subordinate.

The development of capitalism has had effects on both of these features but most importantly on the latter. What has happened is that to a degree the overlap between these two structures has broken down. The market structure, the relationship of classes to the means of production, remains the same; but the work structure, the system of social relationships within the workplace, has changed towards a structure in which there has been a significant increase in the size of the superordinate class. The result of that has been the development of the highly significant intermediate class, which does not own the means of production, but is in a powerful or favoured status-situation in the structure of workplace relationships.

The Professional-Managerial Class

Barbara and John Ehrenreich

'The Professional-Managerial Class', *Radical America*, vol. 11, no. 2 (March–April 1977) pp. 12–17

From our point of view, a class (as opposed to a stratum or other social grouping) is defined by two major characteristics:

1. At all times in its historical development, a class is characterized by a common relation to the economic foundations of society – the means of production and the socially organized patterns of distribution and consumption. . . . The relations which define class arise from the place occupied by groups in the broad social division of labor, and from the basic patterns of control over access to the means of production and of appropriation of the social surplus.

2. However, the relation to the economic foundations of society is not sufficient to specify a class as a real social entity. At any moment in its historical development after its earliest, formative period, a class is characterized by a coherent social and cultural existence; members of a class share a common life style, educational background, kinship networks, consumption patterns, work habits, beliefs . . . . In addition, the social existence of a group of people is determined not only by its experience at the point of

production, but by its experience in private life (mediated especially by kinship relations, which, in turn, are at most only distantly related to evolving relations of production). The relationship between class as abstract economic relationship and class as real social existence has been all-but-unexplored; for our purposes we shall have to limit ourselves to insisting that a class has both characteristics.

Having stated these two general characteristics, we should strongly emphasize that class is an analytic abstraction, a way of putting some order into an otherwise bewildering array of individual and group characteristics and interrelationships. It describes a phenomenon existing most clearly at the level of society as a whole. When, however, the notion of class is called on to explain or predict infallibly the actions, ideas and relationships of every individual, it ceases to be very useful . . . .

We define the Professional-Managerial Class as consisting of salaried mental workers who do not own the means of production and whose major function in the social division of labor may be described broadly as the reproduction of capitalist culture and capitalist class relations.

Their role in the process of reproduction may be more or less explicit, as with workers who are directly concerned with social control or with the production and propagation of ideology (e.g., teachers, social workers, psychologists, entertainers, writers of advertising copy and TV scripts, etc.). Or it may be hidden within the process of production, as is the case with the middle-level administrators and managers, engineers, and other technical workers whose functions . . . are essentially determined by the need to preserve capitalist relations of production. Thus we assert that these occupational groups – cultural workers, managers, engineers and scientists, etc. – share a common function in the broad social division of labor and a common relation to the economic foundations of society.

The PMC, by our definition, includes people with a wide range of occupations, skills, income levels, power and prestige. The boundaries separating it from the ruling class above and the working class below are fuzzy . . . .

The very definition of the PMC – as a class concerned with the reproduction of capitalist culture and class relationships – precludes treating it as a separable sociological entity. It is in a sense a derivative class; its existence presupposes: (1) that the social surplus has developed to a point sufficient to sustain the PMC in addition to the bourgeoisie, for the PMC is essentially nonproductive; and (2) that the relationship between the bourgeoisie and the proletariat has developed to the point that a class specializing in the reproduction of capitalist class relationships becomes a necessity to the capitalist class. That is, the maintenance of order can no longer be left to episodic police violence.

Historically, these conditions were met in the U.S. by the early twentieth century. The last half of the nineteenth century saw: (1) the development of an enormous social surplus, concentrated in monopolistic corporations and individual capitalists; and (2) intermittent, violent warfare between the industrial working class and the capitalist class. The possibility of outright insurrection was taken very seriously by both bourgeois and radical observers. At the same time, however, the new concentration and centralization of capital opened up the possibilities of long-term planning, the refinement of 'management' (essentially as a substitute for force), and the capitalist rationalization of both productive and consumptive processes. In the decades immediately following the turn of the century, these possibilites began to be realized:

1. At the point of production, the concentration of capital allowed for the wholesale purchase of science and its transformation into a direct instrument of capital. Science, and its practical offshoot engineering, were set to work producing not only 'progress' in the form of new products, but new productive technologies which undercut the power of skilled labor . . . .

2. The huge social surplus, concentrated in private foundations and in the public sector, began to be a force for regulation and management of civil society. . . .

3. Beginning in the 1900's and increasing throughout the twentieth century, monopoly capitalism came to depend on the development of a national consumer-goods market. Items which had been made in the home or in the neighbourhood were replaced by the uniform products of giant corporations. . . .

The penetration of working-class life by commodities required and continues to require a massive job of education – from schools, advertisers, social workers, domestic scientists, 'experts' in child rearing, etc. As the dependence of American capital on the domestic consumer-goods market increased, the management of consumption came to be as important as the management of production.

To summarize the effects of these developments on working-class life: The accumulation and concentration of capital which occurred in the last decades of the nineteenth century allowed for an extensive reorganization of working-class life – both in the community and in the workplace. This reorganiozation was aimed at both social control and the development of a mass consumer market. The net effect of this drive to reorganize and reshape working-class life was the social *atomization* of the working class; the fragmentation of work (and workers) in the productive process, a withdrawal of aspirations from the workplace into private goals, the disruption of indigenous networks of support and mutual aid, the destruction of autonomous working-class culture and its replacement by 'mass culture' defined by the privatized consumption of commodities (health care, recreation, etc.).

It is simultaneously with these developments in working-class life (more precisely, in the *relation* between the working class and the capitalist class) that the professional and managerial workers emerge as a new class in society. The three key developments listed above – the reorganization of the productive process, the emergence of mass institutions of social control, the commodity penetration of working-class life – do not simply 'develop'; they require the effort of more or less conscious agents. The expropriation of productive skills requires the intervention of scientific management experts; there must be engineers to inherit the productive lore, managers to supervise the increasingly degraded work process, etc. Similarly, the destruction of autonomous working-class culture requires (and calls forth) the emergence of new culture-producers – from physicians to journalists, teachers, ad-men and so on. These new operatives, the vanguard of the emerging PMC, are not simply an old intelligentsia expanding to meet the needs of a 'complex' society. Their emergence in force near the turn of the century is parallel and complementary to the transformation of the working class which marks the emergence of monopoly capital.

Thus the relationship between the PMC and the working class is objectively antagonistic. The functions and interests of the two classes are not merely different; they are mutually contradictory. True, both groups are forced to sell their labor power to the capitalist class; both are necessary to the productive process under capitalism; and they share an antagonistic relation to the capitalist class. But these commonalities should not distract us from the fact that the professional-managerial workers exist, as a mass grouping in monopoly capitalist society, only by virtue of the expropriation of the skill and culture once indigenous to the working class.

The New Petty Bourgeoisie

Nicos Poulantzas

Classes in Contemporary Capitalism (London: NLB, 1975)
pp. 209–16, 221–3, 301–2, 304–7, 309, 316–18, 321–2, 326

We must now examine the new wage-earning groupings that are referred to as the new petty bourgeoisie . . . . These groupings do not belong to the bourgeoisie, in so far as they have neither economic ownership nor possession of the means of production. On the other hand, they do present the phenomenon of wage-labour, remunerated in the form of a wage or salary. The basic question that is raised here, therefore, is that of their relationship to the working class, a question that can in the first instance be formulated as that of the boundaries and limits of the working class in capitalist relations of production. . . . In the case of capitalism, as Marx puts it, if every agent belonging to the working class is a wage-earner, this does not necessarily mean that every wage-earner belongs to the working class. The working class is not defined by a simple and intrinsic negative criterion, its exclusion from the relations of ownership, but by productive labour . . . .

The productive or unproductive character of labour does not depend either on certain intrinsic characteristics, or on its utility. It is in this sense that one should understand Marx's argument, according to which the definitions of productive and unproductive labour are not derived from the material characteristics of labour (neither from the nature of its product nor from the particular character of the labour as concrete labour), but from the definite social form, the social relations of production, within which the labour is realised. . . . Thus, for example, labour performed in the sphere of circulation of capital, or contributing to the realization of surplus-value, is not productive labour; wage-earners in commerce, advertising, marketing, accounting, banking and insurance, do not produce surplus-value and do not form part of the working class . . . .

It is necessary to emphasize at this point that this distinction between the process of value production and the process of circulation is not the same as the supposed distinction between 'secondary' and 'tertiary' sectors, nor is it one of an institutionalist kind between the types of 'enterprise' (industrial, commercial) in which this labour takes place. Labour involved in the circulation process (sales, advertising, negotiation, etc.) may well be undertaken by industrial enterprises for themselves, but it still remains unproductive labour, and its agents unproductive workers. . . .

Also to be considered as unproductive labour is that taking the form of services, whose products and activities are directly consumed as use-values and are not exchanged against capital but rather against revenue or income . . . .

It is, moreover, essentially in terms of this problem of services that Marx deals with a series of forms of labour that greatly contribute to the reproduction of capitalist social relations, i.e. the labour of the agents of the state apparatuses, the civil servants; it is of course necessary to exclude here that directly productive labour that is performed within the state sector, for instance 'nationalized' industrial enterprises, 'public' transport, and workers in the various 'public services'. . . .

But are the agents providing services themselves exploited? . . . From medicine through to the liberal professions (law, architecture, etc.), and including entertainment, and the media, the agents providing services have overwhelmingly become employees of capital, which has seized hold of their activities. This does not mean that these wage-earners have become productive workers. But they too sell their labour-power, their wages correspond to the cost of reproduction of this labour-power and they even provide a portion of their labour without payment. Surplus labour is extorted from them . . . . Their exploitation is thus of a similar order to that which wage-earners in the sphere of capital circulation experience.

The case of agents of the state apparatuses and those who perform 'public' services is rather more complex (the latter including teachers in state schools, medical personnel in the state sector, etc.); in this case, capital does not intervene directly to subsume labour-power. The capitalist is present not as capitalist but as buyer of services. These agents also provide surplus labour, which is extorted from them, but they are not involved in a transfer of surplus-value in favour of the state as employer. Their exploitation, in the form of extortion of surplus labour, is essentially a function of the unequal situation in the exchange between them and capital, the latter having a dominant position on the market.

I would like to put forward here one major proposition, and deal with certain problems that it raises. Marx's analyses of capitalist productive labour must be rounded off on one key point, which would seem to be co-substantial with the definition of capitalist productive labour. We shall say that productive labour, in the capitalist mode of production, is labour that produces surplus-value while *directly reproducing the material elements that serve as the substratum of the relation of exploitation: labour that is directly involved in material production by producing use-values that increase material wealth. . . .*

These remarks are particularly important in so far as Marxist discussion of productive labour has too often been exlusively oriented to exchange-value, neglecting the process of material production. . . . In fact, the relationship between productive labour and the process of material production which is involved in all productive labour must be particularly stressed in the case of 'science', because of the current spread of various ideologies of the role of 'science' within the contemporary production process. It is seen as intervening more and more 'directly', as such, in the production process ('the scientific and technical revolution'), and the 'bearers of science', in a very broad sense, are seen as forming part of the productive workers and thus belonging to the working class. . . .

But . . . even if capital bends the whole of scientific work to its requirements, enrolling science 'in its service', as Marx puts it (there is in this sense no 'neutral' science), and even if the role of technical innovations is today more important than in the past (intensive exploitation of labour), this does not by itself make scientific work productive. The work of the first category, the scientist proper, is no more directly involved in the process of material production today than it was in the past. . . . This work remains unproductive even if its products assume the commodity form (patents, licences) and have a 'price', for they no more produce value in their own right than do works of art. . . . The basic position is not changed when this labour, and the activities bound up with it, take place actually within industrial enterprises, as is often the case in the present phase of concentration . . . .

The rapid increase of non-productive workers is a real fact, and a major one, in the main developed capitalist countries. . . . The main reasons for this phenomenon, abstracting from the particular features of each individual social formation, are due to the characteristics of monopoly capitalism, in particular its present phase:

(a) the shift in dominance, as far as the exploitation of the working class is concerned, towards the intensive exploitation of labour (which includes the productivity of labour and technological transformations), signifying a decline in the ratio of living labour to dead labour;

(b) the extension of wage-labour by the radical subjection (subsumption) of the labour-power of non-productive sectors to monopoly capital, combined with the present dissolution effects that monopoly capitalism has on other forms of production (decline of the various 'independent' producers);

(c) the considerable, but subordinate increase in activities dealing with the marketing of goods and commodity circulation (diversification of finished products, and with the realization of capital (money-capital, banking, insurance, etc.);

(d) the increase, also considerable, in the number of civil servants (including public services), which accounts for a large section of the general increase in non-productive labour, and which is also related to the growth in the functions of state intervention that is specific to monopoly capitalism and to its present phase. . . .

The most important current transformations in the sector of non-productive wage-labour are as follows:

1. Its marked feminization, which is a function of several factors, including the considerable increase in the number of non-productive employees and the massive entry of women into the 'economic activity' which is subject to the capitalist exploitation of labour. . . . Not only are women the main victims of the reproduction of the social division of labour within non-productive wage-labour, but this is supplemented in their case by various

forms of sexual oppression in their actual work itself, in the relations of exploitation and politico-ideological domination. This element plays a specific role of its own, analogous to the phenomenon of racism which the immigrant workers have to suffer. . . .

2. The relation that has now been established between the wages of productive workers (working-class wages) and the wages of non-productive workers: most writers have seen this as a tendency towards the reduction of the gap between 'average' working-class wages and 'average' wages in the tertiary sector, and as the loss of wage privileges for the whole of the tertiary sector in relation to the working class. . . . But this general tendency, which is also modified by the political factors that enter into wage differentials, does not operate in anything like the same manner for all sections of the new petty bourgeoisie . . . . It operates in particular by effecting a major reduction of the gap between the agents who occupy certain disqualified and subaltern petty-bourgeois places (clerks, lower-level workers in commerce, services and offices, and minor civil servants) and certain strata of the working class. . . .

3. The reproduction of the mental/manual worker division actually within mental labour: this . . . produces certain cleavages within the ranks of the new petty bourgeoisie: the fragmentation of knowledge and standardization of tasks in certain of its sectors and levels, the divisions within the bureaucratized petty bourgeoisie between levels of decision and levels of execution, the process of qualification and disqualification within mental labour that is bound up with the 'rationalization' of their work, etc. . . .

The first fraction of non-productive workers with an objectively proletarian polarization includes (i) the great majority of lower-level workers in the commercial sector (shop assistants, etc.), who are particularly subject to the current concentration in this commercial sector (increase in size of stores); (ii) employees who are affected by the introduction of machinery actually within the non-productive sector, and acutely so by the mechanization of labour (whether they belong to the sphere of circulation and realization of capital, to the service sector, or to the state apparatus); (iii) those employed in certain parts of the service sector – workers in restaurants, cafés, theatres, cinemas, as well as lower-level health workers (e.g. hospital orderlies), etc. In point of fact:

(a) In the social division of mental and manual labour, these are the non-productive workers who are nearest the barrier that separates the new petty bourgeoisie from the working class, in their relation to knowledge and to the symbolic and ideological ritual with which it is surrounded. . . .

(b) In relation to the other petty-bourgeois fractions, these agents are the least affected by the tendency towards the bureaucratization of non-productive labour; this is because they are nearest the barrier of manual labour. . . .

(c) The factor of 'career' and 'promotion' takes on a rather different form here than it does for the other petty-bourgeois groupings, even though it still remains distinct from the case of the working class. Genuine career opportunities are restricted, as a result not only of the organization of work and its fragmentation, but also of the instability of employment characteristic of this sector. The range of earnings and hierarchy is here fairly compressed, particularly in the case of commercial workers, i.e. it is marginal to the bureaucratic hierarchy. The proportion of agents who move upwards, even within their own class (e.g. become 'middle managers') is much more restricted in the case of commercial workers than for those who are classed in the statistics as 'office workers', or for civil servants. . . .

The second fraction of the new petty bourgeoisie with an objectively proletarian polarization is that of the subaltern agents of the public and private bureaucratized sectors; this where the various types of 'office workers' among others, are located. . . . This fraction is quite different from the previous one. We find here a sharper emphasis on the 'mental' aspect of its agents' labour, in opposition to manual labour, as well as certain significant effects of bureaucratization in the relations to which they are subjected. This fraction is also more affected by 'promotion' and 'career', and educational qualifications play here a more important role, as well as promotion according to length of service. These agents also display a relatively more significant tendency to circulate and change their place, during their own working lives and between generations, and both within their own class and upwards into the bourgeoisie. Moreover, 'profit-sharing' and bonuses designed to give employees an 'interest' in the firm play a special role here. . . .

The third and last fraction of the new petty bourgeoisie with an objectively proletarian polarization is that of the technicians and subaltern engineers directly involved in productive labour, the production of surplus-value . . . . This fraction still belongs to the petty bourgeoisie, but the cleavages that mark out its boundaries also cut through the statistical category of engineers, technicians and managers. This is, however, a different case to that of the other petty-bourgeois fractions with an objectively proletarian polarization. Although these agents are directly involved in the production of surplus-value, and thus display certain objective preconditions for grasping the essential mechanisms of capitalist exploitation, they still remain marked by their place in the politico-ideological relations of the enterprise as an apparatus. In recent years the forms of struggle of this fraction have distinguished it from the various groupings of intermediate engineers and managers, but have also shown the ambiguous character of its relations with the working class (since they retain their sense of 'those in charge').

The Global Function of Capital

G. Carchedi

'On the Economic Identification of the New Middle Class', *Economy and Society*, vol. 4, no. 1 (March 1975) pp. 51–2, 56, 58, 61–6

The essential features which distinguish the old from the new middle class are three. First of all . . . the old middle class belongs to the capitalist class (since it is the real and the legal owner) while the new middle class does not. Secondly, the old middle class performs the function of capital individually. It is the individual capitalist, at most helped by a few employees, who is the agent through which capital can realise its self-expending nature. The new middle class, on the other hand, performs this function collectively in the double sense that this function (1) is performed both by the capitalist and by the new middle class and that (2) within the latter, is performed by a great number of agents. Thirdly, and this is of fundamental importance, while in the old middle class the function of capital/exploiter (or oppressor)/non-labourer elements are always dominant, in the new middle class this is no longer so, as they are not the real owners of the means of production. One of the characteristics of this class is that the global function of capital and the function of the collective worker (which is no longer restricted to performing the work of co-ordination and unity of the labour process) are now combined in a varying balance. . . . *This fact, that the new middle class performs the global function of capital even without owning the means of production, and that it performs this function in conjunction with the function of the collective worker, is the basic point for an understanding of the nature of this class.* . . .

Just as the function of capital is performed by a hierarchically organised complex at many levels of which agents perform both the global function of capital and the function of the collective worker, in the same way the function of the collective worker is performed by a collective ensemble hierarchically organised at many levels of which agents perform both functions . . . .

Under monopoly capitalism . . . there is a complex of agents performing both the function of the collective worker and the global function of capital. Thus, the agent performing both functions has his wage determined by the value of his labour-power only in so far as he performs the function of the collective worker. The more this function outweighs the global function of capital, the higher in his income will be the wage components vis-à-vis the revenue component. Conversely, the more he performs the global function of capital, the more he participates in the redistribution of surplus value (not as a labourer but as a non-labourer) the higher will be the revenue component in his income and thus the weaker the relation between this income and the culturally determined subsistence minimum. . . .

What is . . . the essence of the process of proletarianisation of the new middle class? As a first approximation, we can say that it is a process of devaluation of labour-power, from skilled to average labour-power. To understand this point it is essential to realise that the nature of a socio-economic process is never a simple mechanical, sort of cause–effect relationship but the result of an interaction between a basic tendency and a number of counter-tendencies which arise and develop contemporaneously with the basic tendency itself and as a part of the same process. Thus, the basic tendency and the counteracting influences are not be understood as chronologically separated but as parts of a unity, of a whole, the development of which is contradictory because it is a development of both a basic trend and of counteracting factors. If this is understood we have the basis for an understanding of what proletarianisation is and of the contradictory development which is at its origin: the development of capitalism itself, that is the constant tendency to devalue skilled to average labour while at the same time originating an ever increasing complexity in the social division of labour which constantly creates new functions, new strata of skilled labourers.

[Consider] the commercial worker. As capitalism develops, commercial capital develops into a specific branch of activity. . . . As a result a stratum of commerical workers is also called into being. At first the commercial worker is a skilled worker whose labour-power stands above the average because of the necessary know-ledge of commercial practices, languages, etc. Therefore 'in the strict sense of the term', considering purely his place in the economic structure, without considering political and ideological factors, he 'belongs to the better-paid class of the wage-workers'. However, because of the place he occupies in the social division of labour, that is given his higher qualifications and thus his higher than average income, he is more prone than the average industrial worker to middle class ideological and political influence. Therefore as a stratum, the commercial worker cannot be auto-matically classified among the proletariat. Yet, this situation is not static, his 'wage tends to fall, even in relation to the average labour, with the advance of the capitalist mode of production' (Marx, Capital III: 300). . . .

First of all, 'the division of labour within the office [implies] a one-sided development of the labour capacity' (Marx), a fragmentation of tasks, devaluing the labour-power of the com-mercial worker . . . . Secondly, . . . inasmuch as practical knowledge becomes generally necessary for the carrying out of the new functions, the weight of providing that knowledge is shifted from the capitalist to public education which performs the task more cheaply than the capitalists themselves would. Thus, while the general level of knowledge (at least in the developed countries) rises, thus raising the value of the average labour-power, this rise is achieved more cheaply by the introduction and expansion of practical, technical public education. Thus, the value of the commercial worker's labour-power fails, *in relation to the average labour-power*, because it becomes, through this process, more and more similar in labour content to the average. . . .

Thirdly, . . . 'the universality of public education enables capitalists to recruit such labourers from classes that formerly had no
access to such trades and were accustomed to a lower standard of
living' (Marx). The same is true for other types of workers such as
draftsmen most of whom are recruited from the working class. . . .

This process of devaluation of labour-power, from skilled to
average labour-power, we call *as a first approximation*, proletarianisation. Its origin and essence goes back to the social division of
labour, to the constant creation of new skilled functions and, at the
same time, to the constant need of capital to devalue, to down-
grade those functions to simpler and simpler ones. Only if the
contradictory nature of this process is grasped, can proletarianisation be properly understood.

So far we have considered a part of the petty bourgeoisie which
is actually identifiable, on the level of production relations, as
proletariat and which is petty bourgeoisie on political and ideological grounds on the level of distribution relations. The proletarianisation of this section of the petty bourgeoisie actually
means its returning to what it already is on the level of production
relations. But what we are really interested in, is a different section
of the social structure: the new middle class, those who perform
both the function of the collective worker and the global function
of capital; those who are identifiable as middle class rather than
proletariat on the level of production relations. It is the proletarianisation of this middle class which needs now to be
explained. . . .

We know that the new middle class performs both the function
of the collective worker and the global function of capital. The
accumulation needs of capital also mean that there is a constant
tendency for capital to decrease the area devoted to the performance of the global function of capital and to increase the area
devoted to the function of the collective worker. In fact, only
through the latter function can capital appropriate to itself
surplus labour, either in this form or in the form of surplus value.
There is a constant tendency within the capitalist enterprise to
reduce the number (and pay) of those agents who perform the
work of control and surveillance (especially at the bottom of the
hierarchy). Whatever money is paid to the supervisor is not
available for capital accumulation. Yet, to perform the global
function of captal means to be in a position of privilege (including

level of income) vis-à-vis those who perform the function of the collective worker. Thus, the process of devaluation of the new middle class' labour-power is coupled with a constant erosion of the time during which the global function of capital is performed. This class is subjected to an attack on a double front. As far as the function of the collective worker is concerned, the devaluation of this class' labour-power reduces the wage component. As far as the global function of capital is concerned, its constant and tendential reduction reduces the revenue component. Therefore, the tendential decrease in the incomes of the new middle class[1] (or at least of large sections of it, especially of technicians and employees) is a result of this double movement. . . .

We now have all the elements necessary for an understanding of the proletarianisation of the new middle class. This process takes place at the bottom of that section of the corporation which performs both functions, i.e. it means, in terms of production relations, the disappearance of the global function of capital in order to make room exclusively for the function of the collective worker, a function which is performed by agents whose labour-power has been reduced to the average value. Of course, the two parts of this double movement are strictly related. Take, for example, a chemist who, beside performing quality control tests (function of the collective worker) is responsible for a number of technicians in the sense that he performs the work of supervision and management *in its double nature.* The moment these tests can be performed by someone with lower skills, perhaps by those same technicians he used to supervise, (1) the value of his labour-power is reduced to that of a technician (2) he loses his function as co-ordinator of the technicians' labour and (3) consequently, there is no need to assign to him the work of control and surveillance of those technicians. In other words, a process has been started the final outcome of which will be not only the complete disappearance of the function of capital but also the reduction of the labour-power to an unskilled level. *In short, proletarianisation is the limit of the process of devaluation of the new middle class' labour-power, i.e. the reduction of this labour-power to an average, unskilled level coupled with the elimination of the global function of capital. . . .*

A final remark: we should be careful not to confuse proletarianisation with 'becoming proletariat'. The former term only refers to the economic sphere, as we know, is not enough to classify groups and strata within one or another class. When the process of proletarianisation has been completed we have only the objective conditions for a certain stratum to become part of the proletariat.[2] There are, however, also political and ideological conditions which must be met before that stratum or group will actually become part of the proletariat.

NOTES AND REFERENCES

1. Decreasing, that is, in relation to the average wage, i.e. approaching this average wage.
2. As far as the employees are concerned, among the ideologies which hinder their becoming conscious of their objective situation, the myth of 'career making' is one of the most powerful and well known. What is not so well known is the fact that it is the employees lowest in the hierarchical scale, those who have been proletarianised, who fall more easily prey of this myth. . . . Quite clearly, capital concentrates its efforts to prevent the rise and development of a proletarian class consciousness in the potentially more dangerous areas of social stratification. This fact explains . . . why Italian typists, card-punchers and book keepers were at the tail of the great wave of strikes of 1969–70. However, it should be added, other sectors of the employees did participate in the class struggle and have reached a certain degree of class consciousness. An ideology must sooner or later fade away if its material (economic) basis has disappeared.

A Critique

Terry Johnson

'What is to Be Known? The Structural Determination of Social Class', *Economy and Society*, vol. 6, no. 1 (March 1977) pp. 220–4

The extent to which the work of Poulantzas and Carchedi on social class has already penetrated the theoretical consciousness of British Marxists and social scientists represents something of a shift of emphasis away from those issues which have traditionally guided the direction of class analysis. That is not to say that the existing literature has failed to confront the core problem of these texts, that of identifying a class grouping variously referred to – depending on theoretical perspective – as the 'new middle class', 'new petty bourgeoisie', or the 'new working class'. Rather, the shift relates to the problematic within which solutions are sought and the alternative sets of political issues within which they are generated.

Both authors are clear about their aims: what are the structural bases for existing or potential class alliances in the class struggle? What must be known in order to ensure that the working class party follows correct political strategies? Where are the class allies of the working class to be found? These questions have led both Poulantzas and Carchedi to carry out thoroughgoing attempts to theorize the structural determinants of class formation in 'monopoly' capitalism. It is also clear that both authors are, at the same time, engaged in an attack on existing party strategies. This is particularly so in the case of Poulantzas who, in taking up the question of the 'new petty bourgeoisie', is directly concerned to question the strategy of 'anti-monopoly alliance' favoured by the French communist party. These projects arise, then, out of specific political conditions in France and Italy where the existence and present state of mass communist parties raise in an acute form the question of class alliances and their political consequences.

Until recently such theoretical work has remained relatively underdeveloped in Britain where the political conditions have directed attention to issues associated with 'class consciousness'; in particular, to the issue of 'working class consciousness'. As a result, where analysts and political strategists have confronted the problem of the structural location of the 'new middle class' or 'new working class' their dominant theoretical focus has been at the level of 'consciousness' – it is here that the crucial determining factor has been sought. This is the case whether the analysis has been rooted in a simple Marxist economism and its saving concept 'false consciousness' or varieties of normative functionalism or action theory. While in many cases it is perfectly possible to argue that such a focus has been the direct result of empiricist epistemologies, it is also clear that the character of the British trade unions and labour party has conditioned the significance of class consciousness as a primary issue for the left. As a political issue it has, to a large extent, obscured the prior theoretical question of the structural determinants of class which constitutes the conceptual base from which problems relating to the ideological commitment of class groups and factions can be posed. To restate the problem in a form favoured by Poulantzas, to focus on the forms of consciousness exhibited by class *agents* and the associated question of how individuals achieve a class membership through mobility – the institutionalized obsession of British sociology – leaves the prior question of the determination of class *positions* unanswered and, therefore, subject to arbitrary operationalism. The work of Poulantzas and Carchedi is, then, not only a departure but a welcome one.

At the most general level, then, Poulantzas and Carchedi share a common project and the extent to which they exhibit a terminology in common would also appear to promise a coalescence of their analyses. While the terminology derives from the obvious and pervasive influence of Althusser, this indebtedness merely serves to obscure divergences where a received terminology in common hides the slippage of meaning from one usage to another – Poulantzas is the disciple and Carchedi the heretic in this . . . .

Through his utilization of the concepts of the 'collective labourer' and 'economic oppression' Carchedi progressively extends his identification of the working class from those who labour productively in productive industry, to all workers in productive industry excluded from the global functions of capital, to workers in unproductive capitalist industry and finally to all workers in non-capitalist state activities. They are unified by their exclusion from the functions of surveillance and control and their economic exploitation and oppression. Carchedi never discusses whether this extension of a common mode of oppression and subordination in the form of generalized authority relations will give rise to common class interests, except to allow that ideological and political factors may intervene to modify them – so we must assume a uniformity of interest as a result of his economic identifications.

Poulantzas takes a diametrically opposed line. For while the working class is excluded from economic ownership and possession its full determination is not defined by such 'negative' criteria. Rather, its boundaries are formed by the criterion of productive labour. Only those who are directly appropriated of surplus value make up the working class. In fact the definition is narrower than even this may initially suggest for only those positions which are directly involved in material production are working class. For Poulantzas there can be no departure from this golden rule – except one, that is: technicians and engineers.

Poulantzas must admit that the socialization of labour in the extended reproduction of capital gives rise to the phenomenon of the productive collective worker – he has the means, along with Carchedi, of extending the economic boundaries of the working class. Such workers as technicians and engineers are also involved in material production 'which is broadly equivalent' (*Classes in Contemporary Capitalism*, p. 221) to labour producing surplus-value. To follow the golden rule, technicians must be admitted to the working class. However, Poulantzas cannot allow that.

> Economic relations such as the distinction between productive and unproductive labour are not sufficient to delimit the class boundaries between the working class and certain fringe sections of the new petty bourgeoisie i.e. those fringe sections that are themselves directly involved in material production (p. 224).

This is the case with technicians and engineers in whose case the ideological and political intervene to override the golden rule. Technology itself is not a neutral process but 'supports the reproduction of the ideological relations within the process of material production' (p. 287). Technology is the materialization of dominant ideology:

> Technicians and engineers tend to form part of capitalist productive labour because they directly valorize capital in the production of surplus value. If they do not as a group belong to the working class, this is because in their place within the division of labour they maintain political and ideological relations of subordination of the working class to capital (the division of mental and manual labour) and because this aspect of their class determination is the dominant one (p. 242).

The golden rule it appears is no rule at all, for after the long discussion of productive and unproductive labour which concludes that material labour is the line of demarcation we discover that it is in fact the mental/manual division – the ideological instance. Because the productive–unproductive pair are regarded as an insufficient condition to determine the boundary of the working class and new petty bourgeoisie, Poulantzas is forced to introduce a further dichotomizing pair in its place. The first point to be made about the mental/manual division is that in an attempt to overcome certain ambiguities in the concept of productive labour (ambiguities which as Wright has argued might represent actual contradictions in class locations) he does so by placing at the centre of his analysis a pair characterized by infinitely greater levels of conceptual ambiguity, if not downright mushiness; concepts which unlike their predecessors have little in the way of theoretical underpinnings in Marxist literature. But we will return to a consideration of the mental/manual division below.

But have we finally discovered the actual boundary to the working class? It would seem not, for there is also one exception to golden rule number two. This is the aristocracy of labour. The aristocracy of labour, the craftsmen of capitalism are, Poulantzas agrees, capable of exhibiting the ideological characteristics of the bourgeoisie. However, this ideology is 'conjunctural' ideology which since it cannot be known in Poulantzas' theory cannot operate to override or neutralize their economic determination as materially productive labour. This bending of the golden rules leads Poulantzas to attempt to disarm his critics – with reference to the new petty bourgeoisie:

> The fact that examination of political and ideological relations is particularly important in the case of the petty bourgeoisie does not mean that these relations are only important for this class . . . nor is it a sign of conceptual difficulty, such that the Marxist criteria of economic class determination would be 'uncertain' in its case, and the balance would have to be swayed by taking refuge in ideological and political criteria. If these relations have to be stressed, it is because of the real situation . . . (p. 207).

What is the reality of these fluctuating determinations? Is it always the case that there is a clear distinction to be made between all technicians and all craftsmen in the extent to which in their work they 'materialize the dominant ideology'? Can the technical content of occupations be reduced to a pure structure of domination in the case of technicians and a pure structure of subordination in the case of craftsmen? The fact that such questions can be asked re-echoes the general argument with regard to the reductionism involved in the totalizing concepts of the political. We are now tracing the self-same characteristics within the ideological instance.

We might also question the degree to which Poulantzas' conflation of material production with the production of surplus-value has an significance for the 'real situation'. According to Poulantzas, productive labour produces surplus-value and in so doing is directly involved in material production: 'producing use-values that increase material wealth' (p. 216). Here, he appears to be committing a similar error to that of Carchedi in maintaining the duality of the labour process and surplus-value producing process. Where for Marx surplus-value is the product of the exchange of commodity forms. Poulantzas resurrects use-values in order to restrict (rather than extend) productive labour to the production of material objects. If non-material services take a commodity form for exchange on a market, where is the difference in its relation to generating surplus-value?

... And Another: Contradictory Locations
Erik Olin Wright

Capital, Crisis and the State (London: NLB, 1978) pp. 46–53, 59–64, 77–82

There are three basic difficulties in Poulantzas's discussion of productive and unproductive labour: 1. problems in his definition of productive labour; 2. the lack of correspondence between the productive/unproductive labour distinction and actual positions in the labour process; 3. – and most significantly – the lack of fundamentally different economic interests between productive and unproductive workers.

Productive labour, to Poulantzas, is restricted to labour which both produces surplus-value and is directly involved in the process of material production. This definition rests on the claim that surplus-value is only generated in the production of physical commodities. This is an arbitrary assumption. If use-values takes the form of services, and if those services are produced for the market, then there is no reason why surplus-value cannot be generated in non-material production as well as the production of physical commodities.[1]

The second difficulty with Poulantzas's use of productive/unproductive labour concerns the relationship of this distinction to positions in the social division of labour. If actual positions generally contain a mix of productive and unproductive activities, then the distinction between productive and unproductive labour becomes much less useful as a criterion for the class determination of those positions. . . . Consider the case of the material production of the packaging for a commodity. Packaging serves two distinct functions. On the one hand, it is part of the use-value of a commodity. One can hardly drink milk without placing it in a transportable container. But packaging is also part of realization costs under capitalism, since much of the labour embodied in packaging goes into producing advertising. Such labour cannot be considered productive, because it does not produce any use-values (and thus cannot produce surplus-value). . . .

While Poulantzas does admit that some labour has this dual productive/unproductive character, he sidesteps this problem in his analysis of classes by saying that labour is tendentially one or the other. In fact, a large proportion of labour in capitalist society has both productive and unproductive aspects, and there is no reason to assume that such mixed forms of labour are becoming less frequent. The productive/unproductive labour distinction should thus be thought of as reflecting two dimensions of labour activity rather than two types of labourers.

The most fundamental objection, however, to Poulantzas's use of the productive/unproductive distinction goes beyond questions of definition or the conceptual status of the distinction. For two positions within the social division of labour to be placed in different classes on the basis of economic criteria implies that they have fundamentally different class *interests* at the economic level. . . .

It could also be argued that since unproductive workers produce no surplus-value, they live off the surplus-value produced by productive workers and thus indirectly participate in the exploitation of those workers. Taking the argument one step further, it is sometimes claimed that unproductive workers have a stake in increasing the social rate of exploitation, since this would make it easier for them to improve their own wages. This kind of argument is perhaps clearest in the case of state workers who are paid directly out of taxes. Since taxation comes at least partially out of surplus-value, it appears that state workers live off the exploitation of productive labour. There is no question that there is some truth in this claim. Certainly in terms of immediate economic interests, state workers are often in conflict with private sector workers over questions of taxation. The bourgeois media have made much of this issue and have clearly used it as a divisive force in the labour movement. However, the question is not whether divisions of immediate interests exist between productive and unproductive workers, but whether such divisions generate different objective interests in socialism. Many divisions of immediate economic interest exist within the working class – between monopoly and competitive sector workers, between black and white workers, between workers in imperialist countries and workers in the third world, etc. But none of these divisions implies that the 'privileged' group of workers has an interest in perpetuating the system of capitalist exploitation. None of these divisions changes the fundamental fact that all workers, by virtue of their position within the social relations of production, have a basic interest in socialism. I would argue that this is true for most unproductive workers as well. . . .

Poulantzas insists that while ideological and political criteria are important, economic criteria still play the principal role in determining classes. . . . This does not appear to be the case . . . *Any* deviation from the criteria which define the working class is enough to exclude an agent from the working class in Poulantzas's analysis. Thus, an agent who was like a worker on the economic and political criteria, but deviated on the ideological criteria, would on this basis alone be excluded from the proletariat (this is the case for subaltern technicians). In practice, therefore, the ideological and political criteria becomes co-equal with the economic criteria, since they can *always* pre-empt the structural determination of class at the economic level. (This is quite separate from the question of the correctness of the economic criteria themselves as discussed above.) It is difficult to see how, under these circumstances, this perspective maintains the primacy of economic relations in the definition of classes. . . .

Aside from undermining the economic basis of the theory of class, Poulantzas's use of political and ideological criteria has other difficulties. Especially in his discussion of political criteria, it is sometimes questionable whether these criteria are really 'political' at all. The core political criterion Poulantzas emphasizes in his discussion of the new petty bourgeoisie is position within the supervisory hierarchy. Now, apart from the issue of supervision as technical coordination, there are two ways in which supervision can be conceptualized. Following Poulantzas, supervision can be conceived as the 'direct reproduction, within the process of production itself, of the political relations between the capitalist class and the working class'.[2] Alternatively, supervision can be seen as one aspect of the structural dissociation between economic ownership and possession at the economic level itself. That is, possession, as an aspect of the ownership of the means of production, involves (to use Poulantzas's own formulation) control over the labour process. In the development of monopoly capitalism, possession has become dissociated from economic ownership. But equally, possession has become internally differentiated, so that control over the entire labour process (top managers) has become separated from the immediate control of labour activity (supervision). Unless possession itself is to be considered an aspect of political relations, there is no reason to consider supervision a reflection of political relations within the social division of labour rather than a differentiated element of economic relations.

In Poulantzas's use of ideological criteria, it is never clear exactly why the mental/manual division should be considered a determinant of an actual class boundary, rather than simply an internal division within the working class. It is also not clear why this particular ideological dimension was chosen over a variety of others as the essential axis of ideological domination/subordination within the social division of labour. For example, sexism, by identifying certain jobs as 'women's work' and of inferior status to men's work, is also a dimension of ideological domination/subordination within the social division of labour. This puts men as a whole in a position of ideological domination, and yet this hardly makes a male worker not a worker. The same can be said of racism, nationalism and other ideologies of domination. All of these create important divisions within the proletariat; but, unless they correspond to different actual relations of production, they do not constitute criteria for class boundaries in their own right. . . .

Poulantzas's discussion of the class position of managers . . . is inadequate. When a manager occupies a position in the relations of production that is characterized by *both* economic ownership and possession, it is certainly reasonable to categorize the manager as part of the bourgeoisie. The problem arises when a manager occupies a position characterized by possession but not economic ownership. Poulantzas's solution to this situation is to argue that, in spite of the structural differentiation of different functions of capital, the positions remain unitary parts of capital as such. Thus, occupying any such position is sufficient to define the manager as bourgeois. This is an arbitrary solution. It is equally plausible to argue that exclusion from economic ownership defines non-capitalists in capitalist society, and thus managers who are 'mere' possessors of the means of production should be excluded from the bourgeoisie. A third possibility – which will be developed more fully below – is to argue that there are positions in the social division of labour which are *objectively contradictory*. Managers who are excluded from any economic ownership would constitute such a category, even if they retain partial possession of the means of production.

A second problem with Poulantzas's analysis of the bourgeoisie is that he tends to regard economic ownership and possession as all-or-nothing categories. A position either does or does not have real economic control of the means of production (economic ownership), or does or does not have the capacity to put those means of production into operation (possession). In fact, many managerial positions must be characterized as having limited forms of both ownership and possession. Some managers may have substantial control over one small segment of the total production process; others may have fairly limited control over a broader range of the production process. While it is clear that an agent whose control is so attenuated that he/she merely executes decisions made from above should be excluded from the bourgeoisie, there is considerable ambiguity how middle-level managers of various sorts should be treated. . . .

Perhaps the most serious general criticism of Poulantzas's perspective centres on his treatment of ambiguous positions within the class structure. In his analysis of the working class, *any* deviation at all from the pure working-class criteria . . . is sufficient for exclusion from the proletariat; in his analysis of the bourgeoisie, on the other hand, it is necessary to deviate on *all* criteria in order to be excluded from the capitalist class. In neither case is the possibility allowed that positions within the social division of labour can be objectively contradictory.

An alternative way of dealing with such ambiguities in the class structure is to regard some positions as occupying *objectively contradictory locations within class relations*. **Rather** than eradicating these contradictions by artificially classifying every position within the social division of labour unambiguously into one class or another, contradictory locations need to be studied in their own right. . . .

Three clusters of positions within the social division of labour can be characterized as occupying contradictory locations within class relations (see Figure 7.1): 1. *managers and supervisors* occupy a

FIGURE 7.1

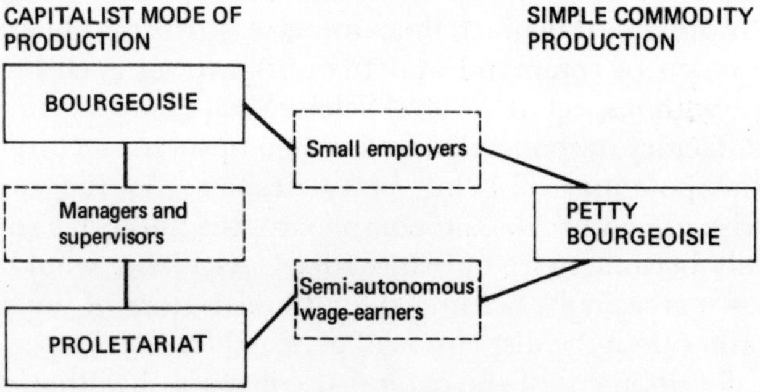

contradictory location between the bourgeoisie and the pro-letariat; 2. certain categories of *semi-autonomous employees* who retain relatively high levels of control over their immediate labour process occupy a contradictory location between the working class and the petty bourgeoisie; 3. *small employers* occupy a contradictory location between the bourgeoisie and the petty bourgeoisie. Our first task is to analyse how these contradictory locations emerge out of the dynamics of class relations in advanced capitalist society. Three interconnected structural changes in the course of capitalist development can help us to unravel the social processes underlying class relations in advanced capitalism: the progressive loss of control over the labour process on the part of the direct producers; the elaboration of complex authority hierarchies within capitalist enterprises and bureaucracies; and the differential of various functions originally embodied in the entrepreneurial capitalist. . . .

The contradictory location closest to the working class is that of foremen and line supervisors. Foremen typically have little real control over the physical means of production, and while they do

131

exercise control over labour power, this frequently does not extend much beyond being the formal transmission belt for orders from above. It is difficult to say whether during the course of capitalist development over the past century, the class location of foremen has moved closer to or further from the working class. On the one hand, the early foreman often participated directly in the production process alongside workers and even defended workers against arbitrary treatment by the boss. On the other hand, the foreman in the nineteenth-century factory often had much greater personal discretion and personal power than today. In the nineteenth century, authority within the capitalist factory was typically organized in much the same as was an army. There was a simple chain of command and the authority at each level was absolute with respect to the level below. Such a system Marx aptly termed 'factory despotism', and foremen in such a factory had at least the potential of being petty despots. As the capitalist enterprise grew in scale and complexity, the authority structure gradually became more bureaucratized. As Weber would put it, foremen increasingly became the administrators of impersonal rules rather than the dispensers of personal fiats. . . .

The development of the capitalist enterprise has thus pushed foremen in two opposing directions: they have moved further from workers by becoming less involved in direct production, and they have moved closer to workers by gradually having their personal power bureaucratized. Superficially at least, it would seem that the first of these tendencies probably dominated during the first part of this century, while the second tendency probably dominates today. In any event, when the control of supervisors over labour power becomes so attenuated that the supervisor lacks even the capacity to invoke negative sanctions, then the position really merges with the working class proper and should no longer be thought of as a contradictory location. This would be the case, for example, of the chief of a work team who has certain special responsibilities for coordinating activities of others in the team, but lacks any real power over them.

At the other end of the contradictory location between workers and capitalists, top managers occupy a contradictory location at the boundary of the bourgeoisie. While top managers are generally characterized by limited participation in economic ownership, they differ little from the bourgeoisie in terms of relations of possession. Again, at the very top of the managerial hierarchy, corporate executives essentially merge with the capitalist class itself.

The most contradictory locations between the bourgeoisie and the proletariat are occupied by middle managers and what can loosely be termed 'technocrats'. Technocrat in this context refers to technicians and professionals of various sorts within the corporate hierarchy who tend to have a limited degree of autonomy over their own work (*minimal* control over what they produce and how they produce it) and a limited control over subordinates, but who are not in command of pieces of the productive apparatus. Middle managers, on the other hand, control various pieces of the labour process; they have control not only over immediate subordinates but over part of the authority hierarchy itself. Both middle managers and technocrats have, in Harry Braverman's words, one foot in the bourgeoisie and one foot in the proletariat. In discussing new technical occupations and middle management, Braverman writes: 'If we are to call this a "new middle class", however, as many have done, we must do so with certain reservations. The old middle class occupied that position by virtue of its place outside the polar class structure; it possessed the attributes of neither capitalist nor worker; it played no direct role in the capital accumulation process, whether on one side or the other. This "new middle class', by contrast, occupies its intermediate position not because it is outside the process of increasing capital, but because, as part of this process, it takes its characteristics from *both sides*. Not only does it receive its petty share of the prerogatives and rewards of capital, but it also bears the mark of the proletarian condition.'[3] Unlike line supervisors and foremen on the one hand, and top managers on the other, middle managers and technocrats do not have a clear class pole to which they are attached. The contradictory quality of their class location is much more intense than in the other cases we have discussed, and as a result it is much more difficult to assess the general stance they will take within class struggle. . . .

The contradictory location between the petty bourgeoisie and the proletariat can perhaps best be understood by returning to the historic process of proletarianization of the petty bourgeoisie. The central dynamic underlying this transformation was the need of capital to increase its control over the labour process. Each step of the transformation involved a deeper penetration of capitalist domination into the labouring activity of direct producers, until in the classic form of scientific management, the direct producer has no control whatsoever over his/her work. This process is constantly being re-enacted within capitalism; it is not a process which was somehow completed at the beginning of this century.

Today there are still categories of employees who have a certain degree of control over their own immediate conditions of work, over their immediate labour process. In such instances, the labour process has not been completely proletarianized. Thus, even though such employees work for the self-expansion of capital and even though they have lost the legal status of being self-employed, they can still be viewed as occupying residual islands of petty-bourgeois relations of production within the capitalist mode of production itself. In their immediate work environment, they maintain the work process of the independent artisan while still being employed by capital as wage labourers. They control *how* they do their work, and have at least some control over *what* they produce. A good example of this is a researcher in a laboratory or a professor in an elite university. Such positions may not really involve control over other people's labour power, yet have considerable immediate control over conditions of work (i.e. research). More generally, many white-collar technical employees and certain highly skilled craftsmen have at least a limited form of this autonomy in their immediate labour process. Such minimal control over the physical means of production by employees outside of the authority hierarchy constitutes the basic contradictory location between the petty bourgeoisie and the proletariat.

While there is some debate on the question, it seems likely that in the course of capitalist development over the past fifty years, this particular kind of contradictory location has been somewhat reduced. It is certainly true that white-collar employees have increased as a proportion of the labour force, but as Braverman has forcefully shown, this expansion of white-collar employment has been combined with a constant proletarianization of the working conditions of white-collar labour. It remains to be shown whether the net effect of these two tendencies – the expansion of white-collar employment and the proletarianization of white-collar work – has increased or decreased the contradictory locations between the working class and the petty bourgeoisie. At any rate, it seems almost certain that the large majority of white-collar employees, especially clerical and secretarial employees, have – at most – trivial autonomy on the job and thus should be placed within the working class itself.

How much autonomy is really necessary to define a position as occupying the contradictory location between the working class and the petty bourgeoisie? Surely the criterion of absolutely any autonomy whatsoever is too broad. While the historical data on the labour process are rather meagre, it is unlikely that more than a small fraction of the working class was ever characterized by the classic image of the fully proletarianized worker, totally under the control of the capitalist through a minutely subdivided labour process governed by principles of scientific management. Most workers, most of the time, have been able to maintain at least some residual control over their immediate labour process. Similarly, it would be inappropriate to restrict the concept of 'semi-autonomy' to positions which, like university professors, have extremely high levels of control over the pace of work, the scheduling of work, the content of work, etc. Clearly, then, a certain amount of arbitrariness will inevitably enter into any attempt rigorously to define the semi-autonomous employee class location.

Provisionally, the minimum criterion for semi-autonomy which I will adopt is that such positions must involve at least some control both over what is produced (minimal economic owner-ship) as well as how it is produced (minimal possession). This means that positions such as laboratory technicians would not be included in the semi-autonomous category since such positions would generally not involve any control over what kind of experiments were done in the lab, even though a technician might have very considerable control over other conditions of work (pace, breaks, techniques used, etc.). A research scientist, on the other hand, would often not simply have autonomy over how he/she performed an experiment, but over what experiments were performed. Research scientists, therefore, would be firmly within the semi-autonomous employee category.

NOTES AND REFERENCES

1. Marx's famous comparison of teaching factories and sausage factories makes this precise point: 'The only worker who is productive is one who produces surplus-value for the capitalist, or in other words contributes towards the self-valorization of capital. If we may take an example from outside the sphere of material production, a schoolmaster is a productive worker when, in addition

135

to belabouring the heads of his pupils, he works himself into the ground to
enrich the owner of the school. That the latter has laid out his capital in a
teaching factory, instead of a sausage factory, makes no difference to the
relation.'
2. *Classes in Contemporary Capitalism*, p. 228.
3. *Labor and Monopoly Capital*, p. 467.

The Political Economy of Class

Rosemary Crompton and Jon Gubbay

Economy and Class Structure (London: Macmillan, 1977) pp. 167–72,
174–6, 178–83, 188–90

We define class situations by locations in the flows of surplus
product, the primary axis of differentiation being control versus
coordinated labour, other axes being capital versus non-capital,
and state versus private ownership. More explicitly, class
situations are initially defined by three elements: (1) whether the
position entails control, coordinated labour or both; (2) whether
the enterprise in which the position is located is a capital, non-
capital, or both (i.e. quasi-capital); (3) whether the capital, non-
capital or quasi-capital is state owned or privately owned. (In
practice state ownership will be confined to quasi-capitals and
non-capitals.) . . .

In capitalist societies there are many tendencies towards
indentification and action as primary classes. There are also
factors working against this, creating individual and sectional
competitiveness. Specific socio-historical studies are required for
any given society to assess the weight and likely changes of these
conflicting forces. We make no prediction that primary class
consciousness and behaviour will inevitably grow, that people
increasingly become aware of their broadest class interests as they
lose their 'selfishness' and 'parochialism'. Nonetheless this is a
possibility, a potential for class polarisation which would present
an acute threat to capitalism as such. The functional dichotomy
between control and coordinated labour *must* be given institutional form in capitalism; any challenge to their separation is also
a challenge to the capitalist order. . . .

The primary class of controllers is fairly firmly wedded to the capitalist social order in attitudes and action, their class consciousness often being expressed in terms of 'order' rather than 'power over', emphasising nationality, law and the 'naturalness' of capitalist market and production relations – challenges to which are seen as leading to anarchy.

Class identifications among the primary class of coordinated labourers are more mixed, fragmented and tenuous, a complex amalgam in varying proportions of acceptance of the above-mentioned dominant values, adaptation to them and rejection of them. . . .

The fragmentation and fragility of working-class consciousness derives in large part from the central dichotomy of control versus coordinated labour, the alternative logical responses to subordination being acceptance, adaptation and rejection, but it is also patterned by other features of class structure.

A major complication to primary class division comes with the recognition that some roles involve *both* control and coordinated labour, a situation we refer to as 'structural ambiguity'. We prefer this rather elaborate term to Carchedi's 'middle class' since the latter incorrectly implies coherent class interests, whereas these positions are characterised by internally inconsistent interests derived from opposed objectives. Under capitalism, the functional distinction between control and coordinated labour tends to be realised concretely in disjunct role complexes, but this separation is not now complete nor is ever likely to be. Those who carry out both control and coordinated labour are in an objectively ambiguous position, whether they are conscious of it or not. Later in this chapter we shall discuss more fully the forces strengthening and weakening the effects of primary structural ambiguity.

Those carrying out both capital and labour functions are faced with contradictory ways of understanding their situation. On the one hand they could identify with the goals of the global capital, viewing labour only as a means to those ends and so seeking to increase surplus labour appropriated by the capital. In this perspective their income is seen as a share of profit, from which low productivity of labour detracts. Alternatively people in this ambiguous position could identify with the collective labourer, regarding the control functions they carry out as purely technical. Income is then seen as wages, with profits being created out of the surplus labour performed by them and others.

In reality those who carry out both functions often adopt an inconsistent and vacillating combination of these two perspectives or synthesise them by regarding their income as a share of total profit which they have contributed to creating.

The primary axis of class differentiation therefore gives rise immediately to three distinct groupings; control, coordinated labour and structurally ambiguous class situations which contain elements of both. As we stated in our introduction to this chapter, the location of the groupings generated by this primary axis can only be grasped if we simultaneously consider sectoral differentiation within the total system of the generation and allocation of surplus product.

The first distinction we build on to our basic model is that between capitals and non-capitals. In practice the great majority of non-capitals will be state-controlled – the health service, national and local government administration, education, etc. Private non-capitals include activities such as churches, charities, and voluntary organisations. . . .

The situation of the controllers in state non-capitals is considerably more complex than in capitals, for one aspect of control is characteristically removed from the enterprise itself and located in government. Olin Wright, following Poulantzas, distinguishes two elements of control – possession and economic ownership.[1] Possession refers to control over plant and equipment together with corresponding supervisory powers over labour, whereas economic ownership refers to the capacity to make long-term strategic decisions, especially over investment and the allocation of resources. In the case of capitals, both elements of control are located within the enterprise itself, typically with economic ownership concentrated in the top echelons. This fact may be responsible for tensions between differentiated functions and levels in a bureaucratic hierarchy, tensions which may also enhance or obscure the primary structural ambiguity of roles involving both global capital and collective worker functions. But in state non-capitals economic ownership is to a substantial degree located outside the enterprise in the government; for it is government which decides the basic shape and size of the health service, the army, the social security system and so on, with the boards concerned only exercising possession. This division of control creates both a characteristic tension between government and internal controllers and, in significant conflicts between control and coordinated labour, the appearance of the internal controllers as 'intermediaries'. On the one hand the fact that those at the top of the managerial hierarchy evidently do not have economic ownership may lead labour in such enterprises to a resigned acceptance that it is pointless bargaining with an 'authority' which cannot deliver, or on the other hand the relative impotence of the internal controllers may give labour's discontents an immediate political flavour.

In discussing non-capitals so far, we have considered only those that are state owned, for we do not regard private non-capitals as part of the capitalist mode of production. Some enterprises appear to be marginal cases, for example, workers' cooperatives and mutual companies (such as insurance companies where ownership is formally vested in the policy-holders). These are clearly *economic* enterprises and the evidence demonstrates that they develop managerial hierarchies, separating control from coordinated labour. Thus as they operate in the market they come to be capitals rather than non-capitals, even though their controllers may be elected or the members subscribe to a cooperative ideology. The most democratic firm can only maintain its viability in the market if the bulk of its members accept no more than market wages and work at no lower productivity levels than comparable enterprises; cooperatives cannot opt out of capitalism.

So far we have related the basic elements of class situation – control/global capital and coordinated labour/collective worker and associated structural ambiguities – to the capital/non-capital distinction. This has inevitably involved building in the state/ private dichotomy, as the significant non-capitals are invariably state owned. Any consideration of quasi-capitals must also simultaneously incorporate the state/non-state dichotomy, since state quasi-capitals may have very different properties from private quasi-capitals. . . .

This conflict of interests between *capitals* over shares of the total surplus product is often presented as a conflict between productive and unproductive *activities* so that, to the extent that this perspective is accepted, productive workers may come to regard unproductive workers as living at their expense. Conversely, unproductive workers may insist that their work is necessary for production to take place, a claim which is of course true in capitalist society. The potential for tensions among different types of collective worker can be seen most graphically where a firm engaged in both sectors is experiencing low profits and reductions in business turnover; for example, sales staff and manufacturing workers may dispute *which* group should make most sacrifices in wages, conditions and jobs rather than combine to minimise total losses. Tensions between types of collective worker is not the result of capitals' conscious decision to 'divide and rule', although any such policy will naturally exacerbate divisiveness, but because the different capital functions require separate hierarchies of authority, conditions of work and systems of payment. The conflicts of interests between factions of capital thus reproduce in more or less attenuated form splits among the primary class of coordinated labour, splits which are institutionalised to some degree in trade union structure in the United Kingdom.

As already mentioned, non-capitals are, like capitals in unproductive spheres, a drain on surplus product so they and their workers are liable to be castigated as an unnecessary luxury. Since the most economically important non-capitals are within the state sector, attacks on 'unproductive activities' often slide into general attacks on state expenditure, including state investment in quasi-capitals. Such criticisms in fact often relate to the potential threat of immensely powerful state competition with private capitals, even though such investment is customarily described as an excessive expenditure of *national* resources.

While such polemics may serve the interests of private capital and divide public sector workers from private sector workers, the supposed association of the state with unproductive activities is fallacious; there are clearly both large unproductive private sectors and productive state sectors. It is of course true that enterprises in the state sector are inevitably pressed into non-capital functions so that there are no pure state capitals, but only state quasi-capitals. This does mean that state enterprises which are predominantly in the productive sphere do, to a greater or lesser extent, absorb as well as generate surplus product. The substantial loss-making nationalised industries like British Railways are a clear case in point. However, this is a rather fine point, for in spite of all the free enterprise rhetoric large corporations are increasingly interdependent with the state.

Whatever the validity of the supposed conflict of interests between private and state activities, it remains true that these arguments to some extent divide coordinated labour. This is again evident in trade union structure.

We have seen how the primary class divisions based on control versus coordinated labour are complicated when taken in conjunction with the other two defining elements of class situation, capital versus non-capital and state versus private ownership. These bases of classification were derived from our general model of flows of value, but the class situations to which they give rise are further complicated by other secondary structural factors. We term these factors 'secondary' because, although they may be extremely important – in particular, in contributing to the *actor's* perception of the class structure – they are not directly derived from the basic framework we have developed above. Furthermore it is a feature of these secondary structural factors that the conflicts between the interest groupings they generate may be resolved without a radical change in the underlying capitalist mode of production, thus they cannot be considered to be *determinants* of social class. . . .

Within the functionally specialised sectors . . . we typically find in developed capitalist society that the many tasks necessary to the creation, acquisition and distribution of surplus value are carried out by specially trained groups possessing the skills relevant to a particular task. . . . Although the capitalist function *is* largely carried out by 'management' because, as we have argued, management also carries out a part of the function of the collective worker, the category of 'management' is not synonymous with that of global capital. Some of the strains and conflicts which can be empirically observed within the differentiated managerial stratum are therefore attributable to the structurally ambiguous class situation of many managers. At the same time conflicts may be generated between different parts of the managerial stratum in the absence of structural ambiguity. Parallel conflicts may also develop within the collective worker/coordinated labour function. . . . .

Wright identifies three processes underlying the social relations of capitalist production: (1) economic or *de facto ownership*, the control of investments and resources, and two aspects of *possession*; (2) the control of the physical means of production; and (3) the control of labour power. Full control in respect of all three of these processes locates an agent unambiguously in the bourgeoisie, total lack of control, in the proletariat. Those managers, therefore, who have more or less full control in respect of economic ownership and the two aspects of possession are to be considered as part of the bourgeoisie, attenuated control in respect of any of these three processes, or control in respect of only one or two of them leads, according to Wright, to a contradictory class location. We will deal with the question of *degrees* of control in our discussion of bureaucracy – the next secondary structural factor we identify. In this section we will evaluate Wright's claim that control in respect of only one or two of the three processes underlying capitalist relations of production places the agent in a 'contradictory class location'.

We would argue, contrary to Wright, that the fact that an agent carries out only a part of the function of global capital – be it economic ownership, control over physical resources, or control over labour power – does not automatically place the agent in a structurally ambiguous (or contradictory) class location in a *fundamental* sense. The carrying out of only a part of the capitalist function by an agent does not make it any the less capitalist, neither does it automatically imply that the agent carries out any part of the function of the collective worker. . . .

The development of bureaucratic hierarchies has certainly had a significant effect in both obscuring and clarifying class relationships. On the one hand the difference between global capital and collective worker is emphasised by a systematisation of authority which separates those who command from those who obey. On the other hand the fact that the different functions and levels within the command hierarchy are themselves constrained by bureaucratic rules and varying degrees of authority is likely to lead to tensions *within* the hierarchy. Although these effects are undoubtedly important, we regard the development of bureaucracy as a secondary structural factor in our analysis of the class structure, rather than an absolutely basic element in its patterning. Particular functions are not transformed by changes in their administration, and if anything the functions of global capital and collective worker are made even clearer by the development of bureacracy. Even though conflicts may well develop between bureaucratically identified groups, such conflicts are susceptible to resolution in the absence of any fundamental changes in the underlying mode of production, and may be analysed as intra- rather than inter-class conflicts, adding further to the complexity of the class structure of contemporary capitalist societies.

In our identification of bureacracy as secondary, rather than a primary, factor in the structuring of class relationships, our analysis again diverges significantly from that of Wright. His approach may be briefly summarised: The carrying out of the different aspects of the capitalist function – the control of investments and resources, control over the physical means of production, and control over labour power – is typically adminis- tered through a complex bureacratic hierarchy. Thus control at different levels ranges from almost full control through partial to minimal. Therefore the *degree* of control – reflected in the position in the bureaucratic hierarchy – possessed by an agent is a crucial factor in *determining* 'contradictory class locations'. Taken together with the number of functions carried out, the degree of control determines class location. For example, if an agent has full control in respect of the physical means of production and labour power, then the class location, although contradictory, will lie very near that of the bourgeoisie. Alternatively an agent with control over labour power, and only minimal control at that, will be located very near the boundary of the proletariat. From this and previous summaries of Wright's approach we can see that Wright identifies two factors which actually *structure* class relations – the differentiation of the functions of capital and the development of complex hierarchies. We have argued that these factors are seondary, rather than primary. Both contribute essentially to intra- rather than inter-class conflicts, and the kinds of conflicts engendered by these factors are technically possible to overcome without radically changing or transcending the capitalist mode of production. We can further develop our criticism by looking at Wright's discussion of [foremen] who have 'moved further from workers by becoming less involved in direct production, and [they have moved] closer to workers by gradually having their personal power bureaucratised'. Whilst we would agree that the fact that foremen participate less in the labour process will move them further from workers, we would not agree that the bureaucratisa- tion of personal power moves them any closer. Even if the foreman only supervises labour in accordance with rules laid down from above, this does not make his control over labour power – or the carrying out of the capitalist function – any less real. A function is not transformed by the *manner* in which it is carried out. Attenuation of control therefore does not change the essential nature of a class situation, although it may further complicate a class situation which is already ambiguous. (For example, a foreman may resent management and *feel* that he is closer to the work-force because he is 'pushed around' in a similar fashion, but he is unlikely to be accepted by the work-force as long as his major task is the administration of delegated authority.)

Although we have been critical of much of Wright's approach, we would stress that in many respects his work represents a significant improvement on many existing strategies of class analysis. Firstly, he locates class relationships firmly in *production*, rather than the market, status groupings, or whatever. Secondly, Wright has identified the differentiation of the capitalist function and the development of bureaucratic hierarchies through a historical analysis of capitalist developments. Logically they are not, therefore, 'the inevitable developments of advanced industrialism', but the *particular* accompaniments of monopoly capitalism.

NOTES AND REFERENCES

1. 'Class Boundaries in Advanced Capitalist Societies', *New Left Review*, 98 (1976).

Part II

The Development and Character of White-Collar Unionism

8 Introduction

White-Collar Unions: Growth, Character and Attitudes in the 1970s

Robert Price

Two interrelated themes have dominated the literature, both academic and popular, on the unionization of white-collar workers. On the one hand, there has been a strong stream of inquiry into the *growth* of white-collar unions; writers have sought to identify those factors which most influenced the decision of workers holding jobs conventionally classified as white-collar either to join or not to join a trade union. On the other hand, there have been those who have been more concerned to evaluate the *character* of white-collar organizations and their impact on the character of trade unionism more generally. At the level of the *organization*, these writers have sought to compare the objectives, methods and policies of white-collar and manual unions. At the level of the *individual member*, they have investigated the variations in attitudes and behaviour of white-collar and manual trade unionists. In Part II, readings in each of these three areas have been selected; and this introductory essay seeks to identify and evaluate some of the main themes and issues which have emerged in the post-war debate about white-collar unionization.

While the two themes of growth and character are clearly distinguishable in the literature, there is a strong theoretical and empirical link between them. In so far as the decision to join a union remains a largely voluntary one for the vast majority of white-collar workers, it is clear that the range of orientations and objectives which prompt that decision will be linked to subsequent behaviour within the organization. This is not to deny the complexity of the notion of union character which, as the later discussions will show, comprises a wide range of behavioural and attitudinal factors. But it is to say that the discussion of why unions grow and decline cannot be divorced from the discussion of unions' goals and priorities, and the methods which they use to achieve them.

Hence, the debate on union growth in Britain in the 1950s and 1960s was permeated by the concern that the character of the union movement at that time was unattractive to potential white-collar members, and that unions were failing to offer the services and benefits that would appeal to non-manual workers. The solution, for those sympathetic to the trade union movement, lay partly in changes in the style and policies of unions – throwing off the 'cloth cap' image – and partly in changes in government policy. Thus McCarthy, writing in an influential Fabian Tract in 1960, warned that if unions were to avoid becoming 'the outdated representatives of a declining industrial minority'[1] it was vital for them to appeal to non-manual workers and to put a special effort into recruiting them. The view that growth and development were dependent on a change of image and character was taken up by a number of union leaderships, most notably by the then newly formed Association of Scientific, Technical and Managerial Staffs (ASTMS). At the end of the 1960s ASTMS launched a number of apparently successful publicity campaigns based on slogans which emphasized the specifically *white-collar* nature of its appeal. Slogans like 'My tragedy was that I picked up a pen instead of a shovel' were designed to present the union, not as just another union which happened to be active among non-manual workers, but as a rather different type of organization with a distinctive commitment to rectifying the economic problems of the white-collar worker.[2]

In the last decade, the remarkable growth of white-collar union membership has focused attention on a different link between union growth and character. It has been argued that the increasing numbers of white-collar workers joining unions have been motivated by essentially 'instrumental' or economic concerns, and that this has resulted in fundamental changes in the internal character of the trade union movement. As the proportion of white-collar unionists within the TUC has grown, so the proportion of union members in Labour Party affiliated unions and paying the political levy has declined. This decline in overt party political commitment has been linked to the less partisan political stance adopted by the TUC in the 1950s and 1960s when it sought to present itself as a major economic pressure group seeking to influence both political parties in equal measure. Other commentators have argued, in a very different and explicitly partisan vein, that the influx of white-collar members has transformed the union movement from 'the moribund carthorse image . . . to a more dynamic and thoughtful movement', which far from being 'moderate' and 'apolitical' in character, is both more aggressive and innovative than traditional trade union policies.[3]

Growth and character are therefore strongly interrelated questions, and the following discussion, although structured around these two themes, seeks to indicate the importance of the interrelationships. In the first section the pattern of white-collar union growth in Britain from 1948 to 1978/9 is examined; and the main issues raised in the readings contained in Chapter 9 on the early history of white-collar unions are then reviewed in the context of a general discussion of the competing theories of union growth. In the following sections, the issue of union character is discussed in the context of the readings in Chapter 10, and the related issue of membership attitudes and behaviour is examined in the light of the structural ambiguities in the position of the white-collar workforce identified by Richard Hyman in Chapter 1. The readings for this section are contained in Chapter 11.

UNION GROWTH AND THE WHITE-COLLAR LABOUR FORCE

The steady shift in the composition of the UK labour force during the twentieth century away from manual towards white-collar occupations has been well documented, and is clearly illustrated in Table 1.1 of Chapter 1. Estimates made in 1975 by the Department of Employment suggest that the 1981 Census will reveal an occupied population in which the manual labour force will be in a clear minority at 48 per cent and non-manual workers will account for some 52 per cent.[4] While these predictions may soon be shown to have been substantially accurate, there are three factors which suggest that the clear trends of the last thirty years cannot be easily extrapolated into the 1980s. The first is the stabilization of the proportion taken by white-collar jobs in the manufacturing sector; this increased slowly over the period

1948–75 (Table 8.1) but has remained relatively static since that date. This development, coupled with a 12 per cent decline in the size of the manufacturing labour-force between 1971 and 1979, means that the number of white-collar workers in manufacturing was in decline after 1975, and was no longer contributing to the expansion of the white-collar share of the total labour force. Secondly, the successive reductions in public expenditure which took place after 1975 resulted in a stabilization of the large white-collar labour force in the public service sector.[5] Thirdly, while the predominantly white-collar private services sector has remained relatively buoyant in employment terms, the introduction of microprocessor technology appears to be threatening many of the routine clerical, administrative and sales jobs in, for example, banking, insurance and parts of the retail distribution sector. Thus the 1980s may witness a major reduction in routine white-collar jobs in this sector which will not be matched by a commensurate reduction on the manual side.

These factors imply that any further major shift in the occupational composition of the labour force towards non-manual jobs is unlikely in the short term, and uncertain in the medium term, but there is little doubt that for the next decade the UK workforce will comprise two roughly equal occupational groups of white-collar and manual workers, with the white-collar group slightly in the majority. It is against the background of this transition to a

TABLE 8.1   *White-collar employment as a percentage of total employment in manufacturing, 1948–79*

1948	16·0
1959	21·1
1964	23·1
1971	27·1
1975	27·8
1979	28·6

SOURCE: These figures are from the annual article published in the *Department of Employment Gazette* which is based on returns made by a sample of employers under the Statistics of Trade Act 1947. The figures include managers, superintendents and works' foremen; research, experimental, development, technical and design employees other than operatives; draughtsmen and tracers; and office employees including works' office employees. See, for example, 'Administrative, technical and clerical workers in manufacturing industries, October 1979', *Department of Employment Gazette*, 87 (December 1979) p. 1249.

majority white-collar labour force that the debate about the growth and character of the trade union movement has been conducted. The larger the proportion of white-collar workers, the more important for the size and representative character of the trade union movement that it should reflect the interests and aspirations of these workers.

Table 8.2 charts the steady growth of aggregate white-collar

TABLE 8.2   *White-collar union membership and density,*
Great Britain (selected years, 1901–78)

	White-collar union membership	White-collar labour force	Density (%)
1901	86	—	—
1911	398	3 433	11.6
1921	993	4 094	24.2
1931	1 025	4 841	21.2
1941	1 613	—	—
1951	2 175	6 948	31.3
1961	2 544	8 479	30.0
1966	2 823	9 461	29.8
1967	2 954	—	—
1968	3 056	—	—
1969	3 211	—	—
1970	3 533	—	—
1971	3 570	10 405	34.3
1972	3 795	—	—
1973	3 966	—	—
1974	4 131	—	—
1978	5 000	11 600	43.1

SOURCES: 1901–74: G. S. Bain and R. Price, *Profiles of Union Growth: A Comparative Statistical Portrait of Eight Countries* (Oxford: Basil Blackwell, 1980) table 2.3.

1978: *Union membership:* membership of wholly white-collar unions from returns made to Department of Employment Statistics Division. Membership of mixed unions from data supplied to the author by these unions.

Labour force: the only source of information on the development of the white-collar and manual groups over time is the Census of Population; consequently, the white-collar and manual figures for 1978 were estimated from 1971 Census data, together with data from the labour force projections developed by the Department of Employment. See, *The Changing Structure of the Labour Force* (London: Unit for Manpower Studies, Department of Employment, 1975).

union membership in Britain since the early years of this century. It also shows the marked lack of union success until the 1970s in raising white-collar union density substantially above the level achieved during the membership boom after the First World War. Although union membership among white-collar workers rose by half a million between 1961 and 1968, density over this period was static at around 30 per cent. The rapid growth of 1969–70 pushed up this figure to over 34 per cent, and this rising trend continued up to 1978 when membership stood at just over 5 million and density at 43 per cent. This decade of dramatic growth produced a major restructuring of the British trade union movement: two million white-collar members were added, but only one million manual members, so that by 1978 the proportion of trade union members in white-collar jobs had risen to 39 per cent from a figure of 30 per cent ten years earlier.

THEORIES OF UNION GROWTH

The dominant theoretical model seeking to explain the growth pattern of white-collar unionism is associated with the work of George Bain. His model was based on data up to 1964 and argues that

> the growth of aggregate white-collar unionism in Britain can be adequately explained by three strategic variables – employment concentration, union recognition and government action.[6]

The implications of this model for the future growth of white-collar unionism were that

> white-collar unions will continue to grow in the future as a result of increasing employment concentration, but their growth will not be very great unless their recognition by employers is extended. The model also suggests that the strength of these unions will not generally be sufficient in itself to persuade employers to concede recognition; this will also require the help of the government.[7]

It should be stressed that Bain's model is essentially associative or correlative in character. By examining the variations in white-collar union density across the economy at a particular point in time, he identified the institutional features which were found in association with relatively high levels of density. These, as we have seen, were employment concentration (or bureaucratic working conditions), employer recognition, and, at some point in the past, government action to support the achievement of that recognition.

The main weakness of this cross sectional type of approach to a model of union *growth* is that it cannot adequately investigate the conditions in which workers actually decide to join unions or the conditions in which employers come to recognize a union. Why, for example, is it the case that, in a *generally* favourable government climate for unionization and recognition, some groups of workers join unions and achieve recognition and some do not? Can it really be the case that the experience of working in bureaucratic and impersonal working conditions is the main reason for workers deciding to join unions prior to employer recognition, or are some other factors not contained in the model also important? A second, and partly related, weakness in the model is that it tells us very little about the process of growth and decline after recognition has been achieved. While recognized unions may generally enjoy a higher level of density than unrecognized unions, there are enormous variations in the patterns of growth and decline; and apart from variations occurring in the level of employment con-centration, there is nothing in the model to explain such variations.

Bain's later work tackles these problems and modifies the original model in some significant respects. In two articles with Price analysing the 1964–70 and 1970–4 periods respectively, a key role in determining the pace and direction of white-collar union growth is ascribed to economic factors – particularly the rate of change of wages and prices. In reviewing the initial upsurge of 1969–70, Bain and Price concluded that

> the membership explosion of 1969–70 was produced by the favourable conjunction of rapidly rising prices and wages with greater public support for union recognition and the extension of collective bargaining.[8]

Four years later, the weight placed upon non-economic factors to explain the continued growth up to 1974 was much reduced. The same authors concluded that 'economic factors have had a dominant influence on union growth between 1971 and 1974'.[9] The favourable effects of a positive government attitude towards union recognition and the extension of collective bargaining in the 1969–70 period were largely absent in the later period following the passage of the 1971 Industrial Relations Act and the consequential deterioration of union–employer relationships. And in a major analysis of long-term union growth patterns in four countries with Elsheikh, Bain elaborates a sophisticated econometric model which demonstrates among other things, that the rate of change of prices and the rate of change of wages have been highly significant determinants of the rate of change of union membership in the UK over the whole period 1892–1970.[10]

The original Bain model can be modified to allow for these economic factors in two ways. First, the evidence strongly suggests that prior to recognition it is economic pressures which provide the major impetus towards unionization within bureaucratized work environments. The existence of a work situation which fosters an awareness of collective interests and of the need to seek collective solutions can be identified as a *necessary* condition for initial unionization; without such conditions, it is likely that priority will be given to individual solutions rather than to the creation of a collective organization. But it is not a *sufficient* condition. For a drive towards unionization to occur within such an environment an important material issue needs to emerge – a decline in real incomes, threats of redundancy, or a reorganization involving demotions or loss of career opportunities. Secondly, following recognition it is clear that economic factors (primarily, unemployment and wage and price movements) exercise a major influence on the success or failure of unions in building up their levels of membership. To explain why membership of the Clerical and Administrative Workers' Union (CAWU) in engineering slumped after recognition by the Engineering Employers' Federation (EEF) in 1921, or why membership of the Association of Supervisory Staffs, Executives and Technicians (ASSET) in engineering failed to increase for almost two decades after recognition by the EEF in 1944, it would not be convincing to refer simply to changes in levels of employment concentration, or to employer policies at the level of the company. General economic factors were highly significant in both cases.

It would be wrong, however, to suggest that employees' reactions to economic pressures of the type mentioned earlier inevitably involve unionization. A wide range of factors can be identified which mediate the reactions of the workers so affected. Bain identifies employer policies and government action as the most significant mediating factors at the aggregate level, and to these could be added others such as the sex, race, age or regional composition of the labour force, which may be important at particular times or in particular countries. Bain classifies employer policies against white-collar unionization into the two categories of 'peaceful competition' and 'forcible opposition', and illustrates how they can, at least temporarily, head off union growth and demands for recognition.[11] Government policies are significant in influencing employee attitudes not only in terms of the legislative framework for union recognition and formal support for the establishment of collective bargaining institutions, but also through the less tangible processes of 'creating a climate of opinion' in which union membership and collective bargaining are viewed either positively or negatively by workers or employers alike. Government also plays an important role in determining the legality of various forms of employer opposition, such as victimization.

As was noted earlier, the decade 1969–78 saw a dramatic upsurge in white-collar union membership and density. Two million members were added, constituting an increase of two-thirds on the 1968 total; density increased by some thirteen percentage points to 43 per cent. By the end of the 1970s nearly 40 per cent of all trade unionists were in white-collar jobs. This rapid expansion in membership in a relatively short period illustrates the processes of union growth and, in particular, the importance of examining the interaction of economic and institutional factors. The period was characterized by historically high, although variable, levels of inflation, rising unemployment, and a series of state interventions into the collective bargaining arena in the shape of incomes policies and cash limits in the public sector. Thus, what Bain and Elsheikh call the 'threat' and 'credit' effects were both working strongly in favour of union growth, especially among white-collar workers.[12] Workers reacted to the erosion of real incomes by joining unions in ever greater numbers; and the apparent success of the unions in defending their members' economic interests reinforced this process. In addition, the two sub-periods of most rapid growth (1969–70 and 1975–8) were also characterized by government support for union recognition and the extension of collective bargaining, and this support further enhanced the upsurge of unionization.

A significant feature of this period in relation to the original Bain model of union growth is that well over one-half of the total increase in white-collar membership occurred in industries and sectors where recognition had been achieved for the unions concerned many years previously. Thus, while that earlier recognition undoubtedly provided the necessary basis of legitimation and bargaining presence for new organizing campaigns at this time, the actual impetus to increased density was derived from the economic and socio-political environment of the 1970s.

THE PROCESSES OF WHITE-COLLAR UNION GROWTH

The three short historical excerpts included in Chapter 9 illustrate the processes of white-collar unionization in the earliest period of union membership among non-manual workers, and underline the strengths and weaknesses of the Bain model.

David Lockwood's accounts of the early years of the Railway Clerk's Association (RCA) and the National and Local Government Officers' Association (NALGO) provide a stark contrast between two 'blackcoated' organisations founded within a few years of each other at the beginning of the century, but which developed in ways which placed them far apart in attitudes, policies and behaviour. The RCA registered as a trade union within two years of its foundation, affiliated to the Trades Union Congress (TUC) four years later, and to the Labour Party in 1909. By contrast, NALGO took fourteen years before becoming a certified union, affiliated to the TUC as recently as 1964, and has not so far affiliated to the Labour Party. The Railway Clerks were in no doubt from the outset as to their *raison d'être*; their activities were unambiguously directed towards issues of terms and conditions of employment, such as salaries, pensions, and sickness insurance. NALGO, on the other hand, operated in its early years largely as a 'social club and friendly society', and although its constitutional objectives included dealing with 'questions of superannuation, security of tenure and others of national importance', very little positive activity was recorded in these areas.

The relationships between these newly established organizations and their employers were also sharply differentiated. The RCA had to face victimization of its active supporters, and a blank refusal to grant any measure of recognition to the union for collective bargaining. The railway employers were notable for dealing with their 'servants' in a highly autocratic fashion, and for their military approach to the running of the railways. The manual worker unions in the industry had to face similar opposition to recognition for bargaining. In the face of the employers' unbending attitudes the Association used the techniques of, 'memorializing, publicity and deputation', and above all, of parliamentary campaigns against various Railway Bills, in order to press for their objectives. Since parliamentary policy on railways, which had been established during the nineteenth century against the dominant doctrine of *laissez faire*, required the approval of Parliament for most major projects which the companies wanted to undertake and for general fare increases, the ability of the unions to hold up Bills in the House of Commons was a highly effective sanction. For the RCA, therefore, TUC and Labour Party affiliation were of direct and immediate value in achieving material gains on freedom of association and on terms and conditions questions.

In contrast to this pattern of conflict and repression, NALGO's policies and behaviour were not considered to 'involve any opposition of interest between the local government officer and his employer'. Recognition was not even considered to be an issue until the attempt to establish a national Whitley Council after the First World War. And the possibility of taking sanctions against the employers was not seriously considered until well after the Second World War.

Despite the very different paths of development pursued by the two unions, they faced similar problems of defining their relationship with the broader labour movement, and of seeking successful strategies to survive, grow and achieve benefits for their membership. What accounts, therefore, for the enormous differences? Lockwood shows that the key mobilizing issues for the RCA were the economic ones of pay and conditions of employment. Salaries were low in relation to clerical earnings in other industries, opportunities for promotion were very limited, and although salary scales were generally in operation, clerks were often held at a particular scale-point for several years. 'Fringe benefits' and other conditions related to issues like overtime and weekend working were also generally poor. The RCA journal, *The Railway Clerk*, contains a steady stream of complaints about low pay, and available earnings data confirm that in the first decade of the century railway clerks were on average no better off than male manual workers. Despite strong employer opposition, the RCA survived and grew, recruiting primarily on the basis of its ability to achieve material economic benefits for the disgruntled railway clerks.

NALGO, by contrast, emerged from an environment in which employment conditions were relatively favourable. In terms of average salary levels, security of employment and opportunities for advancement, the lot of the local government clerk was considerably better than that of his opposite number on the railways or in a manufacturing industry. Not surprisingly, therefore, the establishment of NALGO did not reflect the eonomic pressures which characterized the early years of the RCA. It was set up by a group of relatively senior officers, and for many years the major posts in the organization at both local and national level were held by officers of relatively senior rank. The policies of the young organization, stressing professionalism and social benefits, reflected the community of interest which these senior officers saw between themselves and their employers: a harmonistic view of the employment relationship which was cemented by the ideology of public service.

Thus the foundation and growth of NALGO were based on a distinctive *group consciousness* nurtured by the structured and bureaucratic work environment of local government service, but this collective consciousness was not directed against the employers. The goals of the organization, such as enhanced professionalism and superannuation and friendly benefits were not seen as goals to be achieved in opposition to the employers. Rather, they were a reflection of and validation of the status of the public servant within the wider community. This form of non-conflictual group consciousness has been termed 'harmonistic collectivism'. NALGO's character in this early period reflects, as this phrase indicates, a definite awareness of common employee interests but coupled with a generalized absence of conflict with other groups in defending these interests. The fundamental difference between NALGO and the RCA is in this latter area and can be accounted for primarily by the different economic circumstances of the two memberships.

The early years of the Association of Engineering and Ship-building Draughtsmen (AESD), as described by Roberts and his colleagues, are marked by the acute tension which developed between the effective prosecution of the economic issues which brought about the foundation of the Association and its growth during the First World War, and the strong professional orientation of many of its leading members. While they were concerned to defend real incomes against employer policies and the inflationary pressures of the period, great stress was also laid on ensuring that such policies should not damage the 'professional' image and status of draughtsmen. This strong emphasis on the maintenance of 'professional' standards was not in contradiction with the defence of members' material interests. It was simply another strategy for achieving the same objective; high status would, it was assumed, lead to the social (and employer) recognition that such workers deserved high material rewards. A rather different attempt to use a 'professional' identity to achieve material rewards can be seen in the attempts of the AESD to set terms and conditons of employment unilaterally along the traditional craft and professional lines. Although they were largely unsuccessful in this, the defence of 'professional' entry standards remained part of the collective bargaining strategy of the Association for many years: such 'professionalism' could be used to legitimize high wage demands.

The evidence of the RCA and AESD clearly points to the vital significance of economic factors in white-collar union formation and growth. Both were established in response to perceived injustices and inequities in pay and conditions relative to the expectations of those they sought to organize. The contrast in the methods which the two organizations used to achieve their objectives gave them very different characters: the RCA adopting a strategy which linked it firmly to the parliamentary focus of the central bodies of the labour movement, while the AESD sought to use 'professionalism' and unilaterally established minimum rates as the basis for a relatively aggressive local bargaining strategy. But their fundamental goals were very similar.

The early history of these two bodies also highlights another of the controversial propositions in Bain's analysis of white-collar growth. In reaching the conclusion that 'most white-collar recognition in private industry has come about, directly or indirectly, as a result of government policies and the favourable climate they created for trade unionism',[13] he takes the view that the industrial strength of white-collar unions was 'generally a factor in getting . . . recognition, but it was rarely the most important factor'. This view that very little weight should be placed on the independent action of union organizations in achieving recognition while heavy stress is laid on state policies, has been opposed by Adams,[14] Fairbrother[15] and, almost parenthetically, by Jenkins and Sherman.[16]

It is evident that both the RCA and the AESD were involved in major industrial action for recognition immediately prior to achieving it, and in both cases this action clearly precipitated the recognition decision. However, as Bain has documented in detail for the AESD,[17] and Walkden for the RCA,[18] state support for Whitleyism was of fundamental importance in influencing both the EEF and the railway employers towards recognition, and in predisposing them to accept collective bargaining in the face of industrial action. Although this would generally seem to support Bain's conclusions, it should be remembered that the RCA grew, obtained concessions from employers, and developed a militant consciousness over a twenty-year period prior to recognition, *without* state support, and *against* massive employer opposition. Similarly, the AESD successfully built up its strength throughout the First World War against employer opposition and with only limited state support in the form of recognition by the Ministry of Munitions. It was actually refused recognition by the EEF in 1920 'until circumstances make this course necessary'. The experience of both unions suggests that, although Bain's conclusions are valid, they fail to give sufficient weight to the independent accumulation of membership strength and credibility prior to recognition. For the RCA and AESD to have been in a position to take decisive advantage of the favourable climate for union recognition at the end of the First World War, required them to build to a position where their pressure on the employers could 'tip the balance' in favour of recognition. Thus, although state intervention may be a necessary condition for recognition it is not in itself sufficient. The evidence suggests that formal recognition occurs after a complex and often lengthy process of interaction between independently sustained union action, and state and employer policies. It is therefore likely to be misleading to examine the factors leading to recognition simply within the context of the final recognition episode. It is equally important to take into account the pressures generated by union action over a number of years to make recognition into a live issue and to expose the employers to state influences.

NALGO's foundation and early growth illustrates this point further, and also illustrate a number of other factors influencing the growth of public service white-collar unions founded in the early years of the century. The growth of large-scale public bureaucracies produced groups of employees with a strong sense of collective common interest but a weak perception of employer–employee conflict. A further common feature was a strong individualistic career orientation. These produced the strand of 'harmonistic collectivism' which can be identified throughout the history of white-collar organization; the notions of public service and of professionalism militated against an oppositional form of collectivism, as did the generally favourable economic position which these public servants enjoyed. The main thrust of representational activity, therefore, was directed towards the maintenance of a respectable image which was held to be appropriate for this class of public servant. The maintenance of their professional status, a cut above the ordinary employee, was considered to be the best way of continuing to get the rewards which were associated with such status. Collective representation was necessary to ensure that due regard was given to the legitimate claims of the public servant, but there was no thought that collective organization would imply the use of collective sanctions.

In stark contrast to the RCA and AESD, NALGO's weakness and lack of credibility as an organization able to deploy meaningful sanctions, meant that despite state support for Whitley machinery for white-collar local government staff, the union was unable to keep the employers to the terms of the agreement signed in 1922. Nevertheless, despite the foundering of the Whitley machinery, NALGO was able over the next twenty years to increase its membership, achieve a number of significant material benefits for local government staffs by methods other than formal collective bargaining, and then finally to use the next period of state support for recognition, during and immediately after the Second World War, to achieve full negotiating rights. The case of NALGO further underlines the need, in interpreting Bain's theoretical model, to give due weight to the importance of independently generated and sustained growth prior to recognition. While recognition clearly is a key watershed for many unions in their growth pattern, a model of growth which overlooks *how* unions get to the starting-gate of recognition is only providing half the picture.

As Table 8.2 shows, despite the upsurge of the last decade or so, a majority of white-collar workers are still not in unions. There is thus scope for further substantial growth in membership amongst this group. How far the unionization process goes, however, will depend on a complex interaction of the various factors identified above. It will depend, first, on the extent to which bureaucratized working conditions become established amongst groups of white-collar employees, who are currently either working in small firms or are in a position to bargain individually on a major part of their employment contract. It will depend, secondly, on economic factors which accentuate the need for the collective defence of real incomes and job security. Thirdly, it will depend on the degree to which employer policies are sympathetic or hostile to the development of unionization amongst predominantly non-union groups, such as managers and professional employees. Policies of opposition by paying salaries above the market rate and adopting a variety of manipulative techniques as employed, for example, by IBM, Hewlett-Packard and Mars, will hinder unionization. Fourthly, in this process, government influences on employer policies by pressure through agencies such as the Advisory, Conciliation and Arbitration Service (ACAS) and the Department of Employment will be significant. Government pressure via the legislative framework on recognition and the extension of collective bargaining is equally important in that it sets the parameters within which employers are required to operate.

It is impossible to make confident predictions on how these factors will interact and what the consequences will be for white-collar growth. Much inevitably depends on the relative weights attached to each element of the analysis, but at a general level it seems certain that private sector employer resistance to union membership amongst managerial and professional staffs will be sufficiently strong to require powerful opposing pressures for there to be any major breakthrough amongst these large occupational groups.[19]

Introduction

The concept of union 'character' is clearly not confined in its application solely to white-collar unions. As a shorthand phrase for conveying some of the differences between unions in goals, policies and activities, it can be equally well applied to comparisons between craft and general unions, public and private sector unions, or British and French unions. However, as Bain, Coates and Ellis point out, although many writers have mentioned union character in relation to these types of comparison, it is really *only* in the analysis of white-collar union organization that it has been rigorously developed and applied. The extracts that have been selected for Chapter 10 provide a comprehensive summary of the main strands in the debate on white-collar union character, but in this introduction some assessment should be made of *why* so much attention has been directed at the concept of character in relation to white-collar organizations, and whether it has proved itself to be a useful tool of analysis.

The readings by Strauss and Allen reflect the dominant perspective on white-collar unionism during the 1950s and the early 1960s in Britain and the US. Although they were writing from widely divergent political perspectives and their views were expressed in very different terms, the amount of common ground is substantial. By and large, they both had little difficulty in treating the white-collar category as a unitary mass. Such internal differences as are mentioned are not considered to be very significant by comparison with the elements in white-collar occupations which bind the whole group together. Both writers consider white-collar unionization to be essentially a defensive reaction to declining prestige and status; in Strauss's words, 'White-collar workers join unions, not because they reject their middle-class aspirations, but because they see unionism as a *better way* of obtaining them.' Unionization is viewed in this light as a means of keeping ahead of manual workers rather than an expression of unity with them in fighting for a common cause. Not surprisingly, therefore, both Strauss and Allen consider that white-collar organizations will inevitably want to maintain a separate and distinct identity from manual unions. As far as policies and bargaining techniques are concerned, both writers perceive major differences between white-collar and manual organizations as to their willingness to use industrial sanctions and, in the British case, their willingness to affiliate to a political party. Indeed, Allen suggests that white-collar workers show a 'hostility towards the aspirations of organized labour . . . which presents a barrier to assimilation within the labour movement which might persist long after white-collar workers have realized the need for collective action'.

Thus, the writers included in this reader together with many others who wrote in similar terms, were confident that while unionization might continue to spread amongst white-collar workers, the 'character' of this new union membership would be different from 'traditional' unionism in certain important aspects. The nature and significance of the differences were, however, left imprecise as were the implications of union character for union growth. Blackburn and Prandy's attempt to develop a conceptual framework for union character, which is the third extract included here, seeks to remedy these deficiencies by providing a 'consistent theoretical basis' for the assessment of the *degree* of similarity and differentiation between white-collar and manual unions. They present the concept of 'unionateness' as 'a measure of the commitment of a body to the general principles and ideology of trade unionism'. Seven elements are identified as making up these 'principles and ideology' against which unions are to be tested, and these can be sub-divided into two discrete groups. Four refer to union relations with the wider society and comprise what the authors, in a later paper, have called 'society unionateness'.[20] The remaining three relate to union behaviour within the employment sphere and are described as measuring 'enterprise unionateness'. The degree of unionateness measures the character of the union and is also considered by these authors to provide an 'index of class consciousness' and a 'measure of potential for class action'. This closely follows Lockwood's earlier formulation of the character of white-collar unionism, in which he argued that the *degree* to which clerical workers become involved in trade unionism and come to terms with its 'wider class character' constitutes a measure of their general class consciousness.[21]

Blackburn and Prandy's attempt to formulate systematically a set of objective dimensions of union character is an important contribution since it focuses sharply on two fundamental questions. Do the criteria which they identify constitute an adequate and unambiguous measure of a union's character? Are these really the dimensions along which unions can be differentiated one from another? If not, what alternative or additional criteria are proposed to provide such a measure of character? And secondly, can this particular measure of union character which they propose really be taken as an index of class consciousness? Whatever may be the limitations of the models advanced by Lockwood and by Blackburn and Prandy, it is clear that any adequate formulation of the concept of union character must say something about the wider political and social significance of white-collar unionism. For it is the *nature* of its significance which has been at the heart of the debate about union character since the earliest years of clerical unionism.

The sweeping critique of Blackburn and Prandy's approach made by Bain and his colleagues in the fourth extract in Chapter 10 identifies the principal weaknesses in the earlier analysis. Three points should be highlighted here. First, as a measure of character, it is clear that each of the seven criteria is to some extent ambiguous. A union can score either positively or negatively on each dimension for a variety of reasons, and as a consequence, the implication of its 'score' is indeterminate. The clearest example of this difficulty is the question of TUC affiliation, which in Blackburn's view is 'the most direct way of expressing shared interests and identity with other unions',[22] and which has been a highly controversial issue in many white-collar unions precisely because of its perceived significance as a symbol of commitment to the wider labour movement. Some white-collar unions have affiliated explicitly on these grounds: the Railway Clerks' Association, for example, was in no doubt as to its desire to align itself with the ranks of organized manual labour in its struggle for decent wages, recognition and better working conditions. However, all the recent affiliations by large white-collar unions such as NALGO, the Civil and Public Servants, and the four main organizations of teachers in schools and higher education, have been justified primarily by reference to the role of the TUC in influencing government policies (particularly incomes policies) and in regulating inter-union disputes.[23] While many of the members and delegates of these unions, who were involved in taking the decision to affiliate, may have been influenced by broader considerations of the type identified above, it is clear that the tactical and instrumental arguments were crucial in every case. Thus, to consider TUC affiliation as *necessarily* implying a commitment to 'the general principles and ideology of trade unionism', would certainly be incorrect. This ambiguity of motive and purpose is present to some degree in each of the other six criteria, and makes their interpretation a complex and subtle enterprise.

Secondly, there is the problem of how each of these variables, particularly the continuous ones (such as 'preparedness to be militant'), could be measured and weighted relative to each other, except by 'the researcher exercising his purely subjective judgement'. The later attempt by Blackburn *et al.* to resolve this difficulty is unconvincing; as Carter puts it, 'the purpose of the work seems to be not to show how sociological understanding can be aided by statistics, but how sociology can provide an area in which statistics can be used. The method totally overwhelms the subject.'[24] Whatever statistical sophistication is used, there would seem to be insuperable difficulties in seeking to create a *composite* measure of unionateness from the Blackburn and Prandy criteria which would allow reliable inter-union comparisons to be made.

Thirdly, the implied link between unionateness (as measured by these criteria) and class consciousness can be seen to rest on two faulty premises. The first is the assumption that the manual union 'ideal-type' advanced by Blackburn and Prandy to measure white-collar unionateness is itself a measure of a class-conscious form of worker organization. The evidence marshalled by Bain *et al.* illustrates the extent to which manual worker unionization has in fact been characterized by sectionalism, instrumentalism and accommodation to the capitalist control of industrial and state power. High 'unionateness' scores are therefore fully compatible with a wide range of class attitudes. A second, and related assumption is that a shift along one of the dimensions of unionateness can only occur because of a shift in the class consciousness of the union's membership. But as Bain and his colleagues clearly demonstrate, such shifts can also occur for a range of reasons related to the 'narrowly conceived organizational requirements of the union and the sectional needs of the members'.

Two further points can be made to underline the weakness of the definition of 'unionateness' advanced by Blackburn and Prandy. By proposing a set of 'timeless' criteria, they are making the implicit assumption that the social meaning of, for example, registering as a trade union, affiliating to the TUC, or engaging in some form of industrial action, has remained constant over time. If, as is more plausible, the meaning attached to these actions has varied considerably between different time periods, their implications for both union character and class consciousness must also be variable. More specifically, it can be argued that the institutionalization of trade unionism and its incorporation into the power structures at both company and national levels in the past few decades has significantly reduced the flavour of class opposition to employers and the state, which many white-collar workers clearly attributed to the decision to join a union at the beginning of the century. Similarly, there can be little doubt that the significance attached to TUC affiliation has altered radically as the proportion of TUC membership in white-collar unions has increased. Each successive affiliate has been able to point to the wide range of similar organizations in membership as evidence of the broad, representative character of the TUC, as opposed to the image of it constituting a sectional exponent of the class war.

The second point is closely related. Two of the main criteria advanced by Blackburn and Prandy – TUC and Labour Party affiliation – carry with them the assumption that such affiliations imply a commitment to a broadly similar body of principles and beliefs. In practice, of course, the base of common commitments is a very narrow one and the character of the policies pursued within both organizations by individual unions is extremely variable. If the concept of 'character' as applied to unions is to be at all meaningful, and particularly if it is intended to indicate something about the socio-political perspective of a union and its membership, it is necessary to take into account not simply the fact of affiliation or non-affiliation, but also the nature of the policies pursued. Without this admittedly more complex definitional approach, it would seem that *all* unions affiliated to the TUC and Labour Party must be taken to be of similar character. In the light of the wide differences which exist within the TUC between, for example, the Hospital Consultants and Specialists Association and the Association of First Division Civil Servants on the one hand, and ASTMS and AUEW–TASS (formerly the Draughtsmen and Allied Technicians Association) on the other, such a crude measure of character will be of limited value in an assessment of the socio-political significance of white-collar unionism.

In the final extract in Chapter 10, Rosemary Crompton challenges the concept of unionateness from a very different perspective. As has been noted earlier, the implication of using the concept in the form proposed by Blackburn and Prandy is to measure white-collar organizations against a manual union stereotype; white-collar unions are characterized as being either more or less like manual unions. Crompton's concern with this approach is that it 'makes it difficult to conceptualize different modes of representation as *alternative* strategies. In short, the concept may actually impose limitations on the successful analysis of white-collar unionism if it is used in isolation.'[25] Thus, while the discussion so far in this chapter has focused on the weaknesses of 'unionateness' as a measure of union character, Crompton is more concerned with its inadequacy in explaining *why* white-collar collective representation assumes a range of different forms.

Her critique is based on an explicitly neo-Marxist analysis of the class situation of the white-collar labour force, in contrast to the Weberian approach which characterized the work of Lockwood, Blackburn and Prandy, and Bain and his colleagues. She locates the white-collar labour force in a position of structural ambiguity between the functions of capital and the functions of labour. This intermediate position gives rise to considerable variations in the class situations of different white-collar groups, reflecting the variation in relationships between particular white-collar occupational groups and the capitalist mode of production. These variations in turn give rise to a range of attitudes and patterns of behaviour, particularly in respect of collective representation, which reflect the ambiguity of their class situation.

Crompton illustrates this point by reference to the contrasting experience of unionization amongst technical employees and clerical workers in banking and insurance. It is argued that the class situation of both groups has become less ambiguous as capitalist economies have developed, but while this has generally increased their propensity to organize collectively, the strategies of representation have been very different. Technicians have tended to choose to join the TUC-affiliated unions while bank and insurance workers have continued to join both TUC unions and company-based staff associations. The continued ambiguity of their class position is reflected in contradictory and ambivalent choices concerning collective representation.

There is no substantial area of disagreement between Crompton and those whom she is seeking to criticize – Bain, Lockwood, Blackburn and Prandy – concerning the principal causes of union growth among white-collar workers: bureau-cratization, employer policies and economic pressures are all mentioned. The key difference lies in Crompton's attempt to link these external phenomena to the processes of social and economic change within capitalist societies. She probes behind the categories of work and market relationships which dominate the theoretical analysis of Lockwood and others to identify the structural determinants of the changes affecting those relationships. 'Proletarianization', she writes, 'can only be explained by reference to the development of the capitalist mode of production.'

Although this analysis is interesting and suggestive, it fails to explore in a convincing way the precise nature of the links between the evolution of the class structure and the behaviour of white-collar workers and their unions. Take, for example, the link which is argued to exist between the increased subjection of the white-collar labour force to bureaucratic organization and control, and the character of white-collar collective organization. Both technicians and clerical workers in the financial sector are cited as cases in which such changes have taken place over recent years. But no attempt is made to explain why it should be that technicians have responded to the change in their class situation by joining unions, while in response to similar changes bank and insurance clerks have joined internal staff associations in large numbers. If, as Crompton suggests, 'an understanding of the white-collar class situation is *essential* to any interpretation of white-collar union behaviour',[26] it could be expected that these differences in response would be linked to aspects of the class situation of the two groups. Surprisingly, however, no such link is suggested. Rather, it is argued that 'the heterogeneous and often ambiguous nature of the white-collar class situation is reflected in heterogeneous and often contradictory forms of collective representation'.[27] This leaves the nature of the link between class situation and union character in a highly fluid and unspecific state. Indeed, it appears to imply that it is impossible to go any further than the vague prediction that white-collar organizations will continue to display a variety of different strategies and patterns of behaviour.

Even in this minimal form the argument is unconvincing. The only element of 'heterogeneity' in collective representation that is identified is the distinction between TUC unions and internal staff asssociations. If this is suggested as a measure of the ambiguity in the class situation of British white-collar workers it is hardly a serious problem. In 1978, less than 5 per cent of white-collar unionists were members of staff associations, and the overwhelming majority of such bodies were to be found in the financial sector. They represent therefore a rather idiosyncratic exception to the general rule as far as white-collar collective representation is concerned. And if heterogeneity of organizational type is held to reflect ambiguity of class situation, the conclusion must be that British white-collar workers are in little doubt as to where they stand in the class structure!

WHITE-COLLAR WORKERS AND ATTITUDES TO TRADE UNIONS

The question of union character lies at the heart of any theory of the labour movement. The attention which has been given to the character of white-collar unionism is, therefore, an inevitable reflection of the growing significance (both numerical and in terms of their influence on policy) of white-collar organizations. So far, however, apart from the brave but deeply flawed attempt by Blackburn and Prandy, neither 'industrial relations' nor 'sociological' analysis has sought to come to grips with the complexities of the issues involved. As Bain, Coates and Ellis put it in the conclusion to their book:

> There is a need for a wider and more meaningful specification of union character. Precisely because so much of the literature ... has operated with too simple a notion of character it has focused on peripheral aspects of unionism which do not locate the significant points of difference within unions or between them.[28]

Paradoxically, some interesting and important contributions to the discussion of white-collar union character have been made in the context of much more limited analyses focusing on the attitudes of white-collar workers to trade unionism, and we turn to these in the final chapter of the reader. While none of the contributions in this last section seeks to provide the kind of overarching comparative analysis which is the concern of the writers in the preceding chapter, most of them suggest ways in which the 'wider and more meaningful specification' of union character proposed by Bain and his colleagues might be reached.

As used by Crompton to explain the diversity of organizational forms taken by white-collar collectivism, the notion of class ambiguity is of only limited value. However, it can be more fruitfully applied in exploring the wider concept of union character as discussed here. Crompton's view is, in essence, a sophisticated development of the earlier arguments of Strauss, Allen and others: that white-collar unions are indeed 'different' from manual unions. In her case this view is firmly grounded in a theory of the development of advanced capitalism, from which it is concluded that such differences are likely to continue and to influence the character of white-collar collective representation. But the *nature* and *extent* of these differences are not examined; it is here that the notion of class ambiguity may be useful.

As has already been noted, the range of economic rewards, authority positions, and status/prestige positions within the white-collar labour force is so wide that it is impossible to discuss it in an undifferentiated way. One crude division would be between those who at the 1971 Census were classified in the 'clerical' and 'sales' categories, and who might therefore be regarded as clearly exercising 'the functions of labour' – the white-collar proletariat; and, on the other hand, the groups classified as 'managers', 'professionals', 'technicians' and 'foremen', which covered those jobs which might generally be said to combine employee status with a greater or lesser degree of authority over other employees.[29] The dual functions of these workers, the intrinsic ambiguity of their position in the division of labour, will of necessity affect the character of their collective organizations. But its effect cannot be summarized in a checklist of simple external attributes such as those advanced by Blackburn and Prandy; rather, it has to be identified by the subtle assessment of the type of involvement in job regulation which characterizes these organizations. The type of issues which are given priority; the style and methods by which they are pursued; the nature of their involvement in political life; the relationships of assent and control which exist between leadership and rank and file: all are important aspects of union character, and all will be intimately affected by the nature of the jobs occupied by white-collar workers in this second category. This is not to say that all the elements of the characters of white-collar unions will be peculiar to these bodies; there will inevitably be important areas of similarity with manual unions. But it is to say that the only fully satisfactory way

171

of approaching the analysis of *white-collar* character is by starting from the ambiguities and cross-cutting pressures inherent in white-collar jobs.

The ambiguity of white-collar workers' attitudes to, and involvement in, trade unions is a consistent theme running through the four extracts contained in Chapter 11. This ambiguity of attitude and action is well summarized by Roberts and his colleagues when they write that white-collar workers

> are willing to support either individualistic or collective action, or a combination of both, depending upon the strategy that best fits their situations . . . . White-collar workers can join trade unions thereby endorsing the principle of collective action without their attitudes otherwise becoming any less middle class.[30]

Two essential points are being made here: first the very wide variations that occur *within* the white-collar category in terms of work, market and class situation make it imperative to consider the attitudes and strategies of each group in the context of its particular circumstances; and secondly, no easy equation can be made between union membership and the adoption of a general collectivist philosophy – it will be important to assess the issues on which a collective strategy is held to be appropriate, and those on which individual strategies are seen as valid. The variations in the 'blends' of collective and individual strategies will, of course, have a significant bearing on the question of union character.

Reynaud's thoughtful survey draws heavily on the work of Marc Maurice on the unionization of technicians and *cadres* in France, which links together the motives for union membership and the style and content of the policies pursued by their unions. Noting the rapid growth of union activity among technicians and scientific research workers, he stresses that this cannot simply be ascribed to the material issues of pay, working conditions and career prospects; the growing *self-awareness* of these groups has also to be taken into account. The group becomes aware of itself as a distinct collectivity and seeks to establish this sense of collective identity in a generally recognized 'normative system' which guarantees and underpins their employment status.[31] The rapid pace of economic development in post-war France and the growth of large multinational companies has led to the emergence of this group in bureaucratized working conditions and with relatively limited career prospects. As the earlier discussion of union growth would suggest, this provided fertile ground for the emergence of a 'collective consciousness'; but this consciousness has been of a 'craft' type which is expressed in the demand for national recognition and status, and does not conflict with individualist aspirations for career progression. In short, the collective union-based strategy is seen as a *basis* for specific individual strategies: it does not replace them.

A similar development can be identified in the case of the *cadres* (junior and middle management, above the foreman level), who unionized very rapidly in France during the 1960s and 1970s, both in the conservative, specifically *cadre* organization CGC (Confédération Générale des Cadres), and in the three general labour confederations. As in the case of technicians, the bureaucratization of employment conditions which accompanied the numerical growth of this category of staff, and the relative decline in the security of their employment prospects, are important elements in the explanation for this growth in union membership. But an additional, and very potent focus of mobilization was the growing awareness that these workers were gradually being distanced from the seat of top managerial decision-making. The aspirations of this group to involvement in top management based on their technical and professional proficiency were being frustrated, leading to a strongly expressed desire for greater 'involvement' and 'participation'. While such aspirations and commitments by their very nature involved a degree of collective and group expression, they were far from being the revolutionary demands suggested by some writers.[32] Rather, they were a protest against the 'undermining and redefinition of the status of the group', and an expression of a desire to be re-incorporated into the managerial elite. *Cadre* unionization in France reinforces Reynaud's general argument that collective organization and individualistic aspirations are fully compatible bedfellows, and that in many white-collar cases, the cause of trade union-based collectivism is

> not only (and in some cases not primarily) the net balance of economic life-chances . . . it is also (and sometimes predominantly) the undermining of an existing normative system and the feeling that it is essential to replace it with another.[33]

Reynaud also underlines the danger of seeking to infer the dominant socio-political attitudes of union members from the stated objectives and overt bargaining behaviour of their unions. He points out that the claims of the Communist and conservative *cadre* organizations are virtually identical. It is the context in which those claims are placed, and the argumentation advanced in their support which differ. Thus, a wide range of political attitudes among members is clearly compatible with similar economic objectives; equally, the adoption of collectivist methods for achieving material gains is compatible with a wide range of political and social attitudes which may be strongly antipathetic to collectivism as a general political philosophy.

The survey data on white-collar attitudes to the trade unionism presented by Mercer and Weir, and by Roberts and his colleagues, provide further evidence that the 'partial collectivism' involved in the acceptance of union membership is fully compatible with the values of individualism. Both surveys suggest that white-collar workers across a broad range of occupations and industries can be characterized as displaying, in the words used by Mercer and Weir, 'a limited instrumentalism'. This implies 'a "conditional assent" not to the values . . . but to the possible efficacy of trade unions in obtaining tangible benefits for their members'.[34]

Few white-collar workers in these surveys could be said to display a strong *ideological* commitment to trade unionism, if this is understood to imply an expression of support for collective worker organization as a form of opposition to employers and to predominantly capitalist control of the means of production. While the evidence of both surveys shows that the improvement of terms and conditions of employment was considered to be the principal focus of union activity, Roberts *et al.*'s data nevertheless suggests that this *sectional* concern was located within a *general* concern that unions should act to promote 'social justice'.

Quite what the respondents understood by 'general social justice' is not clear. Nor, at one level, does it really matter. What is clear is that white-collar unionists display an ambivalent and shifting blend of attitudes, combining pure individualism, sectional collectivism and societal collectivism, but with remarkably little explicit ideological content. None of these findings are surprising in the light of the earlier discussion of the factors which promote union growth. If it is true that white-collar workers generally join unions in response to specific economic pressures arising within an employment situation and socio-political environment which make unionization appear to be both a possible and appropriate response, there is little reason to assume that attitudes to union membership will evince a strong general commitment to collectivism. Rather, they can be expected to display an essentially pragmatic and shifting blend of assent to collective organization, in circumstances in which it is judged to be necessary, and an individualistic striving for advancement on the strength of personal qualities. To use Reynaud's terms, there is no incompatibility between a militant commitment by, for example, local government officers, teachers, civil servants or nurses, to ensure that the 'normative framework' within which their pay and grading structure are determined, reflects a 'fair' assessment of their social worth, and a strong individualistic commitment to scramble as far as possible up the hierarchy of grades which are presented as a potential career path.

But it would be a mistake to regard this 'pragmatic' blend of individualism and collectivism as a distinctive feature of white-collar workers alone. Both the extracts included in this reader and referred to above stress the *similarity* rather than the differences between white-collar and manual workers' attitudes to trade unions. This is particularly clear-cut in the work of Roberts *et al.*, where the instrumental and individualistic attitudes displayed by the sample of manual workers were virtually identical to those of the white-collar sample, leading the authors to the view that, on the evidence presented, 'both blue and white-collar workers are willing to support either individualistic or collectivist action, or a combination of both, *depending on the strategy that best fits their situations.*'[35] In both groups, the level of ideological commitment to a thoroughgoing collectivist philosophy to trade unionism as a social movement seeking to modify the existing social order was very small.

This conclusion is, of course, consistent with the findings of a range of attitude surveys, from Goldthorpe and Lockwood's Luton studies onwards, which have built up a picture of the modern trade union member, white-collar or manual, as relatively little interested in unions as ideological or political institutions, primarily concerned with unions as defenders of workers' material interests, and prepared to be militant where appropriate to achieve strongly desired objectives.[36] This picture is as much a criticism of, and reaction to, the romantic stereotype of the manual trade unionist as a committed proletarian collectivist, as it is of the image of white-collar unionists as being somehow 'different' because of their espousal of individualistic and instrumental attitudes. But as a stereotype itself, it presents too generalized a picture to be very useful as a guide to white-collar union attitudes and behaviour.

For if there is, in principle, little difference between white-collar and manual workers in their attitudes to union objectives and behaviour, it is legitimate to ask why it should be that white-collar workers are still significantly less unionized and less militant than manual workers – measured by the admittedly inadequate method of relative recorded strike proneness. This question has already been partially discussed in the earlier section on white-collar union growth, but it can be linked at this stage to the important condition attached to the conclusion reached by Roberts *et al.*, and italicized in the quotation above. While both manual and white-collar groups are prepared to contemplate both individual and collective strategies, the extent to which each will *in practice* be adopted depends crucially on the appropriateness of those strategies to the circumstances of the case.

There are, of course, wide variations in the availability and effectiveness of individual and collective strategies within both white-collar and manual groups; the condition attached by Roberts *et al.* is thus of central significance in assessing the structure of worker attitudes to trade union activity. But, drawing a broad comparison between white-collar and manual groups, it is clear that the degree to which *individual* advance is possible is still greater for the average white-collar worker than for the average manual worker. The expectation of promotion through a grading structure is a relatively common feature of white-collar environments but applies much less often to manual workers. This unequal distribution of opportunities for individual advance reduces the propensity of white-collar workers to opt for collectivist and solidaristic strategies; solidarity is a less 'natural' expression of white-collar workers' experience within the division of labour.

Carter, in the final contribution to the readings, makes a similar and closely related point in his description of many white-collar workers as performing 'high trust jobs' – jobs which provide their holders with a degree of individual discretion, control and initiative. This type of high-trust relationship with the employer on the actual performance of the job has the effect of substantially restricting the perceived need for collective representation on 'job control' issues, and increasing the emphasis on pay issues as the principal locus of collective action. 'Middle class labour performs high trust jobs and its trade unionism as a consequence has less concern with issues of control of working methods because these are less often under attack.'[37] Nevertheless, it is legitimate to query just how far the white-collar category really can be said to be characterized by high-trust and promotion-oriented jobs, particularly in the light of the fact that at the 1971 Census, virtually one-half of the white-collar category were found to be in clerical, secretarial or sales jobs.

Two further aspects of the situation of these particular groups have contributed to a relative preference for individualized responses to employment problems. First, the very high incidence of small firms and particularistic working relationships; and secondly, the high and rising proportion of female labour in these categories. Although the pattern has been changing in the 1970s, there has been a strong historical tendency for women's work to be viewed as involving a relatively short-term and marginal attachment to the labour force, thus discouraging the adoption of collective responses to pay and conditions issues.[38]

Thus, while an ideological commitment to unionism would seem to be a rare commodity among white and blue-collar workers alike, and there would seem to be little difference in principle between the two groups in their willingness to adopt collective *and* individual strategies, it remains true that the employment conditions and day-to-day workplace relationships experienced by white-collar workers are likely in practice to predispose them to a *less* collectivistic strategy than that adopted by manual workers. Put another way, it will in general be true that white-collar workers will define a narrower range of issues as appropriate for collective action, and more issues as capable of individual solution, than would be the case among manual workers, because of the nature of the particular bundle of rights, benefits and expectations attaching to their roles in the labour process. To this structurally conditioned *preference* for individual strategies should be added the structural limitations placed on the *availability* and *effectiveness* of collective strategies for many white-collar workers in many situations. The ability to impose effective economic sanctions on the employer is less often available to white-collar groups than to manual groups because of their position in the production process and the external labour market.

Clearly, we are dealing here with tendencies rather than absolutes. It would be absurd to suggest that there is a clear-cut distinction between white-collar workers, for whom the realities of the workplace stress individualism and fragmentation, and hence a restricted role for trade unions; and manual workers, for whom unionism is a natural expression of workplace solidarity and of conflict with supervision and management. The example of draughtsmen is just one clear case of a white-collar occupational group whose work situation has generally supported and re-inforced group solidarity, and for whom the union has often been as much an expression of a desire for job control as for decent wages. And there are many examples of manual worker groups for whom unionism is remote and weakly connected with the work-place: agricultural workers, many local authority employees, and workers in hotels, catering and distribution. But, in the final analysis, the relationship between workers' attitudes to trade unions and the work situation must be of major significance in exploring the similarities and differences between white and blue-collar workers.

Carter's analysis of the policies and behaviour of ASTMS illustrates the relationship between the work situation of the supervisory and foreman membership of that union, and their conception of the role and functions of trade unionism. Their occupational function of *controlling* the process of production raises a barrier of authority between them and the shop-floor workers whom they are required to manage; and this makes it very difficult in practice to achieve a degree of solidarity and mutual identi-fication between the two groups. The proximity of these workers to management, and their perception of 'higher management as a reserve bank of authority'[39] act to narrow the area of perceived conflict with the employer; pay and job security are generally seen as the most significant issues. This delimitation of the area in which collective organization is seen as appropriate and legiti-mate, supports a view of the union as a service, providing pro-fessional expertise in negotiations, but not involving a major collective commitment by the employees concerned. Above all, Carter stresses the very narrow basis of the 'collectivism' of these white-collar unionists: narrow, in that it is concerned with their own occupational category, and has little interest in the extension of areas of solidarity; and narrow, in its focus on a relatively small number of issues.

Carter's analysis is, however, much less convincing in its attempt to demonstrate a degree of congruence between the narrow view of the union's role taken by these members, and the progressive, even radical, policy positions adopted by the union nationally. He argues that the parliamentary presence of the union, and its stress on legal rights for union recognition and support for collective bargaining activities, are fully in line with the members' desire to avoid the necessity for industrial action in support of their material objectives. While there is some truth in this argument, it can hardly be said that it is this set of policies which have given ASTMS a generally radical image. In fact, the commitment of ASTMS to recognition legislation in particular placed it among some odd bedfellows in the early period of TUC opposition to the 1971 Industrial Relations Act, when the union temporized for a while before deregistering as required by TUC policy. The policies on which ASTMS has taken a genuinely left-wing line are on issues like incomes policies, nationalization, the EEC, private health care, abortion, and the internal organization of the Labour Party. Apart from the union's well-known and strident opposition to incomes policies, which is clearly consistent with the narrow material concerns of ASTMS members as identified by Carter, none of these issues can be said to fit the image of policies which, while more radical than the attitudes of members, help to avoid the need for industrial action. Nor does Carter's analysis explain how such policies come to be adopted and maintained over long periods.

In fact, the relationship between members' attitudes and union policies is an aspect of the democratic systems within British unions which has been generally neglected. Moran's work on the Union of Post Office Workers[40] is one of the very few to seek explicitly to account for the lack of congruence between the views expressed by rank and file members and the policies pursued at national level (over a long period) by the union's Conference and Executive. He concluded that the UPW members in his study were prepared to tolerate the national policies of the union because these did not, by and large, make any demands on the individual members. They did not require them to become involved, nor did they implicate them in any specific form of activity. The conclusions reached by Roberts *et al.* in their study of technicians are remarkably similar.

> The history of technicians' unions suggests that this category of workers is strongly status-conscious, but status is seen in primarily labour market terms. Professional associations that are concerned mainly with non-pecuniary aspects of status do not fully satisfy the strong desires of technicians for higher relative levels of remuneration. On the other hand, appeals to class concepts of trade unionism make little impact. Although the leadership of these unions has tended to be committed ideologically to left-wing Socialism and even Communism, the collective bargaining policy actually adopted has reflected the practical requirements of the membership. The ideological wish of the leadership to attack the capitalist system, and the interest of members in securing immediate tangible monetary gains have come together in a mutually satisfying aggressive policy to secure higher pay and improved conditions of employment.[41]

While this undoubtedly overstates the degree of the dichotomy between leaders and members, their evidence does suggest that many members of DATA and ASTMS were indifferent to the national policy stance of their union on 'political' issues, since the nature of that stance had relatively little impact on the individual member.

The ambiguity involved in tolerating national policies which have little appeal to, or hold over, the individual member, while remaining a loyal supporter of the union in its collective bargaining role, can be seen as a further consequence of the attitude identified by Carter of regarding trade unions 'as external agencies that involve little action on the part of the individual'.[42] Insofar as members regard national policy-making as 'external' to their area of involvement in the union, they may be prepared to allow active members and full-time officers to struggle over the precise nature of the union's orientation with little concern for the outcome. However, when national policies *do* impinge on the workplace role of the union in collective bargaining – as, for example, in opposing or supporting incomes policies – the degree of autonomy from membership opinion which national policy-making bodies can expect to enjoy is likely to be severely circumscribed. Thus, while Carter's argument is couched solely in terms of the foreman membership of a single union, the underlying theme is of much wider relevance. It implies a degree of relative autonomy between membership attitudes in general, and the specific policy stances adopted by white-collar unions *on issues regarded by the mass of the membership as 'external' to their principal interests and which do not imply any consequential membership activity.* There is nothing very surprising, therefore, in the frequent observation of an apparent lack of congruence between the policies of white-collar unions and the attitudes of their members. On the other hand, it also implies that where specifically industrial policies are concerned, leaders' and members' attitudes must remain closely in step if these policies are to be successful.

CONCLUSIONS

The growth and character of white-collar union organization remains under-researched and under-analysed by comparison with 'traditional' manual unionism. Neither academic nor popular stereotypes have yet adjusted to an era in which workers conventionally categorized as white-collar are coming to represent a majority of the organized labour force. The challenge to sociological, industrial relations and political science analysis is clear: the character of white-collar organizations, and the factors shaping and moulding their activities are major elements in the social and political structure of advanced capitalism, and are set to become even more significant as we move towards the turn of the century.

As the later contributions to this reader demonstrate, the critical question is no longer whether white-collar unions are 'different'. The simplistic notion of white-collar bodies changing gradually towards a clear and unchanging model of a 'proper' union has been replaced in modern analysis by the question of *how* and *why* they differ, and the exploration of the structural and contextual factors which determine their behaviour. One crucial aspect of this analysis, but which has been largely ignored so far, is the split between the public and private sectors in the content and significance of union behaviour. More than two in three British white-collar union members are employed in the public sector, and the proportion is even higher in the US, France and West Germany. The public–private split, together with the other factors mentioned earlier – position in the division of labour, the nature of the labour process, the market for labour and for the product, employer policies and government intervention – are the key elements in developing new approaches to the study of contemporary white-collar union organization.

NOTES AND REFERENCES

1. W. E. J. McCarthy, *The Future of the Unions* (Fabian Society Tract 339, 1962) p. 4.
2. C. Jenkins and B. Sherman, *White-Collar Unionism: The Rebellious Salariat* (Routledge and Kegan Paul, 1979) p. 55.
3. Ibid., pp. 1–9.
4. *The Changing Structure of the Labour Force* (Unit for Manpower Studies, Department of Employment, 1975) mimeo.
5. Total employment in education, health and national and local government stood at 4.7 million in June 1976 and 4.6 million in December 1980. See *Department of Employment Gazette*, 'Quarterly series of employees in employment: Great Britain' (October 1977) pp. 1118–19; and ibid. (April 1981) pp. 512–13.
6. George Sayers Bain, *The Growth of White-Collar Unionism* (Clarendon Press, 1970) p. 187.
7. Ibid., p. 188.
8. George Sayers Bain and Robert Price, 'Union Growth and Employment Trends in the United Kingdom, 1964–70', *British Journal of Industrial Relations*, 10 (November 1972) pp. 366–81.
9. Robert Price and George Sayers Bain, 'Union Growth Revisited: 1948–74 in Perspective', *British Journal of Industrial Relations*, 14 (November 1976) p. 353.
10. George Sayers Bain and Farouk Elsheikh, *Union Growth and the Business Cycle* (Blackwell, 1976) ch. 4.
11. *The Growth of White-Collar Unionism*, pp. 131–4.
12. *Union Growth and the Business Cycle*, pp. 81–6.
13. *The Growth of White-Collar Unionism*, p. 181.
14. Roy J. Adams, *The Growth of White-Collar Unionism in Britain and Sweden* (University of Wisconsin, 1975).
15. Peter Fairbrother, 'Consciousness and Collective Action: a Study of the Social Organisation of Unionised White-Collar Factory Workers' (Oxford, D.Phil. thesis, 1978) unpublished.
16. *White-Collar Unionism*, p. 33.
17. *The Growth of White-Collar Unionism*, pp. 151–5.
18. A. G. Walkden, *The RCA and Its Path of Progress* (RCA, 1928).
19. For an assessment of the prospects for managerial unionism in Europe, see Howard Gospel, 'European Managerial Unionism: an Early Assessment', *Industrial Relations*, 17 (October 1978).
20. R. M. Blackburn, K. Prandy and A. L. Stewart, 'Concepts and Measures: the Example of Unionateness', *Sociology*, 8 (September 1974) pp. 427–46.
21. David Lockwood, *The Blackcoated Worker*, p. 137.
22. R. M. Blackburn, *Union Character and Social Class* (Batsford, 1967).

23. For NALGO, see D. Volker, 'NALGO's Affiliation to the TUC', *British Journal of Industrial Relations*, 4 (March 1966); for NATFHE see Sandra Turner, *The Development of the Association of Teachers in Technical Institutions* (unpublished Ph.D. thesis, University of Bristol, 1978); and for the IPCS see J. E. Mortimer and Valerie Ellis, *A Professional Union* (Routledge and Kegan Paul, 1980) pp. 371–4 and p. 424.
24. R. Carter, 'Class Militancy and Union Character', *Sociological Review*, 27 (May 1979) pp. 313–14, n. 3.
25. Rosemary Crompton, 'Approaches to the Study of White-Collar Unionism', *Sociology*, 10 (September 1970) p. 422.
26. Ibid., p. 412.
27. Ibid., p. 423.
28. George Bain, David Coates and Valerie Ellis, *Social Stratification and Trade Unionism* (Heinemann, 1973) p. 158.
29. For an analysis of the Census by occupational category, see Price and Bain, 'Union Growth Revisited', p. 346.
30. K. Roberts, F. G. Cook, S. C. Clark and E. Semeonoff, *The Fragmentary Class Structure* (Heinemann, 1977) p. 134.
31. For a fuller analysis see M. Maurice, 'Professionalisme et syndicalisme', *Sociologie du Travail*, 3 (1968) pp. 243–56.
32. See, for example, Serge Mallet, *The New Working Class* (Spokesman, 1975).
33. J-D. Reynaud, 'Stratification and Industrial Relations' in M. Mann (ed.) *Social Stratification and Industrial Relations* (SSRC, 1969) p. 157.
34. D. E. Mercer and D. T. Weir, 'Attitudes to Work and Trade Unionism Among White-Collar Workers', *Industrial Relations Journal*, 3 (Summer 1972) p. 57.
35. K. Roberts *et al.*, *The Fragmentary Class Structure*, p. 134; emphasis added.
36. John H. Goldthorpe, David Lockwood, Frank Bechhofer and Jennifer Platt, *The Affluent Worker: Industrial Attitudes and Behaviour* (Cambridge University Press, 1968).
37. 'Class, Militancy and Union Character', p. 299.
38. For a comprehensive discussion of patterns of female employment, see Catherine Hakim, *Occupational Segregation*, Department of Employment Research Paper No. 9 (HMSO, 1979).
39. 'Class, Militancy and Union Character', p. 299.
40. Michael Moran, *The Union of Post Office Workers* (Macmillan, 1974).
41. B. C. Roberts, Ray Loveridge and John Gennard, *Reluctant Militants* (Heinemann, 1972) pp. 117–18.
42. 'Class, Militancy and Union Character', p. 315.

9 The Early History of White-Collar Unionism

The Railway Clerks' Association

David Lockwood

The Blackcoated Worker, pp. 155–9

Of all the blackcoated unions that have emerged in the course of the present century, the RCA deserves special notice. Not only has it achieved a high degree of unionization, but its members have displayed a sense of allegiance to the Labour Movement which, going far beyond that of any other organized group of clerks, has in some respects even surpassed the class consciousness of traditional working-class unionism. Its history stands as a living refutation of the charge that blackcoated workers lack the necessary virility for a manly defence of their interests. The study of the development of trade unionism among railway clerks can only lead to a rejection of the common stereotype of the clerk, and to an awareness of the actual variations in class consciousness which that stereotype obscures.

Founded in Sheffield on May 8, 1897, the association grew slowly, after almost collapsing, and by 1904 it had 4,000 clerks and stationmasters enrolled out of a possible total of 60,000. The decision in 1899 to register the association as a trade union instead of merely as a friendly society gave rise to a great deal of controversy. Many members felt that the young organization, by taking this step, would alienate clerical workers still outside who were generally regarded as Conservative and extremely unwilling to be identified with manual workers' associations. Bolder council prevailed and the step was taken. Membership, instead of stagnating, actually trebled in the next three years. The same doubts about the 'progressiveness' of the railway clerk were voiced regarding TUC affiliation which was effected in 1903. Similar arguments were repeated when the question of Labour Party affiliation was raised, and at the annual conference of 1907 the motion for affiliation was defeated by 2,440 votes to 2,006. 'There are 60,000 railway clerks in the kingdom,' noted one member the same year, 'and I think I am well inside the mark when I say that quite 50,000 of them are Conservative in politics'. Affiliation was carried through in 1909, and by the end of the war the member- ship at last formed a majority of railway staffs – 61,000 out of a possible total of 100,000 clerks had joined. At every stage at which working-class association had been sought for the union, then, arguments appeared which every clerical association has had to face in the course of its economic and political development. In the case of railway clerks, each of the steps was taken early in the career of the union and was in the nature of an experiment. The success which attended these moves did much to make those both inside and outside revise their views on the feasibility and nature of blackcoated unionism. This was only the beginning.

In the pre-war years the RCA had still only a minority influence and its policy was informed by this fact. In the industrial field it was largely hampered by the companies' utter refusal to recognize the union. The only means open to it were the traditional 'memorializing' of directors, publicity and deputation. As a result, most of its battles during this period were fought through political action. It launched a vigorous campaign against the injustice of uncompensated Sunday duty, irregularities in the superannuation funds administered by the companies, and pressed for the inclusion of railway office workers within the scope of industrial legislation. These aims were sought generally through political action, which took the form of holding up Railway Bills to secure discussion of their grievances. This was achieved through the Parliamentary Committee of the TUC and the Labour Party. Legislation was secured in 1906 on the question of compensation for accidents, bringing clerical workers within the scope of the new Workmen's Compensation Bill. Similarly, in 1907 as a result of parliamentary action, the Board of Trade agreed to set up a Departmental Committee to 'Inquire into the Constitution, Rules and Administration and Financial Position of the Superannuation and similar Funds of Railway Companies'. This later showed that serious deficiencies in the funds had resulted from the companies' failure to pay their proper share. By the same methods the RCA also secured representation on the Parliamentary Committee instituted to investigate the question of railway agreements and amalgamations. But the idea of a permanent association of clerks was still highly repugnant to the railway companies who were incensed by these interferences, and their reaction resulted in deliberate and determined attempts to crush the RCA. The North Eastern company, from September 1907 onwards, persecuted and penalized men who dared to join the RCA and to continue their membership against the advice of the company's officers. This move was nonplussed with TUC help by a five weeks' blockage of a Bill submitted by the company in 1909 until the embargo on unionism for clerks was withdrawn. Similar efforts were made by the Midland Company to intimidate, interrogate and penalize, including the practice of 'red-ink records' of men who were trade unionists. Effective opposition by the Labour Party to the General Railway Bill of 1913 was necessary to break this opposition. Thus, action aimed at improving the status of railway clerks and defending the association itself was undertaken at this period through political representation, and this was the situation until the outbreak of the war. The experience of these early struggles confirmed the association's wisdom in its industrial and political affiliations, without which it might very well never have survived.

After 1918, the association, heartened by its unionization of the majority of railways clerks and by the general tone of industrial relations set by the governmental sponsorship of Whitleyism, decided to press for recognition as a bargaining unit for clerical workers throughout the railway industry. In the matter of trade unionism the companies had already acquired a reputation for reaction, and in the course of events leading up to the strike of February 1919 it became increasingly obvious that the RCA was being forced into a trial of strength with the employers. The question of policy revolved around the desirability of strike action, and the ability of the membership to make effective use of this weapon. At a hastily convened meeting in London it was decided to issue strike notices. At the eleventh hour the companies yielded and decided to accord recognition, but not before strike preparations and actual stoppages of work had taken place throughout the country and emphatically underlined the solidarity and confidence of the mass of railway clerks. The degree of concerted action was remarkable, especially since this was the first time non-manual workers had been called upon to defend their interests collectively in such an extreme manner. The past traditions of railway service had all been on the side of producing a blackleg rather than a striker. No wonder then that the Journal referred to the experience as a 'rebirth'. . . . Further evidence of the new spirit was manifested the same year during negotiations on national scales when the association was ready to strike again if its demands were not granted. And again, during the NUR strike in the September of that year, clerks resolutely refused to blackleg despite the 'loyalty pay' lavishly offered by the companies.

A new testing time came seven years later with the General Strike. When the miners came out, the transport workers were in the 'front line' of defence, and the RCA could not remain neutral. For the second time in its short existence, the association called on its members to withdraw their labour, this time not in defence of their own immediate interests but in sympathy with the miner's cause. It was one of the very few blackcoat unions that actually called an official strike. Later that year, the president, in the course of his annual address to the conference, strongly justified the action: 'There was only one way in which the RCA could rise to the occasion. Had we failed to go that way we should have forfeited our self-respect; our standing in the trade union movement would have gone, and we should have demonstrated that the blackcoated workers were not fit to belong to the working-class movement.' Of course, the repercussions followed, from within the movement in the form of resignations and protests, and from the railway companies who, several months later, had refused to reinstate hundreds of clerks who had gone on strike. On the whole, however, the membership was solid, and it is perhaps eloquent of their attitude that when legislation altered the status of their political fund, 83% of railway clerks contracted-in to the political levy. Moreover, the RCA's high reputation in the trade union and labour movement was enhanced still further, and unlike other clerical unions its action brought in 3,000 new recruits in the months following the General Strike.

The National and Local Government Officers' Association

David Lockwood

The Blackcoated Worker, pp. 184–94

The growth and composition of NALGO make it perhaps unique in the history of trade unionism, and the difficulty of holding together such a vast conglomeration of disparate grades and divisions through such a period of growth has been partly responsible for the peculiar brand of trade unionism it offers. In particular, its size has made it increasingly an object of interest to the rest of the Labour Movement at the same time as its comprehensive membership has forced it to move slowly and cautiously in defining its relationship to outside associations. As in the case of other clerical associations, the questions of the status of the non-manual worker and his identity of interest with the manual worker have been raised whenever these character-defining decisions have had to be made.

In the nine years between the formation of the National Association and the outbreak of the First World War, its activities were largely those of social club and friendly society, operated through the affiliated guilds at a local level. Dances, socials, picnics, cricket matches, excursions and discount-trading were innocuous enough to secure the growth of the association. The aims of NALGO in 1906 had been stated as follows: to further the interests of local government officers; to federate local and sectional societies of local government officers; to deal with questions of superannuation, security of tenure and others of national importance; to promote legislation for these and other purposes; to give legal assistance to members 'where the National Executive Council shall deem it necessary'; and to encourage the formation and working of local or district associations. None of these goals was held to involve an opposition of interest between the local government officer and his employer. The question of action on the matter of salaries generally did not arise in the members' minds, and certainly, as one writer put it 'anything savouring of trade unionism is nausea to the local government officer'. In reality, the lot of the officer was rather better than that of the general clerk and definitely above that of the manual worker during this period. But in the few occasional instances of salary reductions that occurred before the war it was clear that, before long, NALGO would have to define its policy towards the more material interests of its members.

This decision was brought to a head by the circumstances following the end of the war. Trade unionism was in ascendancy, 'an infection going round the country like influenza', the cost-of-living was soaring, the social distance between blackcoat and fustian had somewhat diminished in the war-time community, and new, aggressive unions, such as the National Union of Clerks, were invading the local government field. In 1918 it was noted that 'the question whether they should join the Trade Union Party has been acute among civil servants and teachers in recent months, and there is a considerable element in the local government service who favour such a step'; but although 'trade unions were undoubtedly of advantage to the masses of workers and to certain classes of workers "by brain" it would be unwise not to realize that public officers are distinct from any other class of worker or professional men'. The ideas of trade unionism and Labour Party affiliation seemed indissoluble to many of them, as was their association of trade unionism with strikes. At the annual conference of 1919 the council published a long report which was unfavourable to any change in the status of NALGO, and in it many of these fears were expressed.

Nevertheless, a motion for registration as a trade union was pressed at the conference. The discussion centred on the question of the best means to achieve the professed aims of NALGO. 'Constitutional' means were contrasted with the 'big-stick' policy of certain allegedly discontented and irresponsible elements of the membership. Others stressed the speed and efficacy with which demands forwarded by trade unions were met, as compared with the delays and postponements which were the fate of local government officers' claims. 'The very fact of having a legal standing gave a trade union a distinction, an idea of strength which was not given by an association'. . . . The motion for registration was heavily defeated, as was a motion that a ballot of the members be taken, and the matter seemed to have been settled.

But only for a short while. The demobilized soldiers were avoiding NALGO and joining what they considered to be 'real' trade unions such as the NUC, the Municipal Employees Association, the Workers' Union, the National Union of Local Government Officers and the National Union of Corporation Workers. Members also began to secede from the associated guilds of NALGO, causing alarm among local organizers. A special conference had been called for January 1920 to approve an increase in subscriptions, and many of the delegates to this meeting held mandates from their branches to say that unless NALGO became a trade union the entire membership would resign. At the meeting the council surprisingly announced that, despite the decision at the previous year's conference, a referendum of members on trade-union registration would be taken.

The referendum was confounded by the three alternatives given to the voters: to become a registered trade union; to become a certified trade union; or to stay unchanged. The pro-unionists, who feared that the council was still unconvinced about unionism, regarded the proposal for certification as a half-measure. When the count was taken the vote was divided: 7,916 were against unionism altogether; 5,002 wanted NALGO to become a certified trade union; and 6,992 wanted registration – 20,322 members voted, out of a possible 35,000. The general policy was clearly in favour of trade unionism, but the issue of registration or certification was still not settled. The council declared itself in favour of certification, but others held that this was defying the opinion of the majority, and at the 1920 conference it was resolved to refer the decision again to the membership. In July of that year certification was carried by 13,707 votes to 9,180.

It had been feared that the decision to make NALGO a trade union would lead to a loss of membership. This followed in isolated cases, and some of the senior officers resigned. But these losses were more than compensated for by the return of members who had left to join other trade unions before the decision, and by the influx of new members. By the end of 1920 membership had risen to 36,500 – nearly 8,000 more than that of the previous year and treble the 1918 figure. This important move in the history of the association had been carried through by a majority of the membership who were in favour of more militant action and in opposition to the views of the leadership who were at that time drawn largely from the senior ranks of local government service.

Motions for affiliation to the TUC followed in 1921 and 1922 but they were heavily defeated. The opinion of conference was also sought on the desirability of establishing a political fund in

1922. Since 67 branches, representing 10,678 members, agreed to this and only 20 branches having 4,438 members were unwilling, it was moved that a fund be established at once to finance parliamentary and local government candidates. But after discussion of all the implications the difficulties of such a step were seen to be too great. The following year it was announced that the best method 'would be to induce one MP from each of the three great political parties to interest himself in the affairs of the Association', and this method has proved its success over the years.

Thus the association was committed to a strictly non-political existence, and the occasion of the General Strike, whilst calling for a definition of NALGO's responsibility, was regarded as a confirmation of the wisdom of this policy. 'As might be expected, the recent industrial strife was of such a nature, and so widespread, that it presented new and perplexing problems to members. It has also demonstrated the soundness of the association's policy in remaining completely non-political. The members individually hold every shade of political belief, but the association rightly holds itself entirely aloof from the world of politics, devoting its energies and force to the carrying out of its objects.' . . . The association thus neither encouraged its members to support nor to break the strike.

After the show of enthusiasm for trade unionism immediately after the war and the defeat of motions for TUC affiliation in 1921 and 1922, the question of affiliation did not seriously arise again until the middle and late thirties. The General Strike had put trade unionism in bad odour with the middle classes generally, and the fall of the cost of living throughout the late twenties and early thirties, plus security of tenure, worked to the advantage of local government officers. Throughout this period NALGO had been working steadily, had achieved superannuation, and was striving to resuscitate the collapsed national Whitley machinery. After 1932, the general trade union movement began to revive and the affiliation issue was raised again.

The division of the membership of NALGO on TUC affiliation, which began at this time . . . arose out of the basic question as to whether affiliation to the TUC implied allegiance to the Labour Party. Those who thought that it did argued in the following vein: 'NALGO includes in its membership public officers who have to advise their councils on many things. These men and women have no right to let their political leanings, even if they have any, enter into their work. It does not require much imagination to see how untenable would an officer's position become if he were a member of an organization which was definitely allied to one political party. Every local government officer would be suspect. It would mean the end of impartial advice and administration, and that would probably lead ultimately to public officers coming into and going out of service with their party.' The demand for 'no party politics' was supported by the president in his address to the annual conference in 1935. . . .

The controversy revived shortly after the outbreak of war. With the National Union of Bank Employees inside the TUC fold, the only two blackcoated unions remaining outside were the NUT and NALGO. Moreover, the status of the TUC had been enhanced by the war-time coalition, and especially by the appointment of Mr Bevin as Minister of Labour. But the National Executive Council was adamant on the question of the political implications of affiliation. Whether the one implied the other 'technically and legally, is a question on which we hope the NEC will give all the information it can. It is, however, worthy of note that if there were any possibility of misunderstanding on the point one could have expected the TUC itself to disavow such an implication (since it must know that the question must arise in organizations such as ours which are not affiliated to it). So far as we know it has never done so. But whatever the technical position may be, the association has hitherto held the view that in practice, and in the public mind, affiliation does carry these implications.' Eventually, at the annual conference of 1942, in the face of an NEC resolution that there was no reason to depart from the 1936 decision, it was decided by 48,719 votes to 32,705 to have a ballot on the problem. This was to prove very embarrassing for the NEC, because when the votes were counted they showed a majority for immediate affiliation:

	Civilian	Forces	Total
For	39·53%	17·7%	33·67%
Against	29·34%	8·52%	23·73%
Not voting	31·13%	73·71%	42·60%

At the next conference Mr Riley, a member of the executive, persuaded the delegates by a remarkable *tour de force* that such a momentous decision was better reconsidered and referred back to the branches for another year. He pointed out that so many voters had been absent in the forces that such a slight majority for affiliation would split the union if affiliation were actually carried out, that NALGO would lose its identity in the TUC octopus as well as many of its present functions, that NALGO was on the verge of a new Whitley Council,, and that the result of affiliation would be to turn NALGO into a class union which would be mainly clerical and lose its senior officers. 'It had the great advantage over other organizations that it represented everybody from junior to chief. It was a weakness of the civil service that it was divided into clerical, executive and administrative associations, with one class set against the other. NALGO on the other hand represented local government officers as a body, and that was its source of strength, for it was better to have chief officers with the rank and file than against them. Did they want to turn NALGO into a clerical organization, with the chief officers forming a separate organization against the interests of the bulk of the service?' By a narrow majority of 47,259 to 45,825 it was decided to postpone affiliation and to refer the result of the ballot to branches and districts, thus deferring the decision for another year. The answer given by this re-reference showed that 159 branches with 43,152 members were in favour of immediate affiliation, 163 branches with 39,326 members wanted the decision deferred, and 71 branches with 12,382 members were definitely opposed to affiliation. It was bitterly complained by the affiliationists that the voice of the branches was not necessarily the voice of the membership as a whole, and at the next conference, which was in 1945, they asked for immediate affiliation and lost the motion by a card vote of 70,885 to 39,375. They sustained a second defeat in 1946 by 56,250 to 43,742.

The following year the NEC, sensing continuing dissatisfaction over the issue, took a new tack and moved that 'it be authorized to explore the possibility of affiliation to the TUC on a basis mutually acknowledged to be solely industrial and not implying allegiance to nor connection with any political party'. In support of this move, which seemed to bring NALGO nearer than it had ever been to a workable affiliation, the president agreed that 'it was completely untrue that affiliation automatically involved a political levy. Of the 194 unions in the TUC only 61, or one-third, were affiliated to the Labour Party.' A deputation was in fact sent to the TUC and a long report prepared by the general secretary for the 1948 conference setting out the pros and cons. But on this occasion the NEC reverted to its previous position and recommended the delegates not to affiliate, as a non-political affiliation was impossible. A counter-motion was heavily defeated by 101,895 to 55,254 on a card vote, but a proposal for another ballot of the membership was accepted, and it was decided that affiliation would be carried out if a majority of the membership voted in favour. Some 70% of the members voted and of these only 35·6% were for affiliation. . . .[1]

Though NALGO has never engaged in strike action, in recent years the problem has been reconsidered on several occasions. In 1948, it was decided that in the event of a strike by manual workers, local government officers should continue their normal employment but should not be constrained to do other duties, and the full support of the association would be given to officers who refused orders to blackleg. But if the authority concerned made a general appeal for volunteers 'and any of the individual members decided to respond to it the Association would not place obstacles in their way'. Whatever individuals decided to do, the general policy was that the local NALGO branch should carefully refrain from taking any collective action which would give other unions the impression that the staffs were prepared to be used as strike breakers.

At the 1950 conference it was reported that, during a strike of manual workers, clerical staff had been approached by the Electricity Board and asked to volunteer for essential duties in the power stations. Members of NALGO felt that they should get guidance from their trade union. The final decision of the meeting accepted this point of view and stated that 'if a section of employees withdraw or threaten to withdraw their labour, whether with or without the support of their trade union, and the authority of an electricity board desires to seek the services of administrative and clerical staffs in order to maintain supplies, the responsibility for deciding whether or not to carry out such duties should not be placed on the individuals but on their trade union'. In turn it was the duty of the local NALGO to confer with other unions involved to secure agreement upon future action.

As regards NALGO's own capacity to strike, the situation was laid bare by a special report prepared at the request of the annual conference. It considered the legal, constitutional, moral and material possibilities of strike action by local government officers, and revealed that NALGO was practically incapable of striking. Some of the grounds adduced are interesting, since they are generally applicable to blackcoated workers. In the first place, superannuation rights would be endangered. Secondly, the length of notice required for certain officials would destroy all element of surprise in a cessation of work. Further, 'the policy of the manual workers' unions is no doubt conditioned by the fact that, in the main, the rates of pay of their members run roughly at the same level. The situation of NALGO members is very different. Their pay runs at very differing levels; their readiness to accept something less than their normal rates cannot be predicted, the hardships in accepting less may be greater for those on the "bread line" represented by the lower reaches of blackcoated employment than for those even on corresponding levels among the manual workers, since their career prospects are usually greater, but this very fact may have induced them to enter into commitments such as the manual worker might not venture upon.' As regards NALGO's resources, 'The situation can be chiefly illustrated by citing a recent statement reported to have been made by the joint general secretary to the London Society of Compositors: "We have got £1,250,000 in the kitty and only 15,000 members. We can stay out a long time on that." NALGO has 235,000 members with some £200,000 at present in its Special Reserve Fund. . . . The Association has obviously not enough in the "kitty" for a strike in a single large branch.' Despite these facts, the NEC did not favour any policy that would preclude strike action in all circumstances. At present strike action can only be taken if 90% of the staff in the branch contemplating such action vote in favour.

NOTES AND REFERENCES

1. In a very real sense the struggle over TUC affiliation was partly a struggle between the higher and lower grades. When it was argued against affiliation that 'many of the chief and senior officers occupied confidential and advisory posts, they not only had to carry out policy, but they had to advise their authorities on questions of policy', this obviously did not apply to the vast majority of clerical grades in the Association. The counter view ran as follows: 'It is now plain that the only reason why NALGO does not apply for affiliation is chief officer opposition. The essence of the argument about our so-called exceptional status is that, as local government officers, we occupy a position of public responsibility and must, therefore, be non-political and

assert the fact unmistakably. But this cannot apply to 95% of us. The only people who might be embarrassed by association with the TUC are the principal officers. But NALGO is not composed solely of chief officers: it consists in the main of ordinary non-policy-making, anonymous meter-readers, transport inspectors, clerks, minor administrative officers and the like, whose political associations cannot possibly conflict with their official positions.'

The Draughtsmen and Allied Technicians' Association

B. C. Roberts, Ray Loveridge and John Gennard

Reluctant Militants (London: Heinemann, 1972) pp. 75, 77–85

Up to 1961 the title of this union was the Association of Engineering and Shipbuilding Draughtsmen. It is a title which more accurately reflects the membership of the organization over most of its history than does its present one. Its evolution as an organization has been structured by the market, technological, and political factors that have influenced the growth of industrial relations in the British engineering and shipbuilding industries during this century. Nevertheless it has specialized in representing an occupational group which stretches across several industries. Draughtsmen, more than any other category of technicians, have developed a craft or professional identity which distinguishes them from other categories of employees in any one industry. . . .

The Association of Engineering and Shipbuilding Draughtsmen was formed in 1913. Most of the earliest aims of the A.E.S.D. did not depart radically from the 'friendly-society' objectives of earlier local associations of engineering foremen and draughtsmen. The leading speaker at the inaugural meeting expressed prevailing opinion in an article written shortly afterwards. 'Amongst the majority of draughtsmen there has long existed a deep-rooted objection to rampant trade unionism, its despotism, its iron-bound regulations and its strife creating propensity . . . any combination amongst . . . must not interfere with the liberty of the subject.[1]

The employers on the Clydeside had come to a 'gentlemen's understanding' not to compete with each other for the services of draughtsmen, and it was their action which had persuaded draughtsmen of the need to establish a nationally based trade union. This was a period of rising prosperity in which draughtsmen could gain rapid wage increases by moving between firms. It was also a period of technological and organizational change, in which technical drawings were becoming less artistic and more standardized. A draughtsman's capabilities could therefore be advanced primarily through his knowledge of a wide range of varying technological processes. Mobility was an increasing characteristic of the ambitious draughtsman; blocked mobility served to bring home his position in the labour market.

From the inaugural meeting onwards, the Association attracted many senior draughtsmen to its ranks. These senior members have always tended to be pragmatic in their approach to unionism, and while favouring collective bargaining have laid stress on the need to maintain 'professional standards'.

The first major negotiations entered into by the A.E.S.D. took the Association no further than the actions of most professional bodies. Yet their effectiveness probably contributed to the dramatic influx of membership between 1914 and 1917. During these first three years of the first world war, membership increased from 300 pioneering members in and around Glasgow, to 10,000 members scattered in drawing-office combines throughout the country. In 1917 Headquarters were moved from Glasgow to London, partly as a result of geographical expansion, but also because the first major body to recognize the A.E.S.D. as a legitimate representative of draughtsmen had been the government departments in Whitehall. For the period of the war, responsibility for awarding national wage increases rested with the Ministry of Munitions, and the success of the Association in gaining a 12½ per cent increase after skilled manual workers had received a similar award gave it considerable stature in the eyes of draughtsmen. Its role as advocate in defending the mobility of members against the imposition of certificates preventing them from changing their employment was also important in bringing about a book membership of 14,384 by 1921.

The Association was recognized for the purposes of representing its members in grievance procedure by the Engineering and Allied Employers' National Federation. In 1924, after two long-drawn-out local strikes to which members gave their total support, the employers' leader, Sir Alan Smith, explained that the Federation's constituent members had wished to maintain close relationship with their own employees, but since A.E.S.D. had chosen 'another course' this was no longer possible. Having refused to recognize the A.E.S.D. between 1918 and 1920, during its more pacific formative years, the Federation were now anxious to discuss an arrangement for the settlement of grievances.

This was signed at a moment when the immediate rush of Association recruitment was over – when in fact membership had been in decline for two years. The Employers' Federation, on the other hand, had just won a significant victory in the lock-out of A.E.U. members enforced in 1922. Though recognition was confined to non-management staff (and it still remains so), and excluded apprentices, it stands as proof of the success of the militant plant bargaining which had preceded it. This tactic of gaining a concession at a number of key plants and then propagating its gain through a national agreement was not to become the hallmark of DATA strategy again until the full-employment conditions after the second world war.

The A.E.S.D. came under increasing labour-market and political pressures during the late nineteen-twenties and early 'thirties. Recruitment to the union came to depend on the attraction of high unemployment benefits, maintained as part of the early 'craft' tradition. The shipbuilding industry was in an extremely exposed position in the inter-war years owing to the decline in the overseas markets. Despite their early initiative, the Association's members in shipbuilding did not adopt an aggressive position. Only two approaches were made to secure recognition at the national level by the Association. A third refusal from the Shipbuilding Employers' Federation in 1940 led to a request for the intervention of the Minister of Labour, Ernest Bevin. For the second time in its history the A.E.S.D. gained 'recognition' through the intervention of the Government.

The rapid expansion in membership which took place during the first world war was repeated on a greatly enlarged scale during the second. Membership of A.E.S.D. expanded from 19,310 in 1939 to 36,661 in 1945. After a long period of depression the return to a high rate of growth had taken place in 1936. The recovery of the engineering industry and the demands of rearmament brought with them a huge expansion in demand for technicians, and in particular draughtsmen. Much of the new growth took place in the South-East and Midlands. At the 1937 Conference a Scottish delegate proposed a committee to investigate the introduction of a control scheme to protect members from the 'perils of dilution'. The committee, which largely consisted of delegates from London and Birmingham, presented a report in 1938. It recommended that, since the DATA minimum rate was being obtained by the 'dilutees' as well as by journeymen, no action should be taken.

This incident, which preceded many similar debates during the second world war, serves to illustrate the dichotomy which had existed between the positions of two groups of memberships within the Association since the first great influx of 'unqualified' dilutees during the first world war. It has given rise to an internal dialogue on bargaining policy, paralleled by an ideological division, which has underlain the argument chosen to legitimate and justify the chosen labour-market strategy.

Basically the choice has been between . . . the 'open' trade union recruiting 'all working at the trade within a workplace' and seeking to impose a common minimum wage by means of collective bargaining; and the 'closed' craft or professional association, whose concern has been to restrict entry to the *occupation* through maintenance of work standards and so to retain a market value for skills embodied in a required apprenticeship. For these latter organizations, collective bargaining was normally to be regarded as establishing a grievance procedure, a 'safety net' against failure by an employer to accept the self-evaluation of the draughtsmen in his employ. For example, as late as the 1939 Representative Council, a proposal that the Association should seek agreement with the Engineering Employers' Federation on minimum rates of pay was opposed by the Executive Committee on the grounds that it was 'dangerous to the standing of the Association'. . . .

The Association has, however, never lost its interest in control over training and work standards. In an Executive Report on Apprenticeship presented to the 1924 Conference it has suggested that the Association should conduct its own examinations and establish these as being the appropriate ones for journeymen. In 1935 the proposal was modified to accord more with reality by providing for 'joint regulation' of an apprenticeship scheme. In fact the Association achieved no more than normal negotiating rights for apprentices and, thirty years later, it acquired representation on the appropriate Industrial Training Boards on the same basis as that of other interested trade unions.

'Closure' of the occupation in a 'professional' sense was, therefore, never accomplished. Its various classes of membership are now based on experience 'in the trade'. But the Association has retained one important link with the 'learned-society' aspects of its early existence. In 1918 a National Technical Sub-Committee was formed for the purpose of selecting and publishing technical papers, particularly those of members. This work continues, together with the production of a series of technical data sheets for use in work.

One of the methods traditionally employed by the craft and professional associations as a means of exerting bargaining pressure was that of the published list of prices or rates at which members of associations would accept work. If employers refused to pay this rate then members who boycotted the employer were sustained in the interim from the funds of the association. Thus the association was able to exert pressure without resort to open conflict with the employer. . . . This model fits the evolution of DATA's collective bargaining policy almost exactly.

Since 1914 a questionnaire has been sent annually to all active members asking for details of earnings and conditions of work. This information is supplemented by the monthly returns of members' earnings made by all Corresponding Members. The results of these surveys are distributed to members in periodic statistical schedules. In this way the DATA (A.E.S.D.) has been able to assess the 'going rate' for draughtsmen. It was decided in 1920 to draw up a scale of minimum rates below which no draughtsman should accept employment. Members are expected to enquire from the union headquarters about the conditions at any office to which they intend to go.

The inadequacy of these attempts at individual job-regulation, supplemented by the Association's policy on training and the setting up of its own employment exchange, became increasingly apparent in the inter-war period. However, the system that was evolved for individual bargaining became the basis upon which the Association was able to build a most effective strategy and organization for collective bargaining in a full-employment economy. In the changed market conditions following the second world war the Association's statistical service became the focus of a network of communications which enabled DATA to become unique in its use of 'pattern bargaining' and in the strategic use of the strike. This form of central 'control', based on the ability to co-ordinate organizational activities, together with a very militant official strategy, made it possible for the Association to boast that it had 'very few unofficial strikes'.

The outbreak of the second world war again brought all the manifestations of rising demand and government attempts to control the resulting market pressures. Dilution increased membership; most of the new members had been promoted from the shop floor with little or no training and had acquired no 'professional' identity. The earnings differentials *vis-à-vis* shop-floor workers were eroded by payment-by-results schemes and over-time payments. Mobility was restricted by government order.

A.E.S.D. tactics, however, were changing. Despite their earlier opposition to nationally negotiated rates, the Executive Council reluctantly entered into talks on this question with the Engineering Employers' Federation in 1939. Strong pressures favouring this development were being generated among delegates to the Representative Council, and finally in 1942 the National Executive was instructed to enter into negotiations for a national minimum rate at age 21; this was achieved in 1944. In 1943 the union sought to secure an agreed minimum scale up to age 25, but this was not to be achieved until 1965.

Although A.E.S.D. had been bargaining at local level for twenty years, these decisions marked a distinct swing towards collective bargaining at a new level – that of a national 'Common Rule' for the whole membership. This development has been said to denote the beginnings of a two-party system in the Association. The influx of dilutees allowed left-wing activists . . . to organize opposition to the piecemeal bargaining policy of the N.E.C. . . . For the 'new men' a policy of 'national advance through national negotiations' was both an alternative market strategy and the basis of a belief in 'trade unionism as class action' which led them to oppose the current 'individualism'.

In 1958 the 'Left' is said to have replaced the 'Right' as a majority on the Executive Committee. By that time most Divisional Organizers were said to be of the Left. The election of Mr G.

H. Doughty as General Secretary in 1952 had coincided with a new aggressiveness in DATA wage claims. During the fourteen years between January 1951 and December 1964, official strikes of DATA members took place at 238 firms. 15,157 members were involved and a total of £910,000 was paid in dispute benefits. During this period the amount paid out in dispute benefits rose to being proportionally higher (in relation to total income) than for any other British union.

For the most part, however, the dialogue within the Association carried out in the Journal and at Conferences during this post-war period was remarkable for dealing with issues ranging from foreign policy to the nuclear deterrent, rather than for its focus on bargaining questions. In the actual carrying out of the Union's negotiating policy, the emphasis had been shifted inexorably by full-employment market conditions back to the local plant level. In this movement the ideological debate at national level appears to have had little more effect than that of enabling and perhaps encouraging the use of local bargaining strength. Since the Engineering Employers' Federation has insisted on settling the national claims of manual unions first, DATA has always been able to initiate its national campaign by local bargaining designed to restore the differentials disturbed by the manual workers' settlement.

Although the founders of the A.E.S.D. recognized 'a deep rooted objection to rampant trade unionism' among draughtsmen, the engineering and shipbuilding craft unions have exercised a major influence on the Association's tactics. Many of the recruits who came to the Association by way of shop-floor jobs or apprenticeships were members of the Amalgamated Engineering Union, and it was rational that early discussions should be held with this union, as with the Boilermakers, on jurisdictional matters. In 1918 these extended into terms for a possible merger. Throughout the first world war, workshops adjacent to the drawing office on Clydeside and other centres of A.E.S.D. recruitment had been gripped by the ideas of Guild Socialism. The A.E.S.D. journal was a strong propagator of such views (and has remained so), the culmination of which, if adopted, could be an 'industrial' structure for union organization.

The majority of delegates who voted for affiliation to the TUC in 1918 were, however, not convinced by ideological arguments for affiliation to the Labour Party. Attempts to set up a political fund failed until 1944. At this conference a campaign committee was set up and, in the ballot of members which followed, a two-thirds majority was secured for establishing a political fund. However, only about 37 per cent of members subsequently contracted to pay the political levy, and this number dwindled both absolutely and proportionately during the 1950s, the most militant years in terms of bargaining. . . . These figures suggest that many ordinary members may regard the actions of the Association in a limited and perhaps calculative manner rather than as an instrument of wider social reform. DATA Journal correspondence columns seem to confirm this impression. . . . The Association did not affiliate to the Confederation of Shipbuilding and Engineering Unions (C.S.E.U.) until 1943, this being 'the logical consequence of the decision of A.E.S.D. to seek national wage agreements'. In 1944 a Joint Consultative Committee of Staff Unions was established under the aegis of the C.S.E.U., in which A.E.S.D. developed strong relationships with the other two technicians' unions, the Association of Scientific Workers and the Association of Supervisory Staffs, Executives and Technicians. The leadership of the Draughtsmen's Association retained a very strong relationship with that of manual unions represented on the Executive Council of the C.S.E.U. Its relations with the other two technicians' unions reached a high point in their joint campaign against the Prices and Incomes Policy of the 1966 Labour Government. Yet neither of the other bodies achieved the same degree of unanimity with the manual representatives in the C.S.E.U. as has been enjoyed by DATA leadership. DATA (A.E.S.D.) has also been much more successful than the others in the co-ordination of its local bargaining strategy with that of blue-collar unions.

NOTES AND REFERENCES

1. J. E. Mortimer, *A History of the Association of Engineering and Shipbuilding Draughtsmen* (A.E.S.D., 1960).

10 White-Collar Union Character

White-Collar Unions Are Different

George Strauss

Harvard Business Review, vol. XXXII (September–October 1954) pp. 73–81

White-collar workers present special problems both to unions and to managements. Unions find it hard not only to organize but also to service a white-collar group. Managements, accustomed though they may be to dealing with organized factory groups, find white-collar unionism confusing and even threatening. What makes white-collar unions behave so differently?

This article will attempt to answer that question by showing that the one important special characteristic of these unions is the middle-class background and orientation of their members. This fact is fundamental to an understanding of why white-collar workers unionize, to the success of organization drives, to high participation in union activities, to satisfactory negotiations and relations between office and shop unions. Just how the middle-class mindedness of white-collar workers affects each of these areas will be discussed; and in conclusion the implications for those who must deal with them, particularly management, will be pointed up.

The study from which the article stems is based on field work with nine union locals and three organizational drives. . . . Five consist primarily of clerical personnel, such as typists, book-keepers, and time-study men; two are made up of professional engineers, representative of industrially employed professional workers; and two consist of industrial insurance agents . . . .

A great deal has been written about the special characteristics of white-collar workers and what they want from their jobs. As other authors have pointed out, they are essentially middle-class in outlook. Many are possessed by the Horatio Alger dream of working up from office boy to president. Even though he may be paid less than production workers, the typical white-collar worker is convinced that his job is higher in status because it is more dignified, closer to the boss, and offers greater opportunity for initiative and discretion.

Actually, in recent years white-collar work has become increasingly routine, opportunities for promotion have declined, and in many cases wages have dropped below the factory level. White-collar workers – particularly those with long service – often feel that their legitimate expectations have been disappointed. Then they turn to unions. However – and this is the thesis of this article – because these middle-class dreams are not completely dissipated, white-collar unions have a character of their own . . . .

In spite of varying approaches and well-financed drives, efforts to organize white-collar workers have not always met with outstanding success. Techniques developed among industrial workers often fail completely; at other times office workers organize themselves with almost no outside assistance. Why should this be so?

Many white-collar workers fear that by joining a union they will lose their middle-class status. To them unions are dirty, noisy, and 'lower class'. . . . joining the union means abandoning hope; it means showing hostility to the boss (whom they may dream of as a close associate and personal friend); it also means throwing away all opportunity to forge ahead on merit. . . .

The words of one worker summarize the common objection of many: 'As I see it, the union will interfere with the individual's opportunity to get ahead. The union will make it impossible for a man to be rewarded for the little extra which makes the difference between a good job and a bad one.' These worries were voiced by all groups, from teen-aged typists to professional engineers. And yet, as mentioned, at times white-collar groups have been easily organized. In most cases this was because they were 'ready' for unions, and union organizers offered a program in tune with the middle-class aspirations of the white-collar worker. . . .

Union organization is often easiest when the middle-class desires of white-collar workers have been rudely frustrated. For instance: in a telephone organizing drive, operators who lived in the wealthy suburbs showed considerably greater interest than those who came from the poorest slums. The girls from the slums felt envied and respected by their neighbors (and thus had no desire to join the union), while those from the suburbs believed they were looked on as 'just working girls'.

The amount of prestige, independence, and initiative given by the job seems to be more important than pay and security in determining a white-collar worker's attitude toward joining a union. To illustrate: in a large engineering firm, the drafting engineers with college degrees became militant union members soon after the firm moved them from their individual cubicles to one large room and put their work on a production-line basis with each man responsible for a single detail. Formerly a draftsman handled one job from start to finish. In contrast, the field engineers of the same firm showed no interest in unionism even though they had fewer benefits than the drafting engineers, worked long hours without extra pay, and were subject to drastic weeding out whenever the work was slack.

Approximately the same situation prevailed in another local of professional engineers where men who worked together in the laboratory were far more active in the union than their professional colleagues who worked alone. In the words of the 'lab' steward: 'Things are a lot different with the other groups. There are only one or two men on a job. They arrive when they want and they leave when they want. If they want to go out and have coffee or buy a suit, they just go. But we have to ask the section head for permission to leave the lab.' . . .

Industrial insurance agents are often told by their employers that they are 'professional'. They are from the point of view of income which often is $6,000 to $8,000 yearly. Yet large numbers of these agents have joined unions. What is the reason?

These men work on a commission basis and are under constant management pressure to 'produce'. Prior to unionization, the company made great efforts to encourage competition; there were endless series of contests in which the winners won all-expense-paid 'educational conferences', while the losers sometimes lost their jobs. Fraternization between agents was discouraged in the interest of making competition keener. Supervisors often accompanied the agents on their 'debits' to make sure they followed the prescribed sales techniques exactly. The agents joined the union as a reaction to management pressure which robbed them of their independence and 'professional dignity'. . . .

In most factories there is a fairly sharp distinction between the 'shop' and the 'office'. But in the shop there is also a group of white-collar men – timekeepers, production schedulers, expediters, time-study men, and so on. In the situations studied, these shop clericals were the easiest to organize and, once organized, they showed the highest participation in union affairs. The probable explanation for this is twofold:

(1) Shop clericals work in close contact with unionized production men and see at firsthand the advantages of unionism. (In contrast, secretaries to executives are typically antiunion while the attitudes of nonprofessional draftsmen and laboratory technicians often depend on that of the engineers with whom they work.)

(2) Many of these men are college trained yet feel they have little chance for promotion. Their pay and benefits compare unfavorably with those of the skilled craftsmen working beside them. In addition, they feel insecure because of the prevailing attitude in the engineering profession that industrial engineering is hardly engineering at all.

What about 'tyrannical' supervision, poor working conditions, and failure to keep up with community wage increases – factors that might be expected to be the primary reasons for white-collar workers joining unions? Of course they play a significant role; or, as one organizer put it, 'It is almost impossible to organize an office unless management has done something wrong *recently* to stir the people up.' However, the importance of such things as low wages depends to a considerable extent on the worker's conception of his job. For instance, the objections of shop clericals to low pay are almost always voiced along with complaints about inadequate promotional opportunities and management interference with their work – as if low pay were considered the last straw, the final proof that the company has no regard for their effort.

We may conclude then that many workers join unions because they see them as an alternate means of obtaining the middle-class dignity and independence which has been denied them by management and the work situation. This is not the only reason why they join, but all in all it is the most important one, and it seems to hold for all the groups studied. . . .

The very characteristic which makes white-collar workers difficult to organize also makes it hard for their unions to negotiate and administer a contract: they object to uniformity of treatment which has no regard for individual merit. . . .

Many white-collar workers are unwilling to abandon their customary ways. Seniority and automatic job progression are directly opposed to the Horatio Alger tradition. As a result, when white-collar locals move toward the traditional trade-union attitudes, as they generally do, they do so unconsciously through a process of trial and error. They protest several cases of unfair promotion, and soon they are advocating seniority; they file grievances against several pay inequities, and before they know it they are proposing job evaluation. . . .

In many ways collective bargaining for office workers is, by its very nature, more difficult than for industrial workers. Job description may take longer in an office since many jobs are unique. Job evaluation is even harder. . . . and since status is so important, petty jealousies and minor disagreements become inflated. White-collar workers are quick to react to slurs on their white-collar or professional status. In filing grievances against unjust acts of supervisors, one local protested that management was not treating the men like 'professionals'. Several engineers complained because they had been ordered to help a laborer clean up a dirty pump. An accountant objected to being ordered to sweep his floor. . . .

The traditional rivalry between the 'office' and the 'shop' often creates antagonisms which are not eliminated when the two become 'brothers' in the union. (This holds true regardless of whether the two groups are in separate internationals, the same international, or even when both groups are in the same unit.) Factory workers object to office workers' special privileges such as no time clocks, morning coffee periods, sick leave, and longer vacations. The white-collar group resents the higher pay which production workers get in spite of their lower educational qualifications.

Additional friction arises because white-collar workers are, in most cases, partially dependent on the production locals for economic support. During negotiations white-collar officers feel a strong pressure to settle under terms acceptable to the factory group. For a number of reasons they find it difficult to win strikes alone:

(1) When industrial workers go on strike, production ceases and the company immediately starts losing money. A white-collar strike may create inconvenience, but in most instances the really crucial functions can be performed by supervisors. (For this reason some unions seek to include lower-level supervisors in their white-collar membership.)

(2) The officers can never be sure their members will quit work when ordered to do so – although in some cases factory white-collar workers have endured long strikes with the same continuing loyalty to their union manual as laborers.

(3) A high proportion of white-collar employees are unskilled young girls, and the company finds them easy to replace.

(4) At times industrial locals may refuse to honor white-collar picket lines, or – where there are separate gates for office and factory workers – the factory local may request that pickets be confined to the office gates, thus making it possible for factory work to continue. . . .

Some white-collar workers are in an ambiguous position. They are half in management, half out. One would expect them to suffer acute conflicts of loyalty; but, actually, active union members say these conflicts are fairly easily resolved.

Certainly this was true in an office local organized by an industrial international in a large factory. Many of the most active members were production schedulers and time-study men. As such they helped determine the earnings and work load of their union brothers engaged in production. The nature of the dilemma (as well as an insight into why white-collar workers join unions) is revealed by the statement of the office local's vice president, a time-study man:

> I'd been pushing the production workers too hard on this new incentive plan. I believed the system would work if it was pushed hard enough; we could make people like it. Top management didn't support us, and I guess I stuck my neck out too far once. Well, anyway the other guy got the promotion, and I was plenty sore at management for a time. . . .

> I decided that if management was going to play that way I
> could play just as hard against them as I was willing to play
> with them. . . . I worked as hard as I knew how, but now I'm
> going to do just the opposite. I'm going to work hard for the
> union.

In spite of this unhappy experience, he still insisted: 'We still think
of ourselves as part of management; many times we have to make
decisions against production people, and that is what we are going
to continue to do.' . . .

There is another illustration of the same attitude in the discussion at an organizing meeting of an antiunion letter which the
personnel director had sent to all white-collar employees. One
expediter said: 'Everyone knows that the CIO strength is among
the expediters. Personally, I think the personnel director's letter is
an insult to the group which is pushing hardest for production.
That is fine gratitude for all the dirty looks we get from production
workers.' . . .

This group found it possible to remain loyal to its union and still
perform functions which were quasi-management. (Naturally,
such attitudes did little to lessen the tension between the two main
groups.) By joining the union the expediters hoped to increase,
not to reduce, the dignity of their job. . . .

American unions owe much of their strength and success to their
ability to adjust to the peculiar characteristics of the industries in
which they are organized. Nevertheless, one of the biggest
stumbling blocks for unions which are now trying to organize the
white-collar field is their failure to realize that, when the union
enters the office, it is coming into contact with people whose
interests and conceptions of themselves are different from those of
the typical factory worker.

White-collar workers join unions, not because they reject their
middle-class aspirations, but because they see unionism as a *better
way* of obtaining them. In other words, they look on the union as a
means of obtaining dignity, prestige, and control over environment, things which are denied them by the increasingly bureaucratic organization of the modern office.

In order for white-collar workers to be organizable their work
must seem to take on some of the characteristics of the factory; but
to be successful the union must also take on some of the charac-

teristics of a social club or professional society. In other words, unions must meet white-collar workers at least halfway. Attempts to throw a new office union into a 'full program' (such as job evaluation and promotion by strict seniority) usually meet sharp resistance. However, as the local grows older, it moves toward traditional union goals by necessity. For instance, it adopts seniority rules, not because it rejects merit as a basis of promotion, but because in practice merit is a lot more difficult to establish than seniority.

The relationship of white-collar locals to factory locals in the same plant is in many ways typical of their relationship to the union movement as a whole. Although their objectives become increasingly similar, the techniques used in achieving them are different. . . . The white-collar worker wants to and manages to maintain his separate identity. This is a persisting situation, and union leaders will have to recognize it as such.

The White-Collar Revolt

V. L. Allen

The Sociology of Industrial Relations (London: Longman, 1971)
pp. 91–8 (first published in *The Listener*, 30 November 1961)

It has been generally believed that militant trade unionism with its methods crudely forged out of force could never be used by white-collar workers and, in any case, was unnecessary for the protection of their economic wellbeing. It was felt that they could solve the problems they had with employers through their own individual efforts but if it should become necessary for them to act collectively then they would do so with dignity and refinement as befitted intelligent men. Not for them the methods of steelworkers, dockers and miners.

Recently, however, we have witnessed the spectacle of school teachers going on strike; of solicitors working to rule; of scientists parading their grievances through the streets of London; of insurance men lobbying the House of Lords; of chemists threatening to leave the National Health Service; of a vicar suggesting a trade union for clergymen. How do we explain this divergence between the accepted image of white-collar workers and their recent behaviour? Is it a temporary phenomenon or does it indicate a revolution in attitude?

It is neither. It is not new for white-collar workers to act collectively. A National Union of Elementary Teachers was formed as long ago as 1870. Clerks formed a union in 1897; local government officials in 1905; many civil service departmental unions were in existence before the First World War, and even the bank clerks, the élite of clerks, formed a union in 1917 and were 50 per cent organized by 1921. Nor is it the first time they have used militant methods. All were particularly aggressive after the First World War. There were strikes among bank clerks in Ireland, insurance agents in Scotland, and school teachers in England and Wales. Various other groups threatened strike action. Civil servants demonstrated in their masses against the Government.

Since the Second World War a number of industrial protests have been made. In 1950 doctors decided to leave the National Health Service but afterwards changed their minds, and in 1957 health service workers imposed a ban on overtime; on various occasions clerks in the motor industry have gone on strike.

But there is a difference between now and the earlier demonstrations. It is one of size and diversity. More white-collar workers from a wider range of occupations than ever before are willing to use the methods of militant unionism to redress their grievances. It seems reasonable that they should do so. They are, after all, members of a permanent employed class in exactly the same way as manual workers. They sell their labour power in a market which, on the one hand, has many sellers struggling to obtain the highest price for their labour power and, on the other, few buyers who are seeking to buy at the lowest cost possible. As individuals they suffer from being in a position of market inferiority.

But this clearly is an inadequate explanation, for despite their market similarity white-collar and manual workers on the whole have responded differently to economic pressures. Whereas approximately 60 per cent of the manual workers in Britain belong to trade unions, only about 21 per cent of the white-collar workers do so. All told almost two-thirds of the unorganized employees in Britain are in white-collar employment. What accounts for this?

Some social scientists seek an explanation in terms of the different conditions under which these two groups work. It is said that because the white-collar workers have often had higher earnings, greater security in their jobs, more congenial working hours and cleaner working conditions, than the manual workers; because they have not had to work tiresomely in factories and soil their hands; because they have been able to wear their everyday street clothes at work, they have not felt the same need to protest collectively.

This explanation presupposes a correlation between material wellbeing and industrial contentment which does not exist. It is incorrect to assume that the better off a man is the more complacent he is likely to be about his work situation. . . . The highest paid manual workers have always been among the most militant of their group, and it has been the doctors and school teachers, not the lowly paid clerks in dingy back-street offices, who have displayed the greatest collective aggressiveness. . . . The point is that a teacher or an administrator does not compare his industrial situation with that of a labourer or a porter in order to assess his satisfaction with it. He compares it with that of men with similar economic and social opportunities in different occupations. This provides vast scope for disgruntlement. We must look beyond the work situation for an explanation of the collective behaviour of white-collar workers.

A prime distinguishing mark of those in white-collar employment has been their striving for prestige. This has always been so. They have possessed social aspirations but have had limited means for achieving them. Unlike the members of the upper class they could not claim prestige as their birthright; nor could they, like the captains of industry, base it on power and authority. So they sought it in the only way left open to them – by concentrating on social differences; by relating prestige to appearances. Already they were separated from the manual group by the stigma attached to dirty work, and they sought to consolidate this separation by segregating themselves both physically and socially from manual workers. They were successful. The separation became a part of our social structure. It was embodied in the educational system and epitomized in the distinctions between elementary education on the one hand and grammar and bought education, often of a low standard, on the other.

The social insularity of white-collar workers was fostered by the privileged treatment they received from employers. White-collar workers were called staff, not hands, operators, or workmen; they were paid salaries, not wages, and were paid by the month, not by the hour, the day, or the week; they received a high degree of formal job security, superannuation, holidays with pay, sickness benefits, social and sports amenities – most of which were denied to manual workers. The staff were encouraged to identify their interests with those of the employers and to regard themselves as having a personal relationship with them. To emphasize this, white-collar workers were paid at individual rates, and so completely did they accept it that they rarely revealed their salaries to each other. They were encouraged to regard trade union representation as being an intrusion into a highly personal affair. In general, manual and white-collar workers were discouraged from mixing at work. Their starting and finishing times were often different. Sometimes they were provided with their own entrances. The separation of staff from workmen was built into the structures of industrial organizations as if the two represented different castes.

As a result of working in a protected and controlled industrial environment and under the influence of vivid external pressures, white-collar workers became involved in a great social pretence. They formed an image of themselves which bore little resemblance to economic realities. They saw themselves as individuals, superior to manual workers and able to progress through society unaided and without protection. They recognized no common interests. This image acted as a barrier to collective action.

But there have always been some white-collar workers who, for a variety of reasons, many of them personal, felt so aggrieved by their treatment at work that no amount of pressure or influence could distract or deceive them. These people constituted those minorities who formed trade unions. The support they received depended upon the extent to which the predominant social image was modified. Some modifications have now occurred, and the factors which have caused them have been relative changes in real incomes, the advent of full employment and the spread of mechanization into manual and non-manual operations.

The effects of relative changes in real incomes are the most obvious. Because the status of white-collar workers has depended largely upon their ability to engage in selective consumption, anything which has reduced their purchasing power has had implications for status. . . . Since 1945 . . . price rises have been consistent and persistent. They have eaten into the real incomes of relatively fixed-income people and have brought about a substantial redistribution of money incomes as between white-collar and manual workers. In addition this period has been marked by a secular rise in living standards, making it possible for a wider range of people than ever before to engage in selective consumption. House ownership and the possession of cars, washing machines, refrigerators and holidays abroad now characterize the lives of some manual workers more than some white-collar workers. When there is an overlap to any considerable extent the prestige value of the commodities concerned is lost. White-collar workers, in the main, have not had the means to escape from this by shifting their consumption to commodities beyond the reach of manual workers.

Full employment has acted on the work situation of white-collar workers in much the same way as inflation has acted on their social position. It has reduced the element of privilege. When labour is scarce most workers have a relatively high degree of security in their jobs irrespective of the formal provisions for it. Inroads have been made into other privileges too, as employers have been compelled by the labour situation and union pressure to concede to manual workers fringe benefits concerning holidays, pensions, and sickness. White-collar workers may still receive bigger and better benefits but they do not amount to privilege.

The spread of mechanization has also altered the image and so reduced the social distance between white-collar and manual workers. Work in offices nowadays often involves the operation of light machines such as calculating machines, dictaphones, and computers, which so dilute the tasks that many of them can be done by what might be called semiskilled non-manual labourers. The mechanization of the production processes has had opposite effects. It has moved from the stage of diluting craft skills to the point where machines operate machines, thus removing the elements of toil and dirt from work. Manual workers are increasingly able to wear light shoes and a tidy suit for work. . . .

Although all white-collar workers have felt the impact of inflation, full employment, and mechanization, some have felt it more than others. Public employees have been most affected by inflation and those in manufacturing industry least. The consequences of mechanization have been experienced most by workers in commerce and finance. Sometimes the incidence has varied within groups, as in the case of teachers where those on the basic scale suffer most from the Government's pay pause policy.

It is clear, then, that white-collar workers are increasingly practising trade unionism because they know they are losing their status and recognize that the causes are institutional ones. They are being compelled to scrutinize their objective relationships with employers and with each other. But this process has been going on for some time, so why the, seemingly, sudden outburst of militancy? The answer is that the conditions I have described are necessary for the rise of trade unionism but are not sufficient in themselves to determine its motion and intensity. Other things have to happen to shock, jolt, or prompt workers into phases of action. These other things are of a philosophical as well as a sociological nature, and for this reason they cannot readily be discerned and most certainly they cannot be anticipated. In the case of the phase of militancy in 1961 it seems that it was the Government's interference with the collective bargaining machinery of certain groups which was the jolting factor, but it could have been a feeling of tension or frustration unrelated to industrial affairs. But, whatever it was, it did not have the power to create an unhesitant urge to take industrial action. Nor could it have that power.

The only militant methods white-collar workers know about are those they have denigrated and deplored in the past. Because they cannot uproot nor readily pass over over the values which had determined their attitudes, they are confronted by a conflict between what is industrially expedient and that which is socially permissible. The consequence is one of utter confusion, marked by much talk, much dither and hesitation, many second thoughts, and an eager search for more palatable ways of redressing industrial grievances. The conflict is worsened by the essential nature of the work engaged in by so many white-collar workers. They have no desire to harm patients, children, or the public, yet they know that their protests will undoubtedly fail unless they do. Because they feel so deeply about this they rarely practise solidarity in the manual workers' sense. Opinions are often sharply divided about what should be done. All the time, moreover, they have an eye on public opinion. They want to avoid appearing offensive, aggressive, or inconsiderate; they want to preserve as much of their social image as possible.

Because so many white-collar workers are government employees or are financed in part by the Government, they are frequently found making political protests when they are aggrieved. They lobby the House of Commons or canvass individual Members of Parliament. They use constitutional methods which are sometimes quite effective. For example, both civil servants and school teachers secured the defeat of the Government in the early 1920s through careful but vigorous political engineering. . . .

Although white-collar workers do not neatly pivot the interests of labour and capital, they do lie between them, contained on one side by a hostility towards the aspirations of organized labour and on the other by a suspicion of big business interests. The hostility presents a barrier to assimilation within the Labour movement which might persist long after white-collar workers have realized the need for collective action. . . . It is likely to be a long time before white-collar workers identify themselves with'the political left, for not only must a substantial erosion of their social image take place but the effects of many years of propaganda about the administrative ineptness of Labour Governments must be wiped out.

In times of dissatisfaction white-collar workers, I believe, are more likely to adopt a negative than a positive political approach; that is, they would abstain from supporting the Conservative Party rather than vote Labour and they would not support the Liberal Party because, though it has many social qualities which appeal to them, it fails in the important respect that it does not present them with an efficient solution to their problems. In times of general crisis, however, there is little doubt that they would prefer a conservative authoritarian solution to their problems.

A Theoretical Approach

R. M. Blackburn and K. Prandy

'White-Collar Unionization: A Conceptual Framework', *British Journal of Sociology*, vol. XVI (June 1965) pp. 111–22

An increasing interest in white-collar unions has accompanied their rapid growth in recent years. However, there appears to be an underlying confusion in all discussions of the subject, with two contradictory views as to the nature of white-collar unions being held alternately, or even concurrently. In the first place, they are generally regarded as being a special type of union, distinct from those of manual workers (hence the special term 'white-collar unions'). Secondly, it is assumed that they are like other unions, so that membership of a union means the same regardless of whether it is manual or white-collar. In this article we propose to examine the nature of white-collar unionism in an attempt to show how this confusion has arisen, and how it may be explained. The article is based primarily on two independent researches in this field, one among bank clerks and the other among scientists and engineers.

Perhaps the clearest way of illustrating this confusion is to present the two contrasting viewpoints. The first, which owes much to Marxist theory, is forcefully expounded by Klingender.[1] For him clerical trade unions are working class organizations just like those of manual workers. Their faults, low membership and ill-advised policies, are a result of a lack of class consciousness among clerks, and are destined to be remedied as true consciousness develops.

Few writers have followed Klingender very closely, but fewer still, if any, have consistently rejected his position, by claiming that white-collar unions are quite different from those of manual workers. To be sure the view that white-collar unions are different is widely held, but with a variety of limitations. While Goldstein[2] argues firmly that unions of salaried professionals are 'significantly different', these are only a small part of white-collar unionism. Strauss,[3] writing under the heading 'White Collar Unions are Different', emphasizes a viewpoint shared by many. At the same time, in common with these other writers, he also observes similarities, although there seems to be no general agreement between writers on the nature of the differences and similarities. Furthermore, the significance of the differences is frequently not clear, for it is common, when comparing unionism in different fields, both manual and non-manual, for writers to measure the extent of unionization solely in terms of membership size.

The most that can be gathered from a review of the literature, then, is that white-collar unions are both the same as, and different from, manual unions. Either view can be upheld with some sound evidence, but consequently each can also be subject to vital criticism. The result has been indecisiveness, due, we hope to show, to the lack of any consistent theoretical basis by which to tie together the opposing hypotheses.

If we are to overcome the present confusion it is first necessary to look at the actual characters of white-collar unions – their policies and activities. In doing so we introduce the concept of unionateness, which is used as a measure of the commitment of a body to the general principles and ideology of trade unionism. The concept can be considered as comprising seven elements.[4]

1. Whether a given body declares itself a trade union
2. Whether it is registered as a trade union
3. Whether it is affiliated to the T.U.C.
4. Whether it is affiliated to the Labour Party
5. Whether it is independent of employers for purposes of negotiation
6. Whether it regards collective bargaining and the protection of the interests of members, as employees, as a major function
7. Whether it is prepared to be militant, using all forms of industrial action which may be effective.

1. Many white-collar unions prefer to avoid the unpopular connotations of the word 'union' by being known as 'guilds' or 'associations'. In banking there is one union for the whole occupation, the National Union of Bank Employees (N.U.B.E.) which started out as the Bank Officers Guild until it joined forces with the Scottish Bankers Association after the war. When the new title was adopted the word union was deliberately incorporated as an unequivocal description of the organization. On the other hand there are a number of staff organizations which exist in most of the clearing banks, each one recruiting solely within its own bank; these are known as 'staff associations', and although the word

'guild' has occasionally been used in their titles, the world 'union' has been avoided completely. Among the scientists the word 'union' has been avoided also. Their desire not to be regarded as the same as the unions of manual workers is expressed in such titles as: Association of Scientific Workers, British Association of Chemists, Gas Officers Guild and, as a variation from the usual association or guild, the Institution of Professional Civil Servants.

2. Registration as a trade union may be taken as another index of an organization's acceptance of its role as a trade union, with the same functions as other unions and so part of the general trade union movement. Among manual unions registration is more or less taken for granted, but many white-collar unions have not felt it desirable to take this step, even though there are certain legal advantages. In banking the division between N.U.B.E. and the staff association is repeated. No staff association has sought registration, whereas N.U.B.E. became a registered trade union shortly after it was founded. Many scientists and engineers are in unions dominated by other white-collar groups, which are for the most part not registered. Of the smaller unions catering more exclusively for this group, most are registered – particularly those recruiting in the nationalized industries.

3. When we consider connections with other unions we again find that white-collar unions are divided in their practices. Some avoid all connection with other bodies as far as possible, while a few are affiliated to the Conference of Professional and Public Service Organizations (C.O.P.P.S.O.) and the National Federaion of Professional Workers. These two organizations do not seem to arouse much controversy nor, it must be admitted, do they have much effect. Only a few white-collar unions, but these include the A.Sc.W. and N.U.B.E., are affiliated to the T.U.C. and such affiliation has been a major source of dispute in many non-manual unions. Whenever a union considers affiliation the membership is divided. It took over twenty years and numerous conference resolutions before N.U.B.E. resolved to affiliate; then there followed numerous conference resolutions for disaffiliation, although the issue seems never to have been in doubt. In the National and Local Government Officers' Association (N.A.L.G.O.) the opposition has been stronger, and until recently this union has remained outside the T.U.C., with the members more or less equally divided. Finally, by a fairly narrow majority the decision to affiliate has been taken, probably to be followed by

a number of unsuccessful attempts for disaffiliation.

Other unions have experienced similar divisions of outlook among their members. Why should this be so? The arguments put forward for and against affiliation are in part quite rational. That most stressed by the supporters is the instrumental advantage to be gained, and they play down the political and ideological connotations. The opponents reject the instrumental argument on the ground that the T.U.C. is an instrument designed to further the interests of manual workers and is therefore not suitable to represent the 'different' white-collar workers. They argue, also, that one of its means is political action, which is undesirable for themselves, particularly when it involves action through the Labour Party. Both sets of arguments have clear ideological overtones, and it is interesting, for example, that the bank staff associations, despite their objections to political action, and criticism of the T.U.C. on this score, associate themselves with the purely white-collar C.O.P.P.S.O., whose objectives are entirely political.

4. From what has been said about political considerations in relation to T.U.C. affiliation, the attitudes towards Labour Party affiliation will be fairly clear. In fact none of the unions with which we are particularly concerned is affiliated, although some white-collar unions are. Among bank clerks and scientists it is believed there are many who do not support the Labour Party; therefore solidarity within the ranks of a union is thought to preclude the possibility of political solidarity with the Labour movement.

5. It is important to consider independence from employers, for the management-controlled 'company union' is very different from other unions. In Britain there are a number of white-collar 'staff associations' representing the staff of just one company, of which those in the banks are among the best known. It is a matter of considerable dispute whether, or to what extent, these staff associations are independent of the employers. In the space of this article it is not possible to settle this dispute, and no attempt will be made. It may be noted, however, that on the one hand the banks played a major part in the creation of the staff associations, continue to give them financial assistance, including paying the salaries of full time officials, and generally favour the staff associations in preference to N.U.B.E.; on the other hand the associations do carry out negotiations with the banks, backed by independent arbitration agreements which give them some formal

independence.

6. Bargaining and associated activities we take to be the definitive functions of trade unions. For many white-collar unions the representation of employees' interests in this way is a major function, as it is for manual unions. This is true of the staff associations which are, therefore, indubitably trade unions for our purposes, regardless of any arguments about their difference from other unions. Certain white-collar bodies such as the Institute of Water Engineers and the British Medical Association, which are commonly regarded as professional bodies, do engage in bargaining and may therefore be regarded as having some union characteristics. However, these activities form a smaller proportion of total activity than in organizations which are more usually classed as trade unions.

7. Finally we must consider militancy, which is basically the extent to which an organization will go in asserting the interests of its members against employers – in fulfilling its function as a trade union. It should be noted that militancy is only one element in unionateness and not, as it has usually been treated, the sole variable in union character.[5] It depends on two distinct factors: one is the real power of the union, determining what in practical terms it is able to do, and the other is the ideology. Power clearly depends on the general work and market situations and also on the completeness of the union. By completeness is meant the proportion of the potential membership who are actually members of a union, and this in turn depends on the situation, particularly the work situation, and the prevalent ideology. We shall return to these points relating to the situation in the next section.

Ideology, here, consists of two contrary elements, class and status, the latter involving an hierarchical concept of the relationship between staff and management while the former entails a concept of conflict. The existence of a bargaining body does in itself imply that, to some extent, there is a conflict of interest which is recognized; this recognition implies some elements of class ideology. However, this is not the same phenomenon as class consciousness, since there remain in white-collar unions, to a varying degree, elements of a status ideology. Basically, this means that the authority of the employer is accepted, that his control is seen as legitimate. This is most obvious when we consider the staff associations, but may also be observed elsewhere, particularly among some of the scientists' organizations. One result of this is that there is an emphasis on 'representation' rather than bargaining – a belief that management will treat workers fairly, and that a 'rational' solution to problems can be found, as opposed to a compromise reflecting relative power. Also there is an emphasis on professional matters. The unions we are considering exist primarily as bodies for staff representation but all enunciate some principle of professional conduct, generally in the form of helping to run the industry properly or maintaining high standards of service to the public. Clearly these elements of a status ideology tend to reduce the level of militancy. . . .

Whilst it is important to be aware of people's attitudes, it would be wrong to attempt to explain in the present case, for example, the nature of white-collar unionism solely by the attitudes of white-collar workers. Rather we would argue that both of these are mainly related to other objective features of the work situation. . . .

Let us, then, consider those factors which bring about a need and desire on the part of non-manual workers to undertake collective rather than individual action. One of the most important is the attitude and behaviour of the employer. The outstanding example of this for non-manual workers in Great Britain is in public employment. In the Civil Service, local government and nationalized industries white-collar workers are organized to a very high degree. Even a union of high status employees such as the Institution of Professional Civil Servants has a membership of about 80 per cent of its potential. There can be little doubt that one reason for this has been the fact that government policy has tended, at least in recent years, to encourage union membership, notably in the case of the nationalized industries.

There are other instances which demonstrate that employers' approval of unionism greatly facilitates a union's efforts to win members. Conversely, opposition from the employer can be an important factor in bringing about the failure of such efforts. The attitude of the employer not only operates to help or hinder the work of the union in obtaining benefits for its members, thus furthering its instrumental appeal, but works also on the ideological level. Where the employer favours a union, or at least does not oppose it, it is easier for marginal or potential union members to reconcile membership with their acceptance of the legitimacy of the employer's claim to authority.

However, these direct and obvious consequences of the attitude of the employer are not the only factors in unionism – clearly many white-collar unions exist, or have come into existence in spite of strong employer opposition. There would seem to be other, more basic factors, one of which is the growth of bureaucracy. The essential feature of a bureaucratic structure, in the present context, is its emphasis on the office rather than upon the individual office-holder. This means that the employee is treated as a member of a category, as one of a group. Salaries are an obvious and relevant example. Salary scales are fixed and known, with extra payments made, as far as is possible, on objective criteria, and with a formal pattern of promotion.

Such an organizational structure inevitably discourages individual action in favour of collective action; since decisions of the employer, about salaries for example, apply impersonally to all members of a group. Not only does bureaucratic organization encourage unionism in this way, but a trade union, by attempting to extend the scope of collective representation, tends to further, or at least to uphold, the impersonality of the system. Trade unionism and bureaucracy are thus mutually supporting.

On this basis one can explain the high degree of unionization in government bodies in terms of the higher degree of bureaucratization which they manifest.[6] The clearest example is in the nationalized industries, where unions of non-manual workers rapidly grew up, covering even managerial personnel. In private industry, too, there are strong pressures towards greater bureaucracy, which have led to a growth of trade unionism. At the same time, employers have tended to offer resistance to these pressures, and thus to restrict the development of trade unions. It can be argued that whereas in public employment bureaucracy has developed because of its functional efficiency, it has been held back in private industry because of the employers' ideological need for loyalty from their employees. In other words, bureaucracy has often been tempered with a measure of 'administrative particularism' whereby the individual is as far as possible treated as an individual and not as just one of a group. Management feels the need to avoid the consequences of greater rationalization, and to preserve with all workers, but particularly with non-manual employees, what it considers to be the natural relationship of harmony between them. Since management must persuade employees of the legitimacy of its authority, it is loth to admit of any structural differences of interest such as would give rise to collective bargaining. Even where conditions have brought about some degree of collective representation, and here banking provides an outstanding illustration, it attempts to restrain its impact by, for example, encouraging staff associations.

Under certain conditions of organization it is difficult for management to treat all even of its non-manual employees in a 'particularistic' manner, and as a result the employees are less likely to identify with management and more likely to realize a conflict of interest with them. Size is clearly one of these conditions. The larger a work group becomes, the less easy it is for management to treat its members as individuals. We mean this not only in the personal sense of 'human relations' but also in the sense of determining earnings and working conditions. Salaries, for example, will probably be determined no longer by reference to personal characteristics but to such criteria as age, qualifications, output or some ostensibly objective form of merit. In this situation collective bargaining is a more effective method of raising earnings than individual action.

Increased size and complexity of organization is often associated also with a reduction in the prospects of promotion to management for those in the lower levels. The diminished opportunities to share in the exercise of authority will tend to reinforce the individual's rejection of its legitimacy.

A further associated factor is the degree of control that an individual has over his work. Rational production requires that each operation be costed, as far as possible. The more important, relatively, the operation becomes, the greater will be the pressure to do so. This must inevitably reduce particularism and the degree of personal control over work. To take technologists as an example, it is obviously difficult to make research work rationally accountable, except perhaps in the very long term, and no work study engineer could prove that a scientist apparently doing nothing is not in fact having his most creative thoughts! In contrast, it is much easier for management to control an engineer doing semi-production work, or even design and development. And it is amongst the latter type of technologist, rather than those in research, that trade unionism is strongest. . . .

Basically, the reasons for the rise of white-collar unions are the same as for the growth of unionism in general. Comparisons cannot be precise, but there is evidence from many studies to show that trade unionism amongst manual workers is associated with large-scale organization and impersonal rationalization. It results from a rejection of the complete authority of management and an expression of a desire for the group to exercise countervailing power. An ideology representing harmony is replaced by one which realizes a conflict of interest.

To this extent, therefore, middle-class or white-collar unions must be considered as similar to all other unions. However, it should be clear that the conditions which lead to the desire for some form of collective representation can be present in any situation in varying degree. . . . The 'amount' of unionization can therefore be measured along a continuum, though not a simple one. . . . White-collar unions are both similar to manual unions, in being the result of the same basic causes, and different, because, for the most part, they are at a different point on the continuum. The conditions of unionism have not affected white-collar workers to the same extent that they have manual workers.

NOTES AND REFERENCES

1. F. D. Klingender, *The Condition of Clerical Labour in Britain* (Martin Lawrence, 1935).
2. B. Goldstein, 'Some Aspects of the Nature of Unionism among Salaried Professionals in Industry', *American Sociological Review*, vol. 20, no. 2 (April 1955) pp. 199–205.
3. G. Strauss, 'The White Collar Unions Are Different', *Harvard Business Review*.
4. As set out here, of course, several of the elements in the concept refer specifically to Britain. We believe, however, that they can generally be translated for other cultural contexts.
5. This emphasis on militancy alone seems to be one more result of the tendency to treat manual and non-manual unions as different phenomena. Amongst the former militancy is on the whole the most important variable because their degree of unionateness is such as to permit little variation in the other factors.
6. It should be borne in mind that the employers' attitudes which we have described above are also relevant in this connection. However, these cannot be regarded as independent of bureaucratization, for, in the first place, in a bureaucratic organization the advantages to management of negotiating collectively with employees are greatest, and, secondly, attitudes towards employees tend to favour or discourage both bureaucracy and trade unionism.

Class, Stratification and Union Character

George Bain, David Coates and Valerie Ellis

Social Stratification and Trade Unionism (London: Heinemann, 1973)
pp. 79–95

In spite of the different social positions of the members of manual
unions, white-collar unions, and professional associations, differences in the character of these organizations are more those of
degree than of kind: for character differences within each organizational category are at least as great as those between each
category. Even these differences of degree in the character of
employee organizations do not seem to be determined by the
differences in their members' social positions. But . . . certain
writers have argued that a union's character is an index of the
class consciousness of its members.

For Lockwood 'the trade-union movement is a working-class
movement, and to the extent that clerical workers become involved in trade unionism they have to come to terms with its wider
class character'.[1] He assumes that the 'class-conscious feeling of
the blackcoated worker is reflected in the degree to which his
union identifies itself with the Labour Movement' (p. 197) . . . . In
short, by assessing the performance of clerical unions against a
number of '*general problems*' faced by every union 'by virtue of its
status as a defensive organization of employee interests',
Lockwood gauges their character and hence the class consciousness of their members (p. 55).

Blackburn has offered a similar but distinctive analysis.
'Unionisation' for him 'is the measure of the social significance of
unionism', an 'index of class consciousness'.[2] He defines unionization as consisting of two variables: union membership and union
character. Union membership is measured by 'completeness' or
density, the proportion of potential members of a union who are
actual members. Union character is measured by what Blackburn
calls 'unionateness'. Character can be 'more or less unionate'
according to the extent to which the organization 'is a whole-
hearted trade union, identifying with the Labour Movement and
willing to use all the powers of the Movement'. That is, 'the level
of unionateness depends on the commitment of an organisation to
the general principles and ideology of trade unionism' (p. 18).

In other words, unionization, the measure of class conscious-ness, is a function of unionateness and completeness, and within certain specified limits, 'by far the simplest satisfactory formula is *unionisation = unionateness × completeness*' (p. 44). Although Black-burn's formula for unionization 'is symmetrical in its two elements' (p. 270), there is little doubt that he considers unionate-ness and the union character which it measures to be the primary indicator of class consciousness. . . .

Completeness is relatively easy to measure; it is by its very nature a quantitative concept. Unionateness is more difficult to measure. But, in Blackburn's view, 'a useful rough measure' is obtained by considering the extent to which the following seven characteristics apply to an organization:

1. It regards collective bargaining and the protection of the interests of members, as employees, as its main function.
2. It is independent of employers for purposes of negotiation.
3. It is prepared to be militant, 'using all forms of industrial action which may be effective'.
4. It declares itself to be a trade union.
5. It is registered as a trade union.
6. It is affiliated to the Trades Union Congress.
7. It is affiliated to the Labour Party (pp. 18–19). . . .

In assessing the above argument it is necessary to determine to what extent the seven dimensions of unionateness indicate a sense of class solidarity as opposed merely to recording responses to narrow sectional needs and interests. It will facilitate the discussion of these seven dimensions if they are grouped as follows: declaration and registration as a union, independent collective bargaining, militancy, and affiliation to the Trades Union Congress and the Labour Party.

Whether or not an organization calls itself a trade union, or registers as such, may indicate something about the class con-sciousness of its members. But equally it may not. A union's reluctance to declare itself as such may stem not from a lack of class consciousness on the part of its present membership, but from an assumed lack of consciousness on the part of a potential membership which it is attempting to recruit. Moreover, a union may not openly declare itself in an attempt to have a stronger appeal for employers and thereby more easily obtain recognition from them. Similarly, there may be legal and other disadvantages

228

imposed on unions by the state, and they may not wish to identify themselves as such in an attempt to escape these.

Similarly, registration[3] is a poor measure of class consciousness primarily because unions often base their decision on factors which are unconnected with any sense of class solidarity they may possess. There are certain legal and administrative advantages to registration and many unions register because of these. For example, the Association of Scientific Workers decided to register following the discovery of 'its weak legal position in negotiating a particular issue'. . . . Moreover, structural factors have sometimes prevented an organization which would like to register from doing so. The British Medical Association took legal advice in 1910 'as to whether it could register as a trade union: the ruling was negative, since it was an association neither of workmen nor masters'.[4] Hence, as Blackburn himself concludes, 'we should not . . . pay too much heed to the legal status of an organisation' as an indicator of its 'sociological character' (p. 37).

Even granted for the moment that an organization's decision to register or declare itself as a union could indicate something significant about the class consciousness of its members, it is difficult to see how these dimensions of unionateness can be operationalized. As Blackburn himself has pointed out, 'it is not easy to decide whether an organisation does or does not declare itself to be a trade union' (p. 36). He originally suggested that an organization's title was a useful indicator in this regard; if it wanted to avoid declaring itself as a union, it would use such words as 'association' or 'guild'. But in fact, less than 50 per cent of the unions affiliated to the Trades Union Congress in 1970 had the word 'union' in their title. This is hardly surprising for, as Commons has pointed out, 'the original word for a union of wage-earners was "society" or "association"', and it was not until the 1830s 'that the term "trade union" came into vogue, both in England and the United States'.[5] . . .

Independence from employers and collective bargaining are so closely related that it is easiest to consider them together. Blackburn argues that collective bargaining 'is basic to the concept of unionateness'. 'If an organisation has no score under this item, it has no score under the other items, i.e. its level of unionateness is zero' (p. 28). Indeed, he calls collective bargaining and the protection of the interests of members as employees, 'the definitive functions of trade unions' (p. 21).

Blackburn's emphasis upon collective bargaining is somewhat surprising for at least two reasons. To begin with, it conflicts somewhat with his stress on independence from employers. For collective bargaining by its very nature involves mutual dependence. In fact, the more institutionalized the collective bargaining relationship, the greater the mutual dependence. . . . Management supports the strength and stability of the union, allows it to take credit for improvements in wages and working conditions, and does not compete with it for employee loyalty. Paradoxically, there is often more dependence upon management where unions are strong and more unionate (in terms of the other six criteria) than where they are weak and less unionate. Indeed, some of the weakest and least unionate unions on Blackburn's criteria enjoy the ultimate independence of not even being recognized by employers. . . .

It is also difficult to see why Blackburn assigns primacy to collective bargaining if the objective is to measure unionateness. For organizations which engage in unilateral regulation have as good, if not better, claim to being committed 'to the general principles and ideology of trade unionism' as organizations which engage in collective bargaining. The early craft unions in Britain and other countries tended to rely almost exclusively upon unilateral regulation. . . . Given that the various methods of job regulation can be equally effective, unions will naturally prefer that method which minimizes the necessity of compromising with external interests. They thus prefer unilateral regulation to collective bargaining which involves compromise and power-sharing. Indeed, such class conscious trade unionists as the syndicalists rejected collective bargaining on principle because this compromise and power-sharing seemed to them the essence of class collaboration. . . .

But it does not necessarily follow that unilateral regulation is any better a measure of class consciousness than collective bargaining. For the method of job regulation adopted by unions is determined not so much by the attitudes of their members as by structural factors external to them. Perhaps the key factors in this regard are employer policies and the extent to which unions can control labour supply. Both of these, in turn, have been crucially dependent upon the nature of the trade or industry. For example, rapid technological change in the engineering industry towards the end of the nineteenth century made it increasingly difficult for unions to maintain their craft controls and increasingly expensive for employers to tolerate them. . . . The creation of a system of collective bargaining was a function of union weakness rather than strength, and it had little, if anything, to do with the class consciousness of union members.

To summarize, there is more than the one trade union method that Blackburn seems to assume. Moreover, the method which a union chooses is not only or even primarily determined by the class consciousness of its members. Rather, union methods vary with bargaining contexts, and these 'vary so much that the methods which may be appropriate in one situation may be completely inappropriate in another'. In short, the equation of collective bargaining with trade unionism is false.

Blackburn defines militancy as 'the extent to which an organisation will go in asserting the interests of its members against employers – in fulfilling a trade-union function' (p. 31). In his view the strike is the ultimate in militant behaviour.

The strike is undoubtedly an example of militant behaviour, but it and other forms of militant action need not necessarily be an indicator of class consciousness. Strikes can very often be for sectarian ends and contribute nothing to wider class or even union goals. . . . Hence before any judgement can be given regarding the social significance of a strike, its objective must be assessed.

Even if militancy did reflect the class consciousness of striking workers, its use as an index of unionateness would require the assumption that all workers had the same cause and the same ability to strike. But this is obviously not so. Employers may be more considerate of some employees than of others. Some work groups enjoy a more strategic position in the process of production than others, and hence the strike may have greater efficacy for them. Paradoxically, such strategic work groups may not need to strike particularly often, if managements are sufficiently impressed by the threat alone. British printing workers are a case in point. Similarly, many professional associations are able to control their members' terms and conditions of employment without needing to resort to strike action or militant behaviour. . . . In contrast, most trade unions have to exercise their power in a highly visible way.

Blackburn himself recognizes the weakness of using militancy as an index of unionateness. . . . Consequently, he suggests that the militancy of an organization should be assessed not 'by the militancy of its actual actions', but by 'the extent to which it is prepared to use militant action . . . the extent to which, when need arises, it displays readiness to take all forms of industrial action which may be effective' (p. 31). But how is willingness to be measured except by actions? . . . As a measure of class consciousness the concept of militancy is not only conceptually and empirically dubious, it is also non-operational.

Blackburn argues that affiliation to the T.U.C. is 'the most direct way of expressing shared interests and identity with other unions'. Affiliation 'entails an open acknowledgement of a trade-union character and voluntary participation in the trade-union movement' (p. 37). This may be the case, but it does not follow that affiliation to the T.U.C. is a measure of class consciousness. For a union's decision to affiliate is often motivated more by its organizational needs than by its degree of commitment to 'the general principles and ideology of trade unionism'.

This is made clear by the affiliation of certain major white-collar unions to the T.U.C. The National and Local Government Officers' Association and the three largest teachers' unions affiliated to the T.U.C. in the 1960s after creating and abandoning a separate white-collar congress, the Conference of Professional and Public Service Organisations. The decision in each case had little to do with any class consciousness which their members may have possessed. Rather, it was a response to the T.U.C.'s presence on the national planning bodies and C.O.P.P.S.O.'s exclusion from them. In consequence, these white-collar unions felt that by staying outside the T.U.C. they would have no access to policy-making bodies which directly affected their bargaining position. . . .

An additional danger of using affiliation to the T.U.C. as a criterion of unionateness is that it forces into the forefront of a union's character a decision normally taken years ago, and which for many unions involved merely the selection of an extra channel through which to pressure government. Thus as an index of class consciousness, this criterion at best distorts by over-emphasising the peripheral and at worst is totally irrelevant.

There are also serious objections to taking affiliation to the Labour Party as a measure of unionateness and hence class consciousness. Certainly the decision of the trade union movement to participate in the formation of the Labour Party had little to do with any commitment by unions to the creation of a socialist society. They were motivated not so much by a class conscious ideology as by their interest, especially after the Taff Vale Judgement in 1901, in legislation that would give them freedom and support in their industrial activities. . . .

There have been periods in which some of the most militant and politically conscious trade unionists have eschewed parliamentary political action altogether. In Britain, as in France, the syndicalists stressed the self-sufficiency of the trade union movement. . . . Since there are many prescriptions for union political action besides the social-democratic one proposed by Blackburn and Lockwood, it is perhaps not surprising that the relationship which exists in Britain between the trade union movement and the Labour Party has no easy parallel in many other countries. . . .

Thus to state that unionateness increases with affiliation to the Labour Party is to close off the whole question of the relationship between political and industrial activity, to assume the primacy of the social-democratic prescription for union politics, to rely almost entirely upon the British political tradition, to grant to the Labour Party an overriding dedication to the interests of organized labour that is hard to maintain before the Labour Government of 1964 and even more difficult to argue after that date, and to fail to bring out that unions face a choice of mode of political activity, a choice constantly to be re-examined in the light of changing circumstances.

The above review of the seven criteria of unionateness suggests that they do not provide an accurate or unambiguous measure of class consciousness. But even granted for the moment that they do, it is still debatable whose class consciousness they measure. To assume that they measure the class consciousness of members is to ignore the political process within unions and to overstate the degree to which the attitudes of the leadership can be used as a guide to those of the membership. Although membership attitudes are no doubt a constraint on leadership behaviour, there is abundant evidence to indicate the lack of congruence between the two. Lockwood documented this for the National Union of Clerks: 'The low degree of political interest displayed by the mass of the membership contrasts strangely with the outlook of the leadership of the NUC which was extremely active in this sphere during the thirties'.[6] Nor is this merely a phenomenon of the inter-war period; it reappeared in the context of unilateralism in 1959.

A national survey found only 16 per cent of trade unionists in favour of a unilateral surrender of nuclear weapons, but at the Labour Party Conference this was backed by a majority of the delegates representing the trade unions. Other examples could be given, but this is probably not necessary. For sociologists are increasingly becoming aware that membership goals differ from leadership goals, and it is the latter which tend to be taken as organizational goals. Hence any class consciousness reflected by a union's character is more likely to be attributable to its leadership than to its general membership.

NOTES AND REFERENCES

1. David Lockwood, *The Blackcoated Worker*, p. 137.
2. R. M. Blackburn, *Union Character and Social Class* (Batsford, 1967) pp. 14, 9.
3. Blackburn advanced his argument prior to the passage of the Industrial Relations Act 1971 which has changed the nature of union registration. Hence his argument is assessed in relation to the situation prevailing prior to the passage of the Act. Paradoxically, it might now be argued that a class conscious union would refuse to register since this has been the central plank in the Trades Union Congress' strategy in opposing the Industrial Relations Act. But it would be unwise to draw even this conclusion without first examining in detail the extent to which such organizational needs as growth or legal protection influence a union's decision to register.
4. G. Routh, 'White-Collar Unions in the United Kingdom', in A. Sturmthal (ed.), *White-Collar Trade Unions* (University of Illinois Press, 1966) pp. 165–204.
5. John R. Commons *et al.*, *History of Labor in the United States* (New York, Macmillan, 1918) pp. 14–15.
6. *The Blackcoated Worker*, p. 167.

A Critique of the 'Industrial Relations' Approach

Rosemary Crompton

'Approaches to the Study of White-Collar Unionism', *Sociology*, vol. X (September 1976) pp. 411–13, 416–26

The work of Lockwood, Blackburn and Prandy, which I have characterized as being in the 'sociological' tradition, has attracted considerable criticism from 'industrial relations' theorizing – in particular, in the writings of Bain and his colleagues. With considerable over-simplification, the criticisms of Bain *et al.* can be described as resting on the fact that the relationship which the sociological approach attempts to establish between social class and trade union membership and behaviour simply does not hold. Firstly, they argue, no consistent link can be demonstrated between social stratification and union membership. Some occupations high in the stratification hierarchy are extremely well organized, conversely, some very low status occupations are hardly organized at all. Secondly, 'the character of a union, at least as developed by Lockwood and Blackburn, is an inaccurate, ambiguous, and inoperable index of any feeling of class or trade union consciousness which its members may possess' (p. 107).[1] That is, 'unionate' behaviour (in Blackburn's terms) is characteristic of many professional or white-collar associations and, Bain *et al.* argue, is better interpreted as a pragmatic reaction to specific circumstances rather than being an expression of any form of class-consciousness. The difference between various representative organizations, they argue, 'are of degree . . . rather than of kind' (p. 107). Finally, they argue:

> far from distinct class or status positions generating simple, coherent, and distinct images of social reality which then shape and sustain markedly different patterns of union growth and character, perceptions of reality (are) demonstrated to be varied, overlapping, and capable of change over time. No easy equation could then reasonably be expected between social position, social imagery, and trade unionism (p. 154).

In fact, the industrial relations critique which I have summarized above hardly does justice to the sociological tradition of analysis, to say the least. For example, Bain *et al.*'s attempted demolition of the link between social stratification and trade unionism interprets 'social stratification' in what can be described as 'status' terms. That is, they emphasize what is essentially an occupation's position in a status hierarchy, and its relationship to patterns of union growth. However, Lockwood, in particular, was careful to emphasize that it was variations in the *work* situation which affected patterns of union membership, rather than the position of an occupation in an overall status hierarchy. Secondly, the critical methodology adopted by Bain *et al.* systematically considers each variable in isolation from other factors – thus failing to grasp, for example, Blackburn's point that character and completeness (or density) are interrelated and cannot, therefore, be meaningfully considered separately from one another. Thirdly, the statement that 'no *easy* equation could then reasonably be expected between social position, social imagery, and trade unionism' (my emphasis), hardly constitutes a criticism of the sociological approach, as I would have thought that analysis and empirical work within the sociological tradition serves to demonstrate just this.

Although I would broadly reject the industrial relations critique of the sociological approach, their criticisms do reveal some serious weaknesses. In particular, the countless examples provided by Bain *et al.* in order to contradict or destroy the relationship between class position and trade union membership or character, which the sociological approach seeks to establish, cannot simply be dismissed as the exceptions which prove the rule. For the pattern of white-collar union membership and activity does show many inexplicable variations which are sociologically embarrassing if we are seeking to establish a more or less coherent relationship between union membership, character, and social class. I believe that a relationship between white-collar union growth and behaviour and class situation can not only be demonstrated, but would go even further to say that I think that an understanding of the white-collar class situation is *essential* to any interpretation of white-collar union behaviour. However, I do not think that this has been adequately demonstrated at the theoretical level by the current sociological approach. In particular, I think that an accurate conceptualization of the relationship between social class and white-collar trade unions can only be achieved by a radical departure from Lockwood's original neo-Weberian framework of class analysis. In the second part of this paper, I will attempt to demonstrate that an analysis of the white-collar class situation derived from Marxist principles is a more effective strategy from which to begin to understand the nature of white-collar unionism.

Lockwood's account of the class situation of white-collar workers is explained by reference to two structures: the structure of market relationships, and the structure of authority relationships within the workplace. The account I will begin to develop here, on the other hand, directs attention in the first place to a structure which. . . . logically precedes both market relationships and work relationships – the capitalist mode of production and its associated relations of production. . . .

In relating the growth of the propertyless middle class to the development of capitalism in the West I have stressed, firstly, the increasing dominance of the capitalist mode of production, secondly, the constant pressures towards accumulation and thus to increase the mass of surplus value, and thirdly, the need to administer and co-ordinate both the increasingly complex production process and the rising mass of surplus value which results. . . . In the following discussion, I will be above all concerned to emphasize the *structural* ambiguity of the middle class situation (or situations). My discussion of these structural ambiguities makes three points:

(i) the fact that the capitalist function is increasingly performed by agents who do not own or control the means of production.

(ii) (which is related to (i) above) the fact that 'white-collar' labour is predominantly employed in sectors of the economy which are peculiar to the capitalist mode of production, and

(iii) the fact that some white-collar workers perform *both* capital *and* labour functions.

I have already referred to the fact that, as capitalism has developed in the West, the capitalist function has been differentiated and diffused. Increasingly, it is carried out by agents who do not legally own the means of production. In this relatively simple point lies a major source of class ambiguity as far as many white-collar workers are concerned. Although white-collar workers share with manual workers a common situation of 'propertylessness', their role within the capitalist mode of production – i.e. as agents of the capitalist function – means that their *class* situation cannot be unambiguously identified with *either* the proletariat (or labour function) *or* the bourgeoisie. However, a minority of the middle class (e.g. top management), even though they may not *legally* own the means of production, have *real* control over the material means of production, labour, and surplus value. Such control can be described as 'real' as opposed to 'legal' ownership, and renders their class situation unambiguous. The majority of white-collar workers, however, cannot be said to have even real ownership.

In my earlier discussion of the capitalist mode of production and its development, I have argued that continuous pressures towards accumulation – increasing the rate of accumulation of surplus value – are an integral feature of the capitalist mode of production. Partly because of these ever-present pressures towards accumulation and profit-making the capitalist mode of production has become increasingly complex and sophisticated. Specialized sectors have been developed which are essential to the *capitalist* mode of production. Here I would mention such activities as accounting, advertising, some state services, finance (e.g. banking in all its aspects, insurance), etc. All of these activities facilitate and enhance the rate of extraction of surplus value. Such activities perform a vital role in the capitalist mode of production as a whole. Although, however, they do perform this vital role, they do not themselves create new values, but acquire a *share* of surplus value actually produced elsewhere. They would, clearly, be superfluous given a hypothetical non-capitalist mode of production, as a large part of the reason for their existence – the frantic drive towards accumulation – would itself be absent. Although employees within these sectors certainly perform *useful* labour within the capitalist mode of production, as they do not create surplus value they cannot be said to be exploited in the manner of the proletariat. The general category of 'unproductive' labour includes, as well as workers in those sectors which I have just identified as peculiar to the capitalist mode of production, employees in fields such as medicine, education, and administration. In a capitalist society, such workers are maintained out of revenue, and do not themselves create surplus value. However, unlike the sectors I have identified as being peculiar to the capitalist mode of production, medicine, education, etc., and the associated workforce, would clearly be needed in any complex society, including a hypothetical socialist society.

As 'unproductive' labour as a whole is maintained out of surplus value, some writers have argued, firstly, that 'unproductive' labour (within the Marxist framework of analysis) exploits productive labour, and secondly, that this fact (i.e. unproductive = exploiter) throws grave doubts on Marx's account of a future socialist society. They argue that as unproductive (as defined by Marx) tasks would be a feature of *any* complex society, and the unproductive exploit the productive, how is exploitation to be avoided in a socialist society? Firstly, I would disagree that 'unproductive' can be equated with 'exploiter', a point to which I will shortly return. In general, however, I would argue that it is theoretically possible to draw a broad distinction between two main categories of unproductive labour – that which I have argued is peculiar to the capitalist mode of production, and that which would be necessary in *any* complex society. I am well aware that such distinctions could justifiably be said to verge on speculation – as all complex industrial societies to date have been developed by and within the capitalist mode of production – but it is fairly obvious to see that while a future socialist society would still need, for example, hospitals, it could well do without the money market.

My main concern in this section is with unproductive labour in the first broad category I have identified – i.e. in those sectors peculiar to the capitalist mode of production. As for the probable persistence of the second category in a hypothetical socialist society, this fact does not present insuperable problems for Marxist analysis. In the absence of capitalist relations of production, the process of exploitation through the expropriation of surplus value would not occur, therefore the productive/ unproductive distinction would not be valid in any case. The class position of 'unproductive' labour only assumes its present form given capitalist relations of production.[2] In the case of the first broad category of unproductive workers, I would suggest that their already ambiguous class situation is heightened by the fact that they *are* employed in sectors specifically developed by the capitalist mode of production.

However, to return to a point raised earlier, does it follow that they are therefore automatically members of the 'exploiting' class? I would reject such an approach as too crude; maintenance out of surplus value is a necessary, but not a sufficient, definition of an 'exploiting' class.

The greater part of this 'unproductive' labour has no more say in the allocation of the surplus value *acquired* through their labour (or their own share in it) than have productive workers over the value *created* through their labour. In addition – and this is the most important respect in which their class situation parallels that of productive workers – as employees, they have no discretion over the use to which their labour is applied. The fact that their labour is used to acquire surplus value, rather than *create* surplus value, has little impact on the organization of labour within the workplace. Although, therefore, unproductive workers cannot be said to be exploited through the extraction of surplus value, I would argue that they are oppressed through the appropriation of their labour.

In many respects, therefore, the class situation of these unproductive workers parallels the class situation of productive workers. A major source of class ambiguity, however, lies in the fact that these workers, besides being agents of the capitalist function are employed in activities which are peculiar to the capitalist mode of production. Within this general category of unproductive labour, not all will be similarly oppressed. Agents who oversee the oppression of others, and/or have overall control of the acquisition of surplus value, must be described as oppressors rather than oppressed.

The third source of class ambiguity to which I would draw attention again refers to differentiation within the capitalist mode of production. The increasing complexity of the labour process means that it is misleading to view production as being carried out by an individual worker, or even an assemblage of individual workers. The work process is co-operative, different workers or groups of workers collect together raw materials, engage in the many stages of production itself, co-ordinate production, test for quality, and so on. These many differentiated activities involve both manual and non-manual work. In Marxist terminology, this real as opposed to formal subordination of labour to capital means that the labour process is now carried out by the 'collective labourer'. This highly differentiated labour process has been developed by and within the capitalist mode of production, but it is still possible to argue that some elements within this process are peculiar to capitalist production, others would be common to *any* complex production process.

If we abstractly consider the production process independently of the capitalist mode of production, we can see that, beyond a very rudimentary level of complexity, *any* production process will have to be co-ordinated or supervised, and techniques of working will be developed, and will continue to be developed. These two elements – co-ordination and technique – may, independently of the capitalist mode of production, be properly ascribed to the labour function. However, in the case of the development of the capitalist mode of production, both co-ordination and technique have been developed by and within the capitalist function. Because both elements have been developed within the capitalist function, it is difficult, if not impossible, to gauge the extent to which either is strictly (a) 'necessary to any complex production process', or (b) 'necessary in order to ensure the extraction of relative surplus value' – i.e. specific to the capitalist mode of production. For example, to the extent that inspection and testing are necessary in order to ensure the delivery of a safe and efficient product to the consumer, then quality control is clearly necessary in the first sense, and can be considered a part of the labour process. On the other hand, to the extent that quality control is part of a battery of devices through which the workforce is controlled and disciplined, it is necessary in the second sense, and can be seen as part of the capitalist function. Perhaps a less ambiguous example of a work role which incorporates elements of both capital and labour functions is that of the foreman, who both co-ordinates the supply of raw materials and tools (necessary work as defined in (a) above), and acts as the front line of managerial authority (necessary work as defined in (b) above). Therefore, to the extent that white-collar workers perform necessary work (in the first sense) in respect of either co-ordination or technique, then they can be considered as fulfilling a part of the function of the collective worker, and are exploited in the same manner as other workers (or agents of the labour function). To the extent to which their work is necessary only to maintain or increase the rate of extraction of surplus value, then they act as agents of the capitalist function. In many cases, and to varying degrees (although the *precise* degree of variation is impossible to indentify), white-collar workers (particularly in industry) carry out the functions of both labour *and* capital.

This discussion of ambiguities in the middle situation is not comprehensive – I have not, for example, looked in any detail at state employees, or professional workers. I have, however, sought to establish some general points. Firstly, with Lockwood, I would argue that the simple fact of 'propertylessness' is not a sufficient basis on which to discriminate between class groupings. On the other hand, unlike Lockwood, I do not think that the fact that the majority of white-collar workers *are* truly propertyless is irrelevant to an understanding of their class situation. Secondly, like Lockwood, the approach I have been developing has revealed considerable variations in class situation within the white-collar sector as a whole – in fact, perhaps it is misleading to refer to the class situation of white-collar workers. However, these differences are not of the order of 'more like' or 'less like' a manual worker stereotype (which, with some oversimplification, can describe Lockwood's approach), but are structural differences reflecting different relationships vis à vis the capitalist mode of production. Thirdly, although '*status* ambiguity' has long been utilized in order to explain white-collar attitudes and behaviour, I would emphasize that the white-collar *class* situation is structurally ambiguous, and these attitudes and behaviour are not simply the result of 'cultural lag'.[3]

Finally, I will briefly indicate how I believe this analysis of the class situation of the propertyless middle class provides a useful starting point for the understanding of patterns of collective representation amongst this loosely defined grouping.

Market situation, work situation, and status situation (the crucial elements of 'class situation' identified by the sociological approach) are important factors in the explanation of white-collar union growth and behaviour. A recent empirical study of technicians can be utilized to illustrate this. The market situation of technicians was declining relative to that of manual workers as the manual workers benefited from the combined effect of organized union pressure and productivity deals. Hopes of upward occupational mobility (another aspect of the market situation) were being constantly frustrated by ever increasing educational requirements and the development of a 'graduate barrier'. The security so long enjoyed by 'white-collar' employees was threatened by the mergers and rationalization current in the 1960s, which, for the first time, substantially affected non-manual as well as manual employees. Within the work situation, the technicians complained about their inability to communicate with management, who 'had increasingly come to see technicians as part of the new mass labour force, as a homogenous group, little different from the manual workers on the pay-roll'.[4]

These changes in the market and work situation of technicians, combined with their resentment at their decline in status as compared to manual workers, led the authors to suggest that the increase in unionization amongst technicians will continue, combined with '(al)though reluctantly, militant behaviour'.[5] In short, within the framework provided by the sociological approach, as the class situation of technicians has changed, so has their attitude to and participation in collective representation.

As far as it goes, this explanation of changes in both class situation and collective representation amongst technicians is satisfactory. However, this example, I would argue, raises more fundamental questions which cannot be adequately treated within either the sociological or the industrial relations framework. In the first place, why did the market and work situations of technicians change so rapidly over such a relatively short period of time? The proletarianization of the technician can, I believe, only be satisfactorily explained by explicit reference to the development of the capitalist mode of production.

As I have argued in an earlier section of this paper, the development of monopoly capitalism has been accompanied by an ever increasing rise in wage labour employed *within* the capitalist function. An increasing proportion of surplus value, therefore, must be assigned to the maintenance of these workers. Nicolaus may have characterized this group as the 'surplus class',[6] but this ignores the fact that the increase in the number of these workers diverts resources away from the process of capital accumulation. As labour costs within the capitalist function become an increasing proportion of total costs, efforts to utilize this labour more effectively will increase. Technicians, as I have argued earlier, perform the functions of both capital and labour. As described by Roberts, Loveridge, and Gennard, the effect of the rationalization of the technical workforce has been to split the technicians' occupational role between, on the one hand, the graduate manager, and on the other, manual workers, whilst downgrading the remaining elements of the technicians' work role. In other words, the extent to which technicians participate in the labour function has been made more explicit, and their participation in the capitalist function drastically reduced.

As the *class* situation of technicians has become less ambiguous – as they have been truly 'proletarianized' – so have their market and work situations changed in the manner described. It is not surprising, therefore, that technicians have shown 'ambivalence or outright antipathy towards company-oriented schemes of consultation and company-encouraged staff associations'[7] and have chosen instead to join trade unions.

The example of the technicians raises a further question – is their experience likely to be repeated or paralleled amongst other occupational groups making up the propertyless middle class, such as bank and insurance workers, the lower professions, etc? The approach to the analysis of the white-collar class situation which I have developed in this paper would suggest not. The need to rationalize labour within the capitalist function has led to the introduction of computers, job evaluation, etc., work is increasingly routinized, subject to division of labour, and increasingly impersonal controls. These changes have certainly brought with them an increased predisposition towards collective action, but also, considerable conflict over the form this collective action should take – most notably as between trade unions and staff associations. I would suggest that this is because, despite rationalization within many white-collar occupations, their class situation still remains ambiguous – and is likely to so continue. That some white-collar workers should see their interests as being best fulfilled by co-operation with management (or the capitalist function) – for example, in staff associations – and others in the same occupation see their collective interests as being best served by identification with the labour function – in trade unions – is, I would argue, perfectly compatible with their ambiguous class situation. The protagonists of neither view can be said to be 'falsely' conscious of their class interests. The varying and often contradictory nature of much white-collar collective representation, I would argue, is a reflection of the ambiguous class situation (or situations) within the propertyless middle class. It is not surprising, therefore, that *alternative* strategies of representation should be developed.

The concept of 'unionateness' has recently been extended and successfully applied empirically. Its usefulness has clearly been demonstrated, and it has not been my object in this paper to deny this. On the other hand, as a concept it is continuum based – organizations are 'more' or 'less' like manual unions. Whilst it is true that many white-collar organizations resemble manual unions to a greater or lesser degree, a preoccupation with 'unionateness' makes it difficult to conceptualize different modes of representation as *alternative* strategies. In short, the concept, although valid, may actually impose limitations on the successful analysis of white-collar unionism if it is used in isolation. For example, implicit in the sociological approach is the assumption that unions will seek to represent employees rather than employers – an element of conflict of interests, however subdued, is present. Although *some* staff associations may recognize the conflict of interest between employer and employee, there is no doubt that many, possibly the majority, explicitly reject this oppositional stance and perceive a basic harmony of interest between the two groups. In 1972, six out of the seven largest staff associations in the insurance industry embraced this 'unitary' perspective in their constitutions – along the lines of the Sun Life Staff Association's constitutional clause which included amongst the association's objectives 'to maintain a close liaison between the Companies and Staff for the purpose of increasing mutual goodwill and for furthering the interests and prosperity of the Companies and the Staff'. Similarly, the Confederation of Employee Organizations (of which many of the insurance staff associations are now members), states as one of its objects: 'To assist employee organizations to develop and maintain positive relations between employees and employers on the basis of their shared interest in promoting the success of their undertakings.'

Such organizations are not simply 'less unionate' than manual trade unions – or white-collar trade unions for that matter. They represent, and are certainly perceived by their members as, a very different approach to collective bargaining than that of trade unions. I would suggest that future empirical research would yield a better understanding of the nature of white-collar collective representation as a whole if these fundamental differences in approach were systematically incorporated into the framework of analysis.

The sociological, and, to an even greater extent, the industrial relations approaches have attempted to construct models of union growth and behaviour which are universally applicable. I would suggest, on the other hand, that the heterogeneous and ambiguous nature of the white-collar class situation is reflected in heterogeneous and often contradictory forms of collective representation. The construction of a universal theory may be academically satisfying, but is prone to the danger of being too general to be particularly helpful, or even positively misleading. I have tried to argue in this paper the need to develop an approach to white-collar unionism which recognizes that there *will* be qualitative differences in both strategy and behaviour between middle class collective organizations, rather than one which seeks to establish similarities between them.

The Development of White-Collar Unionism

NOTES AND REFERENCES

1. Bain *et al.*, *Social Stratification and Trade Unionism*.
2. This discussion raises the whole question of state employees, but space unfortunately inhibits a systematic consideration. Briefly, I would argue that the development of the state, and its increasing involvement in the processes of production and distribution, is a characteristic feature of the development of monopoly capitalism, not least because of the need to control the inherently anarchic tendencies of the capitalist mode of production if the system as a whole is to be preserved. The extent and manner of involvement of the state in the capitalist mode of production differs considerably from that of the private sector (and also between different countries). For example, the state in western monopoly capitalism plays only a minor role in the direct extraction of surplus value (through nationalized industry), and is more concerned with the distribution of surplus value which is acquired through different forms of taxation and levies. However, because the state *is* an integral part of monopoly capitalism, the class situation of state employees parallels that of employees in the private sector – state employees are variously productive, unproductive, exploited (and exploiter), oppressed (and oppressor), etc. – a similar mode of analysis of the class situation of state employees can be applied as above.
3. See D. Lockwood, *The Blackcoated Worker*, p. 125–32.
4. B. C. Roberts, R. Loveridge, J. Gennard, *Reluctant Militants*, p. 321.
5. Ibid., p. 318.
6. M. Nicolaus, 'Proletariat and Middle-Class in Marx', in J. Weinstein and D. Eakins (eds), *For a New America* (Random House, 1970), p. 272f.
7. Roberts *et al.*, *Reluctant Militants*, p. 66.

11 White-Collar Workers and Attitudes to Trade Unions

An International View

Jean-Daniel Reynaud

'Stratification and Industrial Relations: Reflections on the Trade Unionism of Blackcoated, Technical and Managerial Employees', in M. Mann (ed.), *Social Stratification and Industrial Relations* (London: Social Science Research Council, 1969) pp. 148–60

The social groups that are brought together under the label of . . . white-collar workers, certainly possess specific characteristics which decisively distinguish them from manual workers. But are the implications that can be drawn for the nature of their industrial organisation and action always equally obvious?

Let us briefly summarise the characteristics in question. . . . White-collar are differentiated from blue-collar workers by the nature of their work (mental rather than manual) by their conditions of service (salaries as against payment by the hour, security of employment) and by the social welfare advantages that they enjoy (holidays, retirement benefits, etc.). These distinguishing features are not so clear as has sometimes been made out. . . . Nevertheless, at a more fundamental level, the fact remains that white-collar employees are closer to having a management position; if only because they became differentiated from the management group at a relatively late stage, because, on the whole, they still have better promotion chances than manual workers, because they work to a greater extent with symbols and for the most part are engaged in the task of communication; in

247

brief, because their role in the organisation of production and their social status are different. . . .

We should add that the white-collar group is fundamentally heterogeneous and that its internal differences are tending to become more rather than less accentuated. The 'classic' types of blackcoated worker (salesmen or clerks) technicians and *cadres* can be contrasted in many respects: the spread of education is probably undermining the market position of the first mentioned group but not, for the present at least, that of the latter two. Promotion chances are very unequally distributed. The trend of salaries favours the higher grades (and this is certainly true even when taxation is taken into account). More importantly, a substantial part of the rank-and-file is made up of women whose careers are, on the whole, shorter-lived and do not take them so far up the hierarchy; men are still in a much more favourable position . . . . In brief, the situation of the blackcoated workers is perhaps becoming more comparable with that of manual workers, but the same cannot be said of technicians or *cadres*. . . .

Because of their greater promotion chances and because, in the main, they have a better market situation, white-collar workers, it is held, are more favourable to individual competition than to the making of collective demands, and it is this that turns them away from trade unionism. This is certainly true – but with some awkward exceptions. A recent study – carried out among *cadres* in the French aircraft industry – shows that while promotion and salaries remained, in their view, matters for individual bargaining, this was not the case with opportunities for further education and training which they regarded as a matter to be discussed collectively (that is, as one appropriately handled by their unions) nor with questions of security of employment, in regard to which they felt that they should act jointly with other employees. Even more remarkably, scientific research workers, a category with high promotion chances if ever there was one, are in France heavily unionised. Finally, we scarcely need reminding that large numbers of doctors, those extreme individualists, are in fact organised in unions, and that they seem to wield the weapons of collective bargaining with no little expertise.

Similarly, the argument is put forward that white-collar workers, being conscious of their superior social status and anxious to protect it, are often reluctant to join unions 'like ordinary workers' and still more to become embroiled in collective negotiations. This again is certainly true on the whole, if only because the blackcoated workers at least form a stratum with a high rate of social mobility and are thus particularly sensitive to status issues. But here once more, the exceptions are important: if one had to choose the group best illustrating social mobility in France under the Third Republic, one would probably take the primary school teachers. Yet this is also one of the groups with the strongest trade union traditions (it is still today undoubtedly the occupational group with the highest rate of unionisation). Moreover, one can confirm that awareness of status differences in no way rules out solidarity with working class groups in certain cases . . . .

Finally it is held that, as political moderates, white-collar workers, even if unionised, are often opposed to joining the labour movement on account of its association, particularly in Europe, with socialist parties. This again is true, as is shown by the way certain white-collar unions in England keep their distance from the T.U.C. or in Sweden from the L.O. But it is not true in every instance, French civil service unions have scarcely played a moderating role in the history of the French union movement. They quickly affirmed their solidarity with the unions of manual workers and have in no way been put off by the label of socialism (more so, it is true, by that of communism, although with some important exceptions). They have often provided the socialist party with its officials. . . .

Let us first enquire what needs are met by trade unionism. It is a truism to say that trade unionism enables an occupational group to defend its interests – a truism dangerous in its incompleteness. First, because there are other ways for a group to defend its interests, even those that are of a most strictly economic kind: at a time of full employment, and particularly for skilled grades, individual bargaining often produces better results. So we must ask in what cases action through trade unions becomes indispensable. But we should particularly remember that trade union action does not consist in the substitution of collective for individual bargaining. It is not in itself a form of bargaining: it simply provides rules and norms for the concluding of individual agreements for their execution. Its essential feature is . . . the establishment of some form of control over employment through which the operation of the labour market is adjusted or influenced. The need for unionisation arises, then, when it is felt necessary to substitute a normative system, at least partially, for the laws of the market. Thus, so far as white-collar workers are concerned, the question we must ask is under what circumstances such a necessity comes to be recognised. . . .

Sturmthal . . . advances the hypothesis that white-collar unionism may be linked to a disparity between the traditional status of an occupational category and the economic function which it currently performs: either the former ranks higher than the latter and has to be maintained; or the reverse situation holds and is seen as calling for redress.[1]

To generalise is, we believe, legitimate: unionisation and the industrial relations resulting from it are doubtless correlated with specific economic problems. But it is not clear that they stem directly from these problems. What is much more likely is that they result from the inadequacy of some earlier established normative system, of an implicit or explicit kind, which was created unilaterally or rested upon consensus. The probability of unionisation occurring cannot therefore be directly calculated from an analysis of the economic opportunities of an occupational group. In order to determine this probability, one must take into account the normative system that is in operation. There can indeed be little doubt that what A. Sturmthal refers to as 'status' is a collection of rights, advantages and privileges, linked to prestige and deriving from established norms, rather than a strictly economic evaluation. This intervening variable ought to explain some at least of the apparently exceptional cases . . . .

The observer of the French scene is often struck by the amount of union activity among technicians. One may attempt to explain this as follows: the technicians constitute a young and vigorous group whose occupational aspirations are reinforced by their training, who are today often paid at a level incommensurate with their qualifications, and whose careers very quickly come up against a ceiling. But, however plausible these reasons, they are not entirely convincing: in the majority of factories, the same disparity between qualifications and pay is found among office workers; the career structure of draughtsmen, a group that employers often regard as particularly militant, cannot be overlooked; possibilities of moving up into higher-level grades certainly exist (and, at all events, are very likely to be better than those open to the office staff). To bring out the full significance of the characteristics in question, one must, in our view, add one more: technicians as a category have only recently been recognised, and this was brought about in part as a result of their becoming differentiated from another longer-established category, that of the blackcoated workers. The rapid growth in unionisation could then be explained to some extent in terms of their need to free themselves form the normative system governing the situation of the blackcoated workers, and to establish a status of their own. And it is the uncertainty of this transitional phase that accounts for the aggressiveness which the technicians show in union affairs. . . .

The case of the *cadres* is a particularly interesting one. It is often found surprising, not only by foreign observers but equally by employers themselves, that the degree of unionisation among French managerial officials is not inconsiderable . . . . The part played by the *cadres* in some of the strike movements of the last ten years has often been emphasised, to the extent that it has become commonplace to speak of the unrest or *malaise* of the *cadres*.

The explanation of this state of affairs in terms of the economic prospects of this category seems to be particularly unsatisfactory. Their salaries have for the most part increased at an above average rate and comparisons show that the French *cadres* are in no way at a disadvantage in relation to their colleagues in Italy, Germany or the Netherlands. In May 1968, a small minority of them was even to be found protesting against the systematically hierarchical pattern of the salary increases awarded under the Grenelle agreements. Employment is, without question, their main pre-occupation (although the available figures give only very limited justification for such anxiety). But there is little doubt that even if the tendency towards concentration and modernisation threatens a number of established positions, the market situation of the *cadres* remains a very favourable one.

The enquiry of Marc Maurice[2] . . . confirms that although questions of salary hold an honoured place among the recognised interests of *cadres* in the aircraft industry, such questions in fact rank only second in importance. The leading claim of these employees is for increased participation in decision-making – within the enterprise but also in national economic affairs; and their third demand is for the protection of their status in the sense particularly of 'a better distribution of responsibility and a better utilisation of their skills'. It is therefore the definition of their role that is their primary concern. These reasons enable one to understand better the frequently confused and sometimes vehement literature in which their claims are expressed (and to which the revolution of May 1968 has added dramatic, although certainly minority, statements of faith). . . .

Here again, what creates group solidarity, at least among an active minority, and what drives on this minority to seek, through unionism and professional organisation, a new form of normative regulation of their working lives is not a feeling of being unfairly rewarded: it is rather the keen and sometimes passionate awareness of these men that they are the prisoners of a system established long ago which is appropriate neither to their level of ability, nor to the norms in which they share.

To sum up the argument briefly: what encourages unionisation is not only (and in some cases not primarily) the net balance of economic life-chances – what in Max Weber's sense of the term constitutes 'class' – it is also (and sometimes predominantly) the undermining of an existing normative system and the feeling that it is essential to replace it with another.

But the above statement provides only one part of the explanation. There can be other normative systems than that created by trade unionism through organised industrial relations. What is it in particular that leads to this course of action?

A preliminary observation is necessary: professional associations and trade unions have often been taken as representing contrasting forms of organisation and action. The former, it is held, protects, in the first instance, the status of the profession, it is prepared to allow a greater amount of individual competition, and does not favour strikes or collective bargaining. The latter is concerned first and foremost with economic interests, is far more egalitarian and is founded, as a matter of principle, upon collective action. The question would seem to call for a detailed analysis. But it may suffice here to say that, in our view, the contrast rests upon differences in social prestige of a traditional kind rather than on differences of a fundamental nature. . . . In brief, professionalisation, over and above its marked affinities with traditional craft unionism, seems to us to represent one possible orientation of union action rather than an alternative possibility to such action.

In our view, the choice that exists, when a new normative system has to be worked out, is not between professional organisation and union organisation but between the implicit form of such

a system (in which decisions are for the most part made unilaterally because only the employer has a decision-making
apparatus) and the explicit form which depends for the most part
upon the fact that the employer has a union counterpart. The
question then is: in what ways is greater explicitness brought
about?

Certainly, it could be through the employer's resistance;
equally, through the scale of the economic unit. But here again our
answers must perhaps be qualified if our previous analysis holds
good.

An example will help us to be more specific. It has been pointed
out that where no legal prohibitions exist, civil servants have a
greater propensity to join unions than other white-collar workers.
In attempting to account for this fact, A. Sturmthal suggests three
causes: the size of employment units in the public sector is
generally large; the employment relationship is 'one-sided';
unions are able to act more effectively against the government (via
voting power and appeal to public opinion) than against private
employers. Although these explanations are valid in themselves,
we feel that they could be developed: size of establishment is a
factor in unionisation: one certain reason for this is that it is easier
within a large unit to organise employees and to guarantee them
union protection; but there is also another, namely, that in a large-
scale establishment the administration of personnel is likely to
become subject to a set of rules because, in this case, the gap
between classic market principles and the day to day running of
the organisation is so much greater. In other words, because the
very number of problems to be dealt with promotes the development of a normative system, on which trade unionism can readily
take hold. The distinctive character of administrative organisations becomes, then, quite clear: since they do not assess their
results in terms of profitability, they elaborate rules of a more
strictly juridical kind; since they offer more stable employment
(and usually with guarantees of security) they can much more
confidently build up a community which has to be administered
with long-term considerations in mind. The particular power of
the employer stems therefore from the relative permanency of his
decisions, from the fact that these change in the way that a body of
case law changes and not as a result of the organisation of the
enterprise adapting itself to market fluctuations. Consequently,
union methods are not only more effective: they are also more

appropriate to the situation, being directed at an employer whose policy rests upon the same logic. . . .

In conclusion, we may try to answer more precisely the question with which we started. If we can agree to define industrial relations as the working out, by confronting forces, of a normative system which regulates the association between employer and employees, then it is apparent that the study of social stratification can be enlightening in three ways: the first, and best explored, starts with social classes, in Max Weber's sense, and through comparing the economic life-chances that they possess (or, rather, by which they are defined) specifies the actual nature of employment relationships, that is to say, both the advantages and disadvantages that they carry for those involved. From this point of view, the contrast between manual workers and white-collar workers, or at least the better-off among the latter . . . remains important. The second way concerns status groups . . . : the undermining or the redefinition of the status of a group appears to be particularly conducive to awareness of the need for a normative system. From this point of view, there are no systematic differences between manual and white-collar employees; what is important is not the nature of work, nor even chances in the labour market, but ongoing processes of change, whether technological, or organisational in origin or stemming more indirectly from some social movement. Finally, the third way is concerned with power relationships; the process whereby coalitions are formed is not, of course, uninfluenced by the existence of classes and status groups, but it has its own dynamic and the coalitions that are created often have their particular effect on the organisation of the social groups involved and modify their objectives.

NOTES AND REFERENCES

1. A Sturmthal, 'White-Collar Unions: A Comparative Essay', *White-Collar Trade Unions* (University of Illinois Press, 1966) pp. 365–98.
2. M. Maurice, C. Monteil, R. Guillon and J. Gaulon, *Les Cadres et l'Entreprise* (Institut des Sciences Sociales des Travail, 1967).

Instrumental Collectivism and Occupational Sectionalism

D. E. Mercer and D. T. Weir

'Attitudes to Work and Trade Unionism Among White-Collar Workers', *Industrial Relations Journal*, vol. III (Summer 1972) pp. 49–60

The material used in this paper was collected during a study of white-collar workers carried out between 1964 and 1967. This project was designed with a view to providing empirical information 'across the board' about this group of occupations, which had hitherto been subjected to little empirical investigation in Great Britain. . . .

Recently some writers have argued that ongoing trends in the industrial system are producing a situation where the conditions under which manual work and clerical work are done are becoming increasingly alike. This, it is held, and related developments in the sphere of family and community relationships, are likely to result in an increased similarity in the behaviour of members of both groups. Thus, manual workers with higher wages than formerly, better education, more security and in some cases pleasanter physical conditions of work, can adopt a style of life formerly associated with the middle class only, and may also modify their social attitudes and their image of themselves. This process is commonly referred to as 'embourgeoisement'. At the same time, clerical workers, unable to maintain their higher level of earnings and security, and seeing their work become increasingly routinized and lacking in challenge, begin to shift their reference group towards that of the body of wage workers, rather than looking to the managers, and modify their style of life accordingly; they become 'proletarianized'. By either of these processes, or some combination of the two, a point may be reached when it will no longer be possible to distinguish a 'working', and a 'middle' class; convergence will have occurred to the point of fusion. . . .

The white collar workers from which our sample was selected conformed to the following specifications:

(i) They were employed in organizations employing over 500 total personnel in the Hull area.
(ii) Their work was undertaken inside, in offices, and would normally be performed in street clothes.
(iii) Their work did not normally involve producing or working on tangible goods, with the exception of handling paperwork.
(iv) They were in intermediate positions in the authority structure of their organizations. . . .

The occupational groups who were thus chiefly involved in the survey were clerks, local government officials, technicians,[1] and draughtsmen. . . .

Historically trade union membership has not been very widespread among white-collar workers. The restricted interaction between members of large working groups of office workers inhibited the formation of a collective consciousness. Moreover, the kind of relationship which existed between the clerical employee and his employer, reinforced by the ethic of privatization (ie 'keeping oneself to oneself' which obtained outside the work situation, militated against the use of bargaining methods by the clerk in order to improve his conditions of work. Such methods it is argued, were not seen as appropriate for workers of white-collar status. Enjoying the advantages of higher prestige and income than their manual worker colleagues, and the security of a permanent job with the prospect of steady advancement, they did not consider it necessary to take further steps to protect their position.

Given this interpretation, it has been of particular interest to many sociologists and others to observe the developments in white-collar trade unionism which have been a feature of the last decade, and which have been generally associated with the new circumstances in which the white-collar worker finds himself. In some of the literature on white-collar workers trade unionism has indeed been treated as a sort of touchstone of proletarianization. Lockwood observed that it was crucial to his study of the class consciousness of the clerk 'to aim at an understanding of the relationship of the blackcoated worker to the trade-union movement, the main vehicle of working class consciousness'.[2] Inspired perhaps by his approach, subsequent authors have tended to over-estimate the rate of growth of white-collar unionism and to make rather sweeping assumptions about the removal of inhibiting factors. . . . We should be most cautious about the interpretation that we put on trade union membership, in particular the thesis that it has an inevitable connection with class consciousness.

In our own study we were interested in the facts of trade union membership and attendance at meetings, but we found it necessary when considering our results to make a clear distinction between these measures and the concept of union 'involvement'. Here we concentrate on the perspectives of our respondents on trade unionism as a social institution having symbolic and practical value.

In the *Affluent Worker* monographs contrasts are made between the solidaristic attitudes towards unionism, characteristic of manual workers in traditional industries in largely homogeneous working-class communities, and the instrumental and privatized attitudes of the workers studied in Luton. The latter did not display the behaviour and attitudes which might have been expected from the convergence thesis.

We anticipated that, unless the process of proletarianization was indeed far advanced our respondents' attitudes towards unions would be generally negative. In the event, however, while not especially enthusiastic, they were neither as apathetic nor as hostile as we had expected. It would perhaps be accurate to characterize them as displaying a limited instrumentalism, a 'conditional assent' not to the *values* necessarily, but to the possible *efficacy*, of trade unions in obtaining tangible benefits for their members. Hence the emphasis in Table 11.1 on the first class of reasons, on the part of non-members, for objecting to joining a trade union. Such a step was seen by respondents as being almost illogical, and certainly dysfunctional, since it would not achieve anything in the way of improved salaries or conditions, either because this was already taken care of by other processes, or because 'the firm doesn't negotiate with white collar unions'. Where there was a union recognition, however, membership was seen as rational, and also as acceptable in terms of the integrity of the employing organization.

Not surprisingly, the basic figures of union membership varied widely between our four occupational groups. There was practically 100% unionism among the public employees, 66% among the draughtsmen, and 25% among both the technicians and the clerks. With very few exceptions, chiefly among the public employees, respondents had joined the union during their current jobs or very shortly after the date at which they had entered the service of their present employer.

Rather few respondents felt that unionism represented an important aspect of their work situation, and, in fact between 20 and 30% of each occupational group actually nominated 'a strong and active union' as a factor which was 'least important' about a job. The traditional non-political aims of trade unions – the drive for improved conditions of employment and higher wages – were those most strongly emphasized. Well over a third of the clerks, public employees and draughtsmen rated either 'wages' or 'conditions' as the most important concern of a trade union. Although there was little support for the idea that unions should strive towards 'obtaining employees a *direct* share in management', there was an overall belief that unions should maintain 'effective consultation with management at all levels'. This was rated as the most important aim of a trade union by 30% of the clerks, 33% of the public employees, 47% of the technicians, and 28% of the draughtsmen (Table 11.1). A small, but noticeable minority emphasized what might be called the 'friendly society' role of trade unions in 'dealing with the problems of members': this may be related to the tendency to emphasize the personal nature of the white-collar worker's interests and the determination of some respondents to avoid being categorized and to resist being sub-

TABLE 11.1 *'Which, in your view, is (should be) the most important aim of a trade union today?' (% of respondents giving each answer)*

	Clerks	Public employees	Technicians	Draughtsmen
Dealing with the problems of members	9	7	8	13
Higher wages and better conditions	37	44	19	39
Consultation with management on all levels	30	33	47	28
Obtaining a direct share in management for workers	1	2	1	4
Stimulating political con- sciousness	1	2	1	0
Achieving 100% organization	4	4	8	7
Unity between all workers	12	4	12	7
Democracy in union procedures	2	4	3	1

merged in a collectivity.

If the chief support for trade unionism was based on the traditional role of the unions in pressing for higher wages and better conditions, the opposition among the non-unionists was also partly couched in these terms. (See Table 11.2).

TABLE 11.2 *'Could you tell us why you have serious objections to joining a trade union?' (% of non trade-union members who answered this question)*

	Clerks (n=43)	Technicians (n=60)	Draughtsmen (n=24)
Answers referring to 'inability' of trade unions to meet the requirements of white-collar workers:			
'We don't need one' 'The firm looks after us all right' }	28	23	25
'They are not recognized by the firm'	5	5	0
'They are not suitable for office staff'	2	2	0
Answers referring to the internal structure of trade unions:			
'They don't represent the individual'	14	15	13
'They are inefficient'	0	3	4
Answers referring to general antipathy towards trade unions:			
'I don't like strikes'	11	17	13
'They are involved in politics'	5	13	25
'I just don't believe in unions'	11	7	8
'They have too much power'	9	7	8
'They have changed recently'	9	3	4
'They cause trouble'	5	5	0
	99	100	100

The largest single reason for objecting to trade unionism was that 'we don't need one'. It would be tempting to argue that this represents the credulity and the snobbishness derived from the false consciousness of the white-collar worker. But it can also be said to represent a situation in which respondents perceived themselves as enjoying greater economic security and opportunities for promotion, relative to the manual worker groups who most readily came to mind as 'trade unionists'. In most organizations in which we interviewed respondents there were house organizations, staff councils, or staff associations of varying degrees of strength. But respondents generally did not explicitly refer to these bodies in explaining why they 'didn't need' a union.

More frequently they would refer either to their employer's past record of generosity and liberality, or to their relatively advantageous market position compared to other groups of workers.

A substantial group of respondents, concentrated among the draughtsmen, overtly recognized the political stance of trade unionism as a reason for their objections. In the case of the draughtsmen, it may be possible to infer that this was related to the militant political and industrial posture adopted by D.A.T.A.,[3] and that these respondents in particular were talking about their own union specifically, rather than about 'unionism' in general. However, as Table 11.3 indicates, there was also a good deal of general distrust of the notion of strike action as a union policy: to many respondents the cue 'trade unions' invoked the stereotypical reaction of 'strike', and for a further group it was enough that 'they cause trouble'. Again, some respondents harked back to a previous era when the union had been 'a good thing' and had filled a need – but one which changing economic conditions and the advent of the welfare state had now made redundant. Others saw the advance of trade unionism in a threatening light and emphasized that trade unions had now 'overstepped the mark' and 'got above themselves'.

Finally, the individualistic aspect of lower middle-class ideology and the associated dislike of collective institutions was well exemplified chiefly by the feeling that trade unions did not represent the individual. This took the form of doubts about the internal democratic processes of the union. It would, however, be misleading to regard the answers in question as being merely illustrative of wider values and attitudes like 'individualism', 'conservatism' and so on. The context in which these answers were given and the general tenor of the interviews indicated a largely rational approach on the part of respondents to their own situation. As we have already suggested, many individual white-collar workers do, in fact, see themselves as occupying a position in the firm in which some leverage can be exerted on a personal basis.

In addition to questions directly about their attitudes to trade unionism, respondents were also asked: 'Suppose your son wanted to become a full-time trade union official, as a career, what would your attitude be?'. The concern of middle-class people for the career prospects of their children and the tendency to displace their own goals on to them has been thoroughly documented in many studies. It might then be expected that any generalized white-collar aversion to trade unionism would be crystallized by this question into an attitude of disapproval of a career of this kind.

In fact, the expressed opposition was not very widespread, nor did it vary greatly among the occupational groups (see Table 11.3). The strongest disapproval was among the technicians, 26%

TABLE 11.3   *'Suppose your son wanted to become a full-time trade union official, as a career, what would your attitude be?' (% of sample giving each answer)*

	Clerks	Public employees	Technicians	Draughtsmen
I should be pleased, etc.	26	37	25	27
Modified approval	4	11	2	0
I should leave it to him, let him choose his own career	20	4	20	18
Wouldn't mind, indifferent	22	21	21	27
Partial disapproval	7	8	6	5
I should not be pleased, etc.	20	19	26	23
	99	100	100	100

of whom stated that they would 'not be pleased'. The positive answers indicated a wider divergence between the groups: while approximately a quarter of the technicians, draughtsmen and clerks in private industry said that they 'would be pleased', as many a 37% of the public employees did so. Underlying this latter response may be not merely the higher density of unionization amongst the public employees but also the established respectability of union representation in central and local government. Among our groups many answers fell somewhere between definite approval and strong disapproval, responses varying between a reluctance to express disapproval and the view that the son in question should make his own choice of career and that it should be 'left to him'.

Thus, the white-collar workers we interviewed would seem to hold an intermediate position between out-and-out antagonism to unionism and full ideological commitment to it. Their acceptance is based on instrumental considerations, similar to those which predominated when they discussed their orientation to the job itself and to their employing organization. The necessity for negotiation may thus be recognized, but this is again seen in terms which are consistent with their 'functional and consultative' view of the ordering of intra-organizational relationships. This outlook seems obviously related to the tendency for white-collar workers in some areas of industry to prefer staff associations to trade unions proper. (There were, moreover, some indications that, in the organizations we surveyed, staff associations were in the process of assuming a more definite negotiating role.)

The possibility that there will eventually be a development of full-blooded trade unionism among white-collar workers has to be considered in the light of the orientations which we have described. Our interpretation tends to support Bain's view of the importance of recognition at least in the current stage of development of white-collar unionism. Many white-collar workers, while not adverse on grounds of ideology or *general value* commitments to the idea of joining a union, appear to be waiting for the union to receive the stamp of legitimacy represented by management recognition. On the other hand, one may add, some managers[4] who expressed themselves as aware of the necessity for white-collar workers to make formal arrangments for their collective representation were obviously expecting the initiative to come from the workers themselves, in the typical manner of manual workers who have first organized themselves and then demanded recognition. . . .

The white-collar worker's involvement in trade unionism – and his reasons for non-involvement – seem to be based on instrumental as much as ideological considerations. And there is little basis in these attitudes for sentiments consistent with a *proletarian* or even a *collective* type of class consciousness. This view of unionism and its aims may be quite compatible with the values of individualism.

Several recent studies have indicated that changes in the class structure in the direction of the withering away of class differences, especially those which kept the manual and non-manual segments of the industrial work force apart, have not occurred on *either side* of this division to anything like the extent anticipated by some contemporary theories.

It seems to us that the lower level white-collar workers maintain a social perspective which, while it can no longer be equated with the stereotype of the 'middle-class bureaucrat' is far from conforming to that of the 'proletarianized worker'. There is, in this perspective, one may suggest, a general absence of irrational elements, such as might be expected on the basis of theories of either the 'status panic' or 'false consciousness' type. On the contrary it may derive from a quite realistic assessment on the part of the white-collar worker of his essentially intermediate status in the structure of production, rewards and power.

NOTES AND REFERENCES

1. This group of 'technicians' comprises laboratory assistants and technicians, in both engineering and chemical laboratories, as well as work study engineers. The range of qualifications was fairly wide, and it is clear, therefore, that in some respects this group is not very homogeneous. It is also true that some of these workers handled materials other than paper in the course of their work.
2. *The Blackcoated Worker*, p. 13.
3. The Draughtsmen and Allied Technicians' Association, as it was known at the time of the study.
4. Prior to the main body of interviewing we had less formal discussions, on an individual basis, with managers and supervisors in the survey organisations. At a later stage they also had the opportunity to give written views on matters concerning white-collar employees, partly in answer to specific questions put by us, and partly in the form of general unsolicited comments. The opinion that the existence of white-collar unions would facilitate relationships between management and white-collar employees, and would be beneficial to both, was expressed several times.

Trade Unionism Amongst the White-Collar Proletariat

K. Roberts, F. G. Cook, S. C. Clark and Elizabeth Semeonoff

The Fragmentary Class Structure, (London: Heinemann, 1977) pp. 124–34

Whilst some commentators have been arguing that advanced segments of the manual strata are prone to embourgeoisment, others have been alleging that parts of the white-collar labour force are being proletarianised and those who subscribe to this proletarianisation thesis attribute the process to a number of inter-related developments.

First, it is argued that vis-à-vis manual workers, the market advantages of some sections of the white-collar labour force have been seriously eroded. It is important not to exaggerate the extent of any such developments. Despite widespread beliefs to the contrary, the majority of white-collar employees are not lagging behind working, class affluence. Nevertheless, there are undoubtedly some non-manual workers who are low-paid by modern blue-collar standards and who, in addition to this, have seen the relative value of their 'perks' eroded. For the manual worker, job security has improved as a result of the relatively full employment maintained since 1945, while, as a consequence of mergers and office automation, the threat of white-collar redundancy has loomed. Furthermore, the welfare state and trade union pressure have made paid holidays, sick pay and pensions into universal rights rather than white-collar privileges. . . . On average white-collar workers still enjoy superior fringe benefits, but there are certainly some groups of white-collar employees whose market situations no longer clearly distinguish them from the working class.

Second, it is argued that many white-collar workers now face a promotion blockage similar to that which has always confronted blue-collar employers. In the large modern corporation there is a tendency to recruit individuals with degrees and other qualifications directly into careers leading to higher management levels, with the result that the man who starts at the bottom, in the office or laboratory, finds his prospects limited. Again, it is important not to overstate the extent of any changes that have occurred. Compared with blue-collar workers, on average white-collar employees continue to enjoy attractive career prospects and the 'ranks' are often filled by women who, up to the present, have not been expected to demand career opportunities. Nevertheless, there are male clerks and technicians in industry and elsewhere who are now finding that the bottom rung of the white-collar ladder has ceased to lead to anywhere near the top.

Third, it is argued that shop-floor conditions are gradually being extended into white-collar work situations. Open-plan offices, 'pools' of clerks, and drawing-rooms where individuals work alongside dozens of similarly placed peers are replacing the traditional smaller bureaux with their intricate hierarchies. Hence, as amongst manual workers, it is argued that white-collar employees' work situations are increasingly encouraging an awareness of the difference between 'us' and 'them'.

No one argues that the above trends have enveloped the entire middle class. On the other hand, it can be plausibly argued that some white-collar workers are being overwhelmed by these changes and this is the basis of the proletarianisation thesis. It is alleged that as a result of deteriorating market, career and work situations, former sections of the middle class can be expected to regard themselves as no different from ordinary workers and therefore to identify with the working class, and one school of thought interprets the growth and increasing militancy of white-collar trade unions in these terms. . . .

Whatever its plausibility, some researchers who have examined white-collar trade unions have expressed reservations about the proletarianisation thesis. A number of writers have argued that white-collar trade unions are different; that like the leopard, even when he joins a union the white-collar worker does not change his spots. The argument is that non-manual workers join trade unions not for 'working class' reasons but from distinctly middle class motives and, therefore, that their organisations retain a distinctly middle class character. A number of studies have suggested that joining a union does not necessarily imply that white-collar workers feel any solidarity with the working class. Indeed, actual motives often involve a desire to stay ahead of manual workers rather than an inclination to unite with the working class to fight for a common cause. . . .

In explaining why white-collar unions are different, reference is usually made to the individualism that is supposed to characterise the office, in contrast to the collectivism that is normal on the shop-floor. . . . According to this school of thought, white-collar unions tend to be narrowly oriented, conservative interest groups, unconcerned with the pursuit of general social justice, more concerned with specific occupational interests, and preferring co-operation rather than conflict with management.

The *Reluctant Militants* study,[1] covering over 1100 technicians in industrial firms who belonged to a trade union, supports this line of argument. This study found that the technicians were marginal men, situated between management and the shop-floor without fitting easily into either group. But the group the technicians overwhelmingly identified with and used as a reference group was management. The technicians' problem, as they saw it, was that they were being denied their proper status and recognition. They were mostly ambitious and sought opportunities to move into management, and this was a source of frustration for the technicians found their avenues blocked. The majority of the technicians possessed paper qualifications, mostly from part-time study, but they faced a 'graduate barrier' since higher management positions were being filled by people with degrees and more prestigious professional qualifications. The technicians, therefore, regarded themselves as unfairly held down. There were complaints about traditional differentials – the technicians' superior earnings and career prospects compared with manual workers – being eroded. Expressions of solidarity with the manual labour force were conspicuous only by their absence. . . . Hence the phrase 'reluctant militants'. The technicians had . . . become organised like blue-collar workers, but not because they regarded themselves as working class. Their driving concern was to preserve what remained of their middle class privileges and status.

A. J. N. Blain's study of *Pilots and Management*[2] in the British airlines argues a comparable case. Airline pilots are in no sense an economically depressed group even by middle class standards, but trade union organisation amongst the pilots is strong. Furthermore, the pilots have been prepared to use the full weight of their bargaining power militantly and effectively. . . . What irked the pilots, drew them to trade unionism and disposed them towards militant bargaining behaviour was what they regarded as their declining status in relation to airline managements. The pilots in no way identified with the working class. They were drawn mainly from middle class backgrounds and their political orientations were overwhelmingly Conservative. They regarded themselves as an élite group of professionals – systems managers doing a technically complex job – and expected to be treated commensurately. . . . Like the technicians whose militancy was reluctant, the pilots were adopting a working class means in pursuit of a distinctly middle class objective. . . .

One major source of confusion in the debate surrounding the proletarianization thesis has been the article of conventional wisdom that equates individualism with the middle class, collectivism with the working class and regards these orientations as mutually exclusive. However, . . . when the evidence is squarely examined the aims of both white and blue-collar trade unionists

appear to embrace a similar mixture of individualism and collectivism, and the results of our own enquiry endorse this
conclusion.

Respondents in our investigation were asked to name any
occupational associations to which they belonged and their
answers, presented in Table 11.4 from which the self-employed
are excluded, may at first sight appear to endorse the notion that
white-collar workers are the less disposed to collective organisation. Within the blue-collar sample 78 per cent belonged to a TUC
affiliated body, whereas only 36 per cent of the white-collar
respondents were unionised – less than half the manual density.

However, interpreting this relatively low density of union
membership amongst white-collar workers as proof of an aversion
to collectivism is unwarranted. Membership or non-membership
of a trade union is no valid test of this issue. First, account must be
taken of occupational associations other than TUC affiliated
bodies. White-collar workers have a range of organisations available for the pursuit of collective interests. For example, member-

TABLE 11.4   *Employees' membership of occupational associations (%)*

	White-collar (n=204)	Blue-collar (n=213)
TUC affiliated unions	36	78
Staff associations or other trade unions	11	2
Professional bodies	20	1
No membership	33	19

TABLE 11.5   *Trade unionists' stated reasons for joining a union (%)*

	White-collar (n=90)	Blue-collar (n=168)
Closed shop	22	49
Ideological/ethical	11	8
Pursuit of specific occupational interests	54	38
Other	12	5

ship of staff associations and professional bodies was considerably higher amongst our white as opposed to blue-collar respondents . . . .

Second, some allowance must be made for the closed shop arrangement that operates in many manual occupations. All trade unionists in our sample were asked their reasons for joining and, amongst manual respondents, the most frequent explanation referred to the closed shop despite its illegality at the time of the enquiry (see Table 11.5). Those who believe blue-collar trade unionism to be an expression of working class solidarity would find questioning members about their motivations a sobering experience. It is not just that the majority of members are in no sense activists. Apart from this, amongst the rank and file expressions of solidaristic attachments are highly untypical. It is surprising how many members do not even know the names of their unions. For many members the trade union is rather like an occupational pension scheme; you have to join, you pay your dues and eventually become entitled to certain benefits.

Trade unionism is sufficiently traditional in many manual occupations to have become, in effect, a condition of employment, while amongst white-collar employees this type of inertia joining remains less common. The operation of the closed shop amongst blue-collar workers must exaggerate their apparent greater preference for trade union representation that membership figures indicate. In many of the relevant cases, 'closed shop' was probably the respondents' immediate reason for joining. Some would no doubt have become members in any case and it would be extravagant to infer that 49 per cent of the blue-collar members in the sample were reluctant unionists. Nevertheless, blue-collar vis-à-vis white-collar membership figures must overstate manual workers' apparent greater ideological commitment to trade unionism.

If respondents who explained their membership in closed shop terms are excluded and if all occupational organisations are taken into account, then white rather than blue-collar respondents can be portrayed as the more favourably disposed towards collective representation. While confirming that blue-collar workers are the more likely to belong to trade unions, therefore, our evidence does not support explanations of this in terms of any prevalence of individualism and consequent resistance to the principle of collective organisation amongst the white-collar strata.

To the extent that they were unionised, was there any evidence that white-collar respondents were carrying attitudes into their organisations that would give them a qualitatively different character compared with blue-collar unions? . . . Expressions of ideological, ethical or political commitment to a trade union 'movement' were rare amongst both groups. White-collar unionists mainly explained their membership in terms of pursuing individual or sectional interests, but if this is interpreted as evidence of individualism then blue-collar unionists are shown to be no less endowed with this attribute.

Respondents who did not belong to a trade union were asked their reasons for not joining . . . . Amongst white-collar respondents there was a relatively widespread indifference to the entire subject – the issue of joining had simply never arisen, whereas more blue-collar workers were waiting to be pressured, maybe by encountering a closed shop situation. However, there were more objections to trade unions 'on principle' amongst the blue as opposed to the white-collar non-members. This evidence, therefore, hardly suggests that white-collar workers are especially opposed on ideological grounds to the type of representation that trade unions offer.

We addressed two 'forced choice' questions in order to probe our sample's preferences as regards trade union goals and tactics. . . . First, we asked whether respondents believed that trade unions ought to pursue general objectives (promote social justice) or whether they should concern themselves solely with the sectional interests of their members. . . . . The white and blue-collar unionists gave almost completely identical answers. Second, as regards preferred trade union tactics, we asked members to choose between co-operating with management so as to produce bigger shares for all, and bargaining with employers in order to increase the workers' proportion of the cake. In this instance the white-collar unionists proved the more likely to favour co-operative tactics [87 per cent], but . . . 75 per cent of the blue-collar sample felt likewise.

Investigators seeking to test the embourgeoisment thesis have sometimes worked with rather exaggerated notions about what constitute typical middle class attitudes and likewise, in testing for signs of proletarianisation amongst white-collar workers there has been a tendency to exaggerate the proletarian character of the typical blue-collar employee. It is as well to remember that very

269

few blue-collar trade unionists are class conscious in the Marxist sense and that although unrest may dominate newspaper headlines, 60 per cent of manual unionists have never been on strike. Furthermore, many blue-collar unions are highly concerned with differentials. Indeed, the craft unions' main historical concern has been not so much to unite the working class as to keep their members ahead of the less skilled. So when we find white-collar trade unionists who are concerned about their declining status and who hope to use trade unions as an instrument to keep themselves up the ladder, it is a mistake to imagine that this is a peculiarly middle class phenomenon. Both blue and white-collar unions contain instrumentally oriented members and, alongside broader socio-political objectives, seek to protect their own members' sectional interests.

Density of trade union membership amongst white-collar workers appears to depend upon exactly the same factors that apply amongst the blue-collar strata. . . . White-collar unions are encouraged by exactly the same conditions as blue-collar unions and, given favourable circumstances, it does not appear especially difficult for white-collar unions to recruit. The relatively low overall density of membership amongst white-collar workers, therefore, appears due not so much to non-manual workers being the more resistant to the principle, as to their circumstances of employment being less likely to offer trade unions the chance to organise and operate effectively.

Overall, the evidence suggests that both blue and white-collar workers, whether they identify with the middle or the working class, are willing to support either individualistic or collectivist action, or a combination of both, depending upon the strategy that best fits their situations. The relationship between trade unionism and social class is more complex than some previous writers have assumed and these complexities must be taken into account before the validity of the proletarianisation thesis can be assessed. As regards this thesis, the implication is that the evidence concerning white-collar trade unions needs re-interpreting. White-collar workers can join trade unions thereby endorsing the principle of collective action without their attitudes otherwise becoming any less middle class, while, at the same time, white-collar unionists who display sectional, instrumental and sometimes highly individualistic motives are less unlike blue-collar unionists than has been conventionally supposed.

NOTES AND REFERENCES

1. B. C. Roberts, Ray Loveridge and John Gennard, *Reluctant Militants* (1972).
2. A. J. N. Blain, *Pilots and Management* (Allen and Unwin, 1972).

Conservative Militants – The Case of ASTMS

R. Carter

'Class, Militancy and Union Character: a Study of the Association of Scientific, Technical and Managerial Staffs', *Sociological Review*, vol. 27 (May 1979) pp. 297–316

This article is an attempt to examine critically the main sociological analysis of white collar trade unions and, by a detailed examination of one particular union, the Association of Scientific, Technical and Managerial Staffs (ASTMS), to suggest an alternative approach. . . .

The most important and influential sociological contribution to the study of white collar unionism is undoubtedly that of Blackburn and Prandy.[1] What sets their work apart from that of others in the field is its ambitious and explicitly theoretical attempt to differentiate white collar unionism from manual unionism. They start from a position that any examination of white collar unions should not simply be a head counting exercise but should also examine the nature and policies of the unions that members of the middle class are joining. What distinguished white collar workers from manual workers, for Blackburn and Prandy, was not that they were less willing to join unions but that the character of the unions they joined was different. . . .

Blackburn and Prandy's criteria for 'unionateness' led them to concentrate on comparisons between the official policies of the various unions, ignoring trade union activity at lower levels. This restriction to the formal objectives of the unions weights the comparisons in favour of similarities between white collar unions and manual ones. What it cannot reveal is the relationship of union members to those policies. . . .

There is a disjuncture between the formal objectives of trade unions and the activity in which members of unions engage. With middle class members, moreover, the disjuncture is different from that displayed in manual unions. Middle class workers are members of trade unions for purposes of collective representation but conflict with their employers is less frequent and more likely to centre around pay than in the case of manual workers. Middle class labour performs high trust jobs and its trade unionism as a consequence has less concern with issues of control of its working methods because these are less often under attack. What conflict there is tends therefore to be more formal and is likely to be conducted on their behalf by full-time officials. The membership of a trade union by middle class workers does not involve a change in relationship inside the factory. Their roles remain dominated by the implementation of orders downwards, rather than by conflict with the people above them.

The work of full-time officials in middle class unions, by contrast, is dominated by negotiations and representations to employers. They are only called in when their members have grievances against the employer about which they feel reasonably strongly. The full-time officials therefore, although party to compromises, work in a situation where conflict with the employer is clear. As a result, full-time officials are more likely to have ideas of a sharp conflict of interests with the employers than are the membership most of the time. This attitude that management is clearly opposed to the interests of union members is represented in official union policies, whereas much of the membership see higher management as a reserve bank of authority that can be drawn upon to support their supervisory rôles. The views of officials and official union policy are therefore often more radical than much of the membership.

The position is more complicated when it comes to manual worker unionism. There is a disjuncture between the shop floor and both the branch life of the union and its full-time officers. But this cannot be characterized as one stemming from lack of self activity at shop floor level, on the one hand, and officially organized conflict, on the other. It is simply that much conflict at work is unorganized and unharnessed by the official trade union procedures. Branch life and full-time officials tend to represent the more formalized struggles. Full-time officials, whatever their political hue, who conclude settlements with employers, find it hard to maintain a favourable image with workers who have taken industrial action and got less than they asked for. In short, there tends to be a much larger number of unofficial strikes and conflict between official policies of the union and the activities of shop floor workers. . . .

Blackburn and Prandy . . . note some very general features, such as governmental encouragement of collective bargaining and the growth of bureaucracy and rationalization, which feed the growth of white collar unionization, but these are not linked to any analysis of class. Nor is any indication given as to how these features effect relations in production. Despite their original aim of relating unionization to social class, Blackburn and Prandy end up denying it in practice. White collar unions are destined to function like manual ones, but with no change in the class position of their membership. Correctly denying that there are two distinct types of unionism, Blackburn and Prandy fail to distance white collar unionism from manual unionism on the continuum they have constructed.

It is, however, possible to locate significant differences between white collar unions and manual ones as a result of their different class compositions. In order to do so it is necessary to have a different conception of middle class labour to that offered by Blackburn and Prandy, who equate middle class with white collar, and assume the wearing of a white collar produces a common class situation. But if middle class labourers are defined by their functions in production, their active relations with both employers and other workers, then they are seen to be much more heterogeneous and to have a contradictory class location. The more authority that is exercised by middle class labour the closer the employee approaches the position of the controller of the enterprise. The less authority exercised, the more the middle class labourer is supervised and the closer he or she will be to the working class. Attitudes to trade unionism will therefore vary both with positions within the hierarchy of control and also with conjunctural factors. Many members of this section of the workforce are trade unionists, but their consciousness is dominated by their day-to-day roles as supervisors, foremen, ratefixers, or lower management. For most of the time they carry out a management function and their own membership of a trade union is incidental to their superintendence and control relationship with other workers. When asked about trade unionism their first reactions are often ones of hostility, stemming from the resistance and obstruction they encounter from other trade unionists when trying to carry out their management function. Being members of a union has not stopped foremen requesting the removal of trouble-some shop stewards, although on occasions it has resulted in the request being backed by a threat of industrial action if not acceded to by management.

The ambivalence shown towards trade unionism by middle class labour is paralleled by other trade unionists' attitudes towards middle class trade union organization. There has been considerable hostility towards white collar unions from the wider trade union movement. . . . What is being questioned is the very organization of employees who are not regarded as members of the working class. Solidarity with their struggles is expressed reluctantly, if at all . . . .

Any attempt to delineate the character of a particular union is beset with major difficulties, and characterizing ASTMS is no exception. Indeed the Association presents more of a difficulty than most other unions because its public image is so paradoxical. It appears as superior and middle class on the one hand and yet has a reputation of being 'left-wing' on the other. . . .

It can be stated that the vast majority of ASTMS members are within a supervisory category, although the amount of time spent on supervision by individual members varies. ASTMS also has in its membership employees such as testers, clerks and some technicians, who undertake no supervisory work and could not be defined as middle class. These groups are unambiguously working class and represent a greater potential for militancy and industrial action within the union. National union policy is obviously influenced by these members as well as by supervisory grades so it is not possible simply to attribute stances taken by the leadership directly to the union's middle class membership.

The influence of the middle class membership, however, is undoubtedly dominant in ASTMS and there are a number of reasons why this is so. Firstly, as already stated, middle class members constitute a majority in the union. Secondly, although ASTMS was formed by an amalgamation of the Association of Supervisory Staffs, Executives and Technicians (ASSET) and the Association of Scientific Workers, it is the structure and style of the supervisory association that has been continued and developed by ASTMS. Many of the leaders of ASTMS, including Clive Jenkins, the General Secretary, worked for or were lay members of ASSET, a union that itself had grown out of the

National Foremen's Association. . . . Finally, as the union has merged with other unions, and staff associations, in new areas, some major sections . . . have been given a large degree of autonomy and until recently have felt no need to bring pressure to bear upon the union for policy changes. . . . Very often also these new areas of membership have little tradition of collective bargaining and take the mode of operation of the union as a whole as the norm. It is characteristic of some of these areas, for example amongst university technicians and insurance members, to have senior staff members, that is members with supervisory roles, as the leading lay officials, despite having large numbers of non supervisory members.

None of these complexities can be grasped by using Blackburn and Prandy's framework. ASTMS would be regarded as highly unionate and, indeed, may even be considered more unionate than some manual unions. . . .

Neither is it true that ASTMS lacks 'completeness'. There are areas where it is relatively weak, for example amongst managers and professional engineers, but this is in large part due to its enormous ambitions to recruit outside its traditional areas and is a situation common to all unions setting themselves up as general ones, be they manual or white collar. Within the engineering industry, members of the Engineering Employers' Federation insist upon over 50 per cent membership in an area before recognition is accorded and there is not one major Federation firm that does not now recognize ASTMS. More generally ASTMS's rapid growth from 70,000 in 1968 to over 400,000 in 1978 testifies to the willingness of people to join it.

Using Blackburn and Prandy's framework, it would have to be concluded therefore that ASTMS is no different in character from manual unions. To suggest otherwise, it is necessary to go beyond the criteria of 'unionateness' and look at the behaviour of the union leadership, their policies on major issues and how these relate to the composition of the membership.

ASTMS is affiliated to the Labour Party and has a close relationship at leadership level with the Tribune Group of MPs. The leadership has not, however, been able to secure, to any great extent, the membership's direct support for the Labour Party, even after issuing leaflets and publishing articles in its Journal on a regular basis. At the end 1975, there were 315,000 members of the union but fewer than 50,000 chose to pay the political levy to the Labour Party. Nevertheless, in the same year ASTMS affiliated the equivalent of 185,000 members to that body, by charging those paying the levy considerably more than the Labour Party affiliation fee.

It is not for idealistic reasons that ASTMS seeks to counter the decision of most of its members not to affiliate. It is seen by the leadership as a necessary investment, allowing ASTMS a much greater influence at Labour Party Conferences. After the 1974 General Election, ASTMS had twenty-five members elected to the House of Commons, thirteen of whom were Ministers. In addition, it also had active members in the House of Lords. By 1977, the Annual Report was able to list thirty-eight members of the ASTMS Parliamentary Committee. This committee has regular meetings, produces regular minutes and all members are allowed to attend. It organizes Parliamentary lobbying, meetings with Ministers, the sponsoring of Private Members' Bills, and the asking of questions in the House. In short, it is taken very seriously within the union. . . .

It is not because ASTMS is weak in any organizational sense that it has retained and expanded its political activities. Nor can its political involvements be explained by reference to the importance of its public sector membership. The central political positions taken by the union – for import controls, free collective bargaining, support for the National Enterprise Board, for a legal right of recognition – are much more relevant to their private sector membership than to their, in any case, very small public sector membership.

ASTMS's political involvement is part and parcel of the way the leadership manages the union. Running through ASTMS policy is the reflection and reinforcement of lack of self activity of much of its membership. Its use of Parliamentary pressure group politics is an example of this. It sees progress through political connections and lobbying as an alternative to mobilizing its membership and engaging in industrial action. The attempts to avoid industrial action are not always successful, but there is a real fear amongst the leadership that militancy that goes beyond rhetoric would frighten away actual and potential members. This is why the leadership have been such strong supporters of a legal right to recognition, through ballots and arbitration, rather than through collective action when employers have refused recognition. It assesses, probably quite correctly, than many people would not join the union if recognition had to be fought for through industrial action. . . .

The majority of ASTMS members undoubtedly do not subscribe to the views of the Tribune Group, but as yet there has been only one clash within the union over a major policy item. Attempts by the ASTMS leadership to support nationalization of banks and insurance companies have been thwarted by finance members, who were able to force a special conference about the issue. These members regarded nationalization as a threat to their job security in a prosperous industry. This revolt by a section of the membership is very much the exception. . . .

The union's demands for import controls to stem redundancies rather than concentrating on traditional trade union action at shop floor level, further illustrates its preference for seeking political solutions. A healthy and prosperous British industry is seen as the best way to obtain advances for the membership and therefore the leadership has led a major campaign of opposition to the European Economic Community rather than directing its attention squarely to British employers.

It is this desire for a healthy and prosperous British industry that makes ASTMS such a supporter of the restructuring of British industry and rational planning. These calls for restructuring and planning, attacking as they do private ownership, further add to ASTMS's radical image. In reality, what underlies these attacks is the belief that if only the old inefficient owners and controllers of capital would step aside and let the people who really know take control, then British industry would be the best in the world. Those people are, of course, ASTMS members. There is no hint that manual workers have anything to contribute, no idea of the workforce as a whole taking control and eliminating some forms of the division of labour. The policy is a reflection of the interests of ASTMS members, reinforcing their role as specialists.

This can be illustrated by Clive Jenkins's views on the Bullock Report on Industrial Democracy:

> I predict that the groups most likely to want to play a part in Board decisions include, in the vanguard, white collar workers, middle managers, teams of highly skilled people in technically advanced industries, and entire staffs in banking and

insurance. These are the sort of people who have the confidence that can make an impact on company policy and the desire to do it – based upon their own critique of their company's progression.'[2].

Industrial democracy is conceived as allowing ASTMS members their rightful place on the Board of Directors. . . .

ASTMS's bolstering of its members' superiority over manual workers is also evident in its salary bargaining strategy. The union's claims for differentials are central to its perspectives in private industry and fully incorporate the aspirations and ideology of large parts of its membership.

In principle, its support of differentials is no different from similar craft union demands. They are both products of élitism. There are, however, important differences in the operation and significance of the two similar policies. Since World War II, shop floor workers have found it advantageous to mobilize around the twin demands of differentials and parity. The 'leapfrogging' involved resulted in higher wages for both sets of workers involved through a situation of almost continual bargaining.

What is significant about ASTMS claims for differentials is that they rarely result in subsequent demands for parity or narrowing of differentials from the shop floor. . . . The union's policy on differentials often exacerbates existing frictions and reinforces the views of other trade unionists that ASTMS is a 'middle class' union. In order for its members to be accepted as part of the working class movement, ASTMS would have to adopt policies that emphasized its members' common situation with other workers. It cannot do so because it attracts membership by stressing the superiority of professional, technical and supervisory workers. The ASTMS membership card announces that members have joined 'the élite of white collar workers'.

This is a quite conscious strategy of the leadership. At one meeting addressed by the General Secretary, it was suggested from the floor that the union placed too much emphasis on the differences between the ASTMS membership and shop floor workers, and that more efforts should be made to stress the common problems that both groups faced with employers. Clive Jenkins replied in his colourful manner that the union recruited by telling prospective members that they were handsome and suntanned and that the union would make them even more handsome and even more suntanned. . . .

In fact, Jenkins's light-hearted analogy is not altogether a good one. People confident of their suntan and handsome appearance are not the people who move most readily to the union. Prospective members are more likely to have fading suntans and to be anxious about shop floor workers approaching their terms and conditions of employment. The union steps in and offers to manage that anxiety. It does so by operating with a model where ideally salaries and benefits are neatly graded throughout society, according to expertise and responsibility. But by placing such emphasis on 'the delicate framework of relativities and differentials' ASTMS walks a narrow path between support for shop floor wage claims and hostility to them because they undermine the status and differentials of its members:

'The skills and expertise that scientists and engineers have acquired painfully over many years are not being rewarded by remuneration, security of employment or promotional prospects. The professional, whether a man or woman, whether a scientist, engineer or computer specialist, has seen other less skilled, less qualified groups of workers catch up with and indeed surpass his or her salary, whilst at the same time enjoying more secure employment. This is not to say that others do not deserve their wages and salaries; what it does say is that the time is approaching when skill, qualifications and responsibility will also have to be adequately rewarded.'[3]

Despite the disclaimer, the overwhelming impression is that other workers do not deserve their improved payments and conditions. But the fact that ASTMS makes the disclaimer at all is important . . . .The potential hostility towards other sections of workers must be contained, or it would threaten ASTMS's relationship with the wider trade union movement. The main focus of union propaganda might be on the status anxiety of prospective members, but it must be organized by the union against the employer.

Making differentials a key plank around which it organizes, ASTMS develops little in the way of identification of its members with other workers' grievances. Moreover this policy also has consequences within ASTMS itself. Members overwhelmingly identify with their own occupational category, and the union operates with a structure that both reflects and reinforces it.

Branches are composed of several different groups and sub-groups, which are drawn around particular occupations within a workplace, such as professional engineers, testers, foremen. These groups meet regularly at the workplace to enable people with distinct and separate problems to discuss them in detail and can therefore encourage a high degree of involvement. But at one and the same time, these groups render the branch all but unnecessary for those other than group representatives and members with wider political motivations. The structure thus insulates groups of members from one another and minimizes the likelihood of collective identity within the workplace, or branch, even between ASTMS members.

The formal policies of ASTMS which are responsible for its left wing image are more radical than most of its membership. . . . How is it then that the union is not torn apart by political divisions? It is because the policies do have a certain congruence with the membership's wishes, not in terms of their ideological content, but in their avoidance of the need for industrial action.

This is a central feature of the union running through its policies on recognition through ballots and legal intervention, the extension of the legal rights of trade unions, and negotiations by full-time officers. It is also central to the leadership's conception of trade unionism:

'If you feel unwell you visit a doctor; if you have a toothache you visit a dentist; if you are involved in litigation you visit a solicitor; if collective bargaining needs to be done, workers approach a trade union. We live in the age of the professional and in the case of trade unions this applies not only to the negotiators, but also to their research, legal and educational staffs.'[4]

Trade unions are here regarded as external agencies that involve little action on the part of the individual and demand no changes in the roles of the union members in the workplace. Everything is done for the members on their behalf. . . .

Just as the equation of white collar with middle class needs to be rejected, so too does that which equates the white collar trade unionist with working class. There is no inevitable development of solidarity and identification between supervisory workers and the people they supervise, whether the supervisors are unionized or not. Proletarianization of middle class workers may be taking

280

place but their adoption of trade union defences does not mean they accept their eventual equalization with the position of manual worker. What it can mean is that their feelings of separateness from and superiority to other workers are being organized and represented.

This is not to suggest that ASTMS is holding back its members from developing solidarity with other workers. This lack of identification with other workers stems primarily from their day to day relations inside the workplace, not from the union. The union policies do, however, reflect in a less sharp form the contradiction that much of its membership lives out daily.

NOTES AND REFERENCES

1. R. M. Blackburn and K. Prandy, 'White-Collar Unionization' (1965).
2. *Financial Times*, 8 February 1977.
3. 'Professional Scientists, Engineers and Technologists', ASTMS brochure.
4. C. Jenkins and B. Sherman, *Collective Bargaining* (Routledge and Kegan Paul, 1977) p. 2.

Index

Index

Index